Greed
&
Grace

One Woman's
Faith-Filled Journey to
Freedom from Generational Deceit

A Memoir

Dena McCoy

Trilogy Christian Publishers
A Wholly Owned Subsidary of Trinity Broadcasting Network
2442 Michelle Drive
Tustin, CA 92780

Cover design by: KR's group
Cover photo by Dena McCoy
Author Photo by Sara Corwin Photography

For information, address Trilogy Christian Publishing
Rights Department, 2442 Michelle Drive, Tustin, Ca 92780.
Trilogy Christian Publishing/ TBN and colophon are trademarks of Trinity Broadcasting Network.

For information about special discounts for bulk purchases, please contact Trilogy Christian Publishing.

Manufactured in the United States of America

Trilogy Disclaimer: The views and content expressed in this book are those of the author and may not necessarily reflect the views and doctrine of Trilogy Christian Publishing or the Trinity Broadcasting Network.

10 9 8 7 6 5 4 3 2 1

Library of Congress Cataloging-in-Publication Data is available.

ISBN 978-1-63769-074-1 (Print Book)
ISBN 978-1-63769-075-8 (ebook)

To my children, whose unconditional love, strength, and integrity have inspired me to keep moving forward despite heartbreaking circumstances. You are wise beyond your years, and I'm so proud to be your mom. I love you.

May 3, 2021
New York, New York

I think sometimes, when you have great pain in your life, you have to seek God in a great and intense way because you just really don't have anything else.

Joyce Meyer

Contents

Author's Note

This is a work based on my recollections of my personal life experiences and observations. All dialogue may not be exactly verbatim, rather included to provide a re-creation of the nature of some conversations. Some of the language is based on what has been recounted by others as well as what I have drawn from memory, my notes, texts, or emails. Other sources include photographs, handwritten letters, voice mails, legal documents, bank statements, personal journals, and various other references. There are some events where I may not have been present, and in those instances, information came to me through communication with trusted family, associates, and family friends. Some names and identifying details have been changed.

I intend to recount what I believe happens when otherwise good people become vulnerable to evil through greed, a desire for power, and the devastating effect that can have on a family. With a faithful and humble spirit, my intention is not to hurt anyone, rather to use examples of how challenging trials in life can ultimately be used for a higher, godly purpose.

It is important to note how much my family means to me. For most of my life, I have enjoyed a great closeness with those who raised me, however in recent years, I have struggled with how to balance love for my family of origin while also learning how to love and protect myself when so much pain and misunderstanding divided us. Writing this book has been an important part of my healing process as it has allowed me to finally put order to some emotionally complex events. It has also provided a chance to find my voice when so many times I felt silenced and unable to be heard. Most importantly, it has been an opportunity to deepen my faith through dependency on the Word of God when normal societal structures of support fell short. My hope is to bring awareness to the healing and comfort God's Word has for us even during life's most unexpectedly painful moments.

When I was growing up, my mother used to say to me, "The greatest way to be heard and to reach the largest audience is through the power of the pen."

Through the Holy Spirit, I found my pen. Thank you to those who listen.

Greed brings grief to the whole family, but those who hate bribes will live.

Proverbs 15:27 (NLT)

And the God of all *grace*, who called you to his eternal glory in Christ, after you have suffered a little while, will himself restore you and make you strong, firm and steadfast.

1 Peter 5:10 (NIV)

Submission

Trust in the Lord with all your heart and lean not on your own understanding; in all your ways submit to him, and he will make your paths straight.

Proverbs 3:5-6 (NIV)

My first memorable test of faith came after my daughter, Lily, was born. She came into the world with bright eyes and an energetic spirit, yet with only one functioning kidney. During my second trimester, we learned about the diagnosis of a genetic disorder whereby cysts and structural abnormalities prevented normal function of the kidney, which could ultimately cause the organ to fail. It was a condition that required frequent monitoring and testing with plans for eventual surgery to remove the diseased kidney sometime after she was born.

There was concern that both kidneys could eventually be affected, and the entire situation, even with New York's finest doctors available to her, was one of great uncertainty. We were to watch her carefully during the first year of her young life, and upon her first birthday, it was decided that she would have the dead kidney removed because she would be old enough to endure the procedure. Needless to say, it was a very stressful time that brought constant distress to her father and me.

As a mother, it was unbearable at times to contemplate the worst-case scenarios. The desire to control the outcome consumed me, and yet I knew it was impossible to do so. Still, I looked everywhere for understanding and wanted to fix it for her but knew I couldn't. Although the doctors had no guarantees, I leaned on them as I constantly sought answers. Against their advice, I spent late nights pouring over the Internet for hours, which created endless fear, exactly as they said it would do. As I fed the beast of fear, my list of questions grew. This endless cycle ultimately caused me so much stress that I finally stopped and went back to worrying alone and praying. She would eventually have to have the surgery, and we would hope that her healthy kidney would not also be affected. It was a daily exercise of worry and self-torture over trying to change the unfixable.

Finally, one day while on my hands and knees in tears of desperation, I was faced with a painful decision. The emotional burden was becoming too much to carry, and I was crushed under the pressure of it all. Ironically it was that unbearable strain that helped me finally hit rock bottom where the fork in the road became clear. I could keep trying to carry the impossible emotional load, worrying over how to save my daughter, or I could release her to a higher place. The latter meant I would have to let go of wanting to be in control.

Through my tears and pain, I finally found the courage to fully submit and accept the outcome of her situation. "Heavenly Father, I trust you and trust that what you have chosen for my daughter is your will. If you must call her to heaven sooner than we want, I ask for the strength to understand and give her fully to your care. If it is your will for her to survive and be made whole, I will never forget such a miracle. With a full and open heart to you, I submit to your will. Amen."

My prayer was for God to give me the grace to accept His plan, whether it was for her to survive and live a long life or for her to be called to heaven much sooner than we wanted. It was something I had to reconcile in my soul with God. It was the first time I remember actually putting my belief into action and leaning completely on Him in a way where I trusted the outcome no matter what it would be. Once I did, I immediately found a peace I had never known before. It was an emotional exhale that gave trust to the seemingly impossible situation and allowed me to focus on the present moment with Lily rather than worry about the future, which was completely out of our control.

Some months later, when I took her to a pre-op appointment, her doctor, who was one of the top pediatric urologists in the country, sat across from me at his desk and looked very serious with a wall of medical books behind him, some of which had his name on the spine. "There is no medical explanation for what I'm about to tell you," he said. "In all of my years of practice in this field, I have never seen a complete recovery of a kidney that was diagnosed to be dead tissue and something the body was ultimately expected to reject." It was at that moment, as I held Lily and looked into his eyes, that I realized the answer.

I told him the outcome wasn't in the medical books or anything that would make logical medical sense. I calmly said that I believed God had touched her and healed her. I didn't care what he thought of me or how it sounded because I knew deep in my soul that was what had happened. He smiled at me and said he was happy to say that he wouldn't need to see her or us again. He said that the once dead kidney was nearly one hundred percent functioning and could sustain her life even if something were to happen to her "healthy" kidney.

I promised myself to always tell that story throughout my life because I believe with all my heart and soul that my daughter was touched by a miracle. Spiritual submission took on a new meaning from that point forward, and for the first time, I learned what it meant to live what I believed instead of just being a believer. It was an epiphany for what it meant to put one's beliefs into practice. Little did I know that it would become the cornerstone of how to face future painful events in my life and a situation I would have to constantly remind myself of when future life circumstances seemed impossible.

Blood in the Water

Enemies disguise themselves with their lips, but in their hearts they harbor deceit. Though their speech is charming, do not believe them, for seven abominations fill their hearts. Their malice may be concealed by deception, but their wickedness will be exposed in the assembly.

Proverbs 26:24-26 (NIV)

February 2016, I boarded a flight from JFK to Portland, Oregon. I was headed to my home state to seek objective professional advice. The reasons for the impromptu trip were to review some personal financial matters, gain needed clarity on a family business issue, and hopefully put my growing fears to rest. Something within me wasn't settled, and I knew I had to quietly step out on my own to verify new information I had learned through studying some financial papers and rereading some documents with fresh eyes. I say quietly because I was raised in a close-knit family of four, where I see now how my mother and I often innately found ourselves asking permission to do things instead of just making decisions on our own. Normally I would have told my parents or brother that I was going home, but I realized I didn't always need to ask permission, and it felt new and good. This patriarchal family system was all I had ever known and wouldn't recognize as outdated and stifling until it began to hinder me as an adult.

A few months earlier, I had signed an important legal agreement between my younger brother, Gary, and me. We were new fifty-fifty partners in a family LLC, which was originally created by my grand-father and his sons. Later, my father took it over and became majority partners with my mother while my brother and I were smaller share-holders. As the years went on, larger shares were gifted to us in stages during the final steps of my parent's estate planning. A new operating agreement had been drawn up to formalize my father's relinquish-ment of his last five-percent share of the company and secure each partner's new equal share of ownership.

Gary and I had often joked that our dad kept the last five-per-cent share to make sure he had some control over us getting along as majority partners. "It will be very important that the two of you work well together because this is your nest egg and your future," he would often say to each of us. "I've worked my whole life to be able to pass this along to you and your brother, and if you take care of things well together, you will be able to create something you can hand down to your own kids." It was a time where Gary and I were very close and appeared to be on the same page about our future, as well as our rela-tionship as siblings and business partners. We humored our father and let him keep the last percentage until he lectured us enough and was finally ready to let go.

My father and brother had co-managed the LLC, a property management business, for a number of years before my brother took over as the sole general operating manager. At the time of my signing the new operating agreement, Gary was the person I trusted more than anyone at that moment in my life. We were in constant communication about evolving details regarding the partnership as well as our growing frustrations with our aging parents, who were slowly handing over the reins of their assets to their two grown children. It was a change of the guard for them, and they were understandably struggling with finally letting go, yet I believed they had every reason to trust us and feel confident that their intentions would be fulfilled. It was a new chapter and one Gary and I readily accepted.

Daily emails, calls, and texts flowed between us from New York to the Bay Area during the evolution of the transfer. I felt our relationship as siblings as well as new business partners was as solid as ever. However, during this time, I had made myself unknowingly vulnerable because I was also quietly contemplating a divorce. My brother was my most trusted confidant during this time, which for me was filled with enormous personal uncertainty, pain, and fear. I shared everything with him because I believed without a doubt that he, above anyone, truly had my best interests at heart. Questions surrounding housing, finances, legal advice, the kids, and my personal future were privately discussed between us as to be expected between trusting siblings during times of change and crisis. My two teenaged kids would soon be coming home from boarding school for Christmas, and the stress of my personal life was at an all-time high at that moment. Gary was my rock, my confidant, my only sibling, and now my full-fledged business partner. He was everything to me then, and I trusted him implicitly with all the personal and professional details of my life.

Communication between my parents and me started to take on a third voice, as Gary appeared to be a peacemaker for me with them. They wanted me to stay in the marriage until Lily, the youngest, would leave for college. Wasn't this my decision? Certainly, as I look back now, it didn't feel like it was then. They worried about my financial future and, of course, the family business and legal costs. Gary was trying to quell their fears and support me at the same time, so I habitually gravitated toward him as he appeared to be a trusted voice of stability. Tensions at home with my husband, Randy, were growing, and emotions were high with so much pending change. Stress was mounting, and my immediate focus was more on how to get through the holidays and into the new year without breaking down in front of my kids.

To say it was a painful time is an understatement. What I didn't know then was that it would be the beginning of a nearly five-year nightmare. I had no idea that the person I trusted the most would seemingly use my vulnerability for his long-term advantage. My naïveté in believing siblings would watch out for one another through thick and thin was a lesson I would learn the hard way. If I had known then what lay ahead, I would have never thought I could face it, but with God, all is possible. As my world began to implode, there would be difficult choices to make, and one of the biggest was whether to lean on my own understanding or to reach higher.

When I look back now, it seems clearer to me than ever that Gary likely had a plan for himself, and I did not realize it then. He appeared to be in the driver's seat of the LLC, and it felt like his was the only voice my parents wanted to hear during my time of personal uncertainty. He was my go-to as well as theirs, and he seemed to navigate the situation well for both, yet ultimately acting, likely for himself. Trying to calm the rising fears of my parents and helping me figure out the next steps of my life, Gary appeared to be the man in charge.

The new operating agreement had been in the works during the months leading up to my split with Randy. The evolution of the new business partnership, holiday tension, financial pressure, and my crumbling marriage seemingly became a perfect platform for Gary to find me at my most vulnerable and entice me to sign the agreement. I remember him gently yet persistently encouraging me to sign the documents so that he could move forward with opening a new bank account for the LLC before the end of the year. The urgency, as I recall, was to remove our parents as partners, thus allowing the bank to proceed with the new paperwork for a new account which would reflect only Gary and me as new joint owners of the company. His argument sounded reasonable enough, and I had little reason to question his judgment. Even so, the new operating agreement sat on my desk for a good month, and I would pick it up and read and reread it and put it down unsigned. Something held me back from signing it, but I didn't exactly know what. There was a nagging feeling that I should speak to the attorney for the LLC before I formalized it with my signature.

I had been copied on various emails between my brother and the attorney, but most of the negotiations were taking place between the two of them while I was in New York at the height of my nearly thirty-year marriage coming to an end. Looking back now, the irony of this all isn't lost on me, but at the time, it was overwhelming. It wasn't exactly clear, but it was there, and upon reflection now, I can see it was very likely the Holy Spirit telling me to slow down to protect myself. Instead, I missed the signals and allowed my unwavering iron-clad trust in my brother to overpower that thought and continued to proceed with some of the motions.

"Is it okay if I call the lawyer and run a few questions by him before signing?" I look back now and realize how childish I was to feel I had to ask permission from my brother to speak to the company attorney who represented the LLC. The patriarchal nature of my family had ingrained this into me, so I habitually complied when Gary told me that he would answer my questions. I remember his reason was that he had spent a lot of time and resources with the lawyer and didn't want to use more company funds to have him answer my questions. Gary claimed he could just as easily do so, and that would save us money. It was the naïveté of that moment when I look back on it now that astonishes me. Entering into an agreement with my only sibling, whom I trusted, still should have warranted an hour or so alone with the lawyer representing the LLC, but I fell on familiar habits—blind trust and loyalty to a close family member.

At the time, I didn't believe I had the money to pay for the legal time myself and couldn't go to my Randy for it because tensions between us were so high. In retrospect, it was one of the most vulnerable moments of my life, but the complete trust I had in my brother then was steadfast, and I now see it blinded my better judgment. As Proverbs 28:26 (NIV) says, "Those who trust in themselves are fools, but those who walk in wisdom are kept safe." My unwavering trust had been in the bond I thought I had with my brother. I looked to him for guidance on more than the new agreement between us and had become unknowingly vulnerable. It would take time before I realized the terrible mistake I'd made, thinking my only sibling would treat me fairly, but at that moment, I believed he did. I trusted him with my life as he calmly went over my questions and answered them accordingly until I believed I was as satisfied as I could be and then signed on the dotted line.

God had actually intervened and given me a chance for another look, but I didn't notice it at the time. "I can't believe it, but the copy you signed was the draft, not the final," Gary communicated to me a day later. "I hate lawyers," he continued in exasperation. "Let me get ahold of the final copy, and then you can sign it," he said with impatience. Had I been living more closely to my faith on a daily basis, I am absolutely certain today that I would have seen God's attempt to get me to see the trap that now appears to have been laid before me. I always had a faith-filled heart and was a believer, but I had failed to seek God first in making decisions.

I didn't realize how much this single decision would impact my life so greatly, either positively or negatively, depending on my understanding of what I believed to be true. At the time, my upcoming divorce felt more worrisome and life-altering, but I was wrong. Proverbs 3:6 (TLB) says, "In everything you do, put God first, and he will direct you and crown your efforts with success." The word "direct" stands out now more than ever in that scripture as I ultimately see how I should have let God direct my path but was instead steering myself alone and leaning on my own understanding, which at the time was veiled with anxiety, stress, and an unwavering trust in my brother, whom I loved.

Everything was coming at me at once: talk of divorce, how and when to separate, how to get through Christmas, legal considerations, concern about the kids, money issues, my parents and their confusing advice, moving, and this agreement, which was another spoke on the wheel about to spin out of control at the wrong time. I was overloaded and feeling fear rise up within me over the changing landscape in front of me, and yet my trust in my brother was undeniably steadfast. I wanted to attach to something and someone who seemed to have my best interest at heart and who knew me well.

On November 9, 2015, I signed on the dotted line of the official final copy of the new operating agreement. That single act of putting pen to paper, believing I had been guided by a trusted partner, whose answers to my questions appeared at the time to be just, would forever change the course of my life.

Years later, the consequences of not first seeking spiritual then legal guidance on this moment would be very detrimental to my financial, emotional, and physical health. Neglecting to see the second chance, I had to pause after signing the draft of the agreement while anticipating signing the final original copy was failure to witness an opportunity to avert disaster. What I missed was seeing how God was handing me a gift, a moment of contemplation, and yet my inability to recognize that vital warning was my ultimate demise.

I believe that my perfect storm had become an ideal situation for my brother to take advantage of me. It felt as if he ultimately did so through my extreme vulnerability and unwavering trust in him as my only sibling and confidant. In doing so, I signed a huge part of my life over to him without realizing it. That single signature would alter the course of my life forever. The trip to Portland months later became my first glimpse into the depth of apparent greed and evil I believe existed in what later felt like a well-executed plan. To expect that trust between a brother and sister could and should be sacred was foolish. In my case, I couldn't have been more mistaken. What was worse is that I believe he didn't act alone with his agenda.

Tango with
the Devil

I have known terror dizzy spells
Finding out the secrets words won't tell
Phoenix—"If I Ever Feel Better"

A few years earlier, I traveled outside the country and experienced a small yet powerful foreshadowing of things to come. As an isolated incident, none of it made sense but looking back, I can see how it was a piece to a larger puzzle I would be spending a lot of time trying to construct and understand.

It was 2012, and I was on an annual trip with a fitness group from New York. My friend Louise and I had decided to spend a couple of days together before meeting with our friends who would fly in later that week. We always tried to see as much of a new city as we could in the days before or after our retreats. Historical and tourist sites mixed with a little shopping, lots of walking and dining was how we enjoyed spending our free days. It was a break we looked forward to together, and for a number of years, we enjoyed these adventures. This particular trip began in Buenos Aires, and we explored the city with our usual curiosity and excitement.

Ironically, my son, Jaylen, was on a spring break service trip on the same continent with a group from his high school, while at the same time, I was in Argentina. His class was volunteering in a village in the rainforests of Ecuador. Lily and Randy were in New York, and Gary and his family were vacationing in Honolulu while my parents were in Europe. As the plane traveled due south from New York and dropped below the equator, I visualized where my family members were on the globe. It was my first time below the equator, and my point of perspective felt obviously yet strangely different. For some reason, I was comforted knowing my son was at least on the same continent as me. I had never felt concerned about physical or geographic distance, but this trip and location made me feel very unsettled for some odd reason. I remember fixating from time to time at how geographically spread out we were, yet also connected as a family.

The last night on the town in Buenos Aires with Louise was festive and fun as we decided to go to a traditional Argentinean steak dinner and tango show. It was a memorable evening, and the feeling of time and place being with my friend and enjoying the beginning of a new adventure was exciting. I started to relax and think about the week ahead. Everyone who knows me knows I love to dance, and seeing the tango performed in Buenos Aires was incredible. But as the night went on, the tango dancing and the rich food mixed with the champagne and dessert, flashing colored lights, and heavy air swirled around as my head became foggy.

When the show ended, Louise and I perused a small boutique in the lobby, and I carefully selected a handmade silver chain bracelet from the jewelry case as a beautiful reminder of the evening. While there, we enjoyed meeting New York designer Betsy Johnson who was also in the audience and later in the same shop. Every time I wear that bracelet, I think of the tango show and the fun we had, but it also reminds me of something else from that evening I wish I could forget.

We headed outside the lobby and found a taxi. Since we had an early shuttle boat to Montevideo, Uruguay, the next morning to meet our group, sleep was paramount on our list, so we headed straight for bed.

We got to our room and quickly packed for the early morning departure, then fell into our beds. I dozed off quickly, but it wasn't long before my sleep was abruptly interrupted by a sensation of the walls closing in and my strong urge to run outside of the hotel. I had never felt this way before, and it terrified me because I seriously thought about how to navigate exiting our room for the openness of the street in the middle of the night. I felt like I needed the sky over-head and fresh open air. Our hotel room was built closely up against another building, and there was no light and little air circulation in our room. It was stifling and quickly became uncomfortable.

We were told by our travel agent and tour guide that Buenos Aires wasn't particularly safe after dark, and I was so accustomed to New York City where one could go around rather freely. Even though I knew this about Buenos Aires, and the real desire in that moment of walking out the door and down the long hallway to the lobby and out onto the street where I could see the sky and get fresh air was powerful, my conscious mind knew it was ridiculous. I seriously con-templated it for a moment and envisioned myself exiting the hotel as the urge to get out of the building was immediate and strong. I knew it would cause a major stir both in and outside of our room, and I was dumbfounded by how panicked my thoughts were and how strong the desire to flee became. I took a deep breath and tried grounding myself, and decided I would have to stay in the room.

After talking myself out of the crazy idea of exiting the building, I quietly made my way to the bathroom, being careful not to wake Louise. I sat fully clothed in the bathtub without water. Thinking of this now sounds so absurd, but the cold porcelain against my skin and pajamas settled me. Somehow the confinement of the tub made me feel strangely secure. My heart was still pounding out of my chest, and breathing was an extreme effort. I reached for my cell phone, which in itself was an enormous feat because even the tiniest movement felt like an earthquake. Moving as much as one inch or taking a breath seemed to make me believe I might die. Never in my life had I felt this way, and I was surprisingly terrified. Longing to hear a familiar voice and one that would console me, I called my husband.

"I know this sounds crazy, but I need you to stay on the phone with me. I can't breathe, I don't know what's happening, and I'm really scared. I've never felt this way before, and it sounds so stupid, but it's impossible to move. Please just talk to me until I calm down; please stay here and don't leave." I clung to the phone and to Randy's familiar voice and needed him to tell me I was okay. He was a lifeline, and I was so grateful to have his presence with me as I struggled to get a handle on my circumstances. We stayed on for a while before he finally had to go to sleep, and I had to then face the decision to go back to bed or remain in the tub.

As silly as it sounds now, I stayed in the bathroom and quickly focused my attention on the small television at the end of the bathtub. I had never realized that a bathroom television would be such a great diversion, but it was. My anxiety waned and then increased as I thought of Louise waking up and finding me looking foolish lying fully clothed in the bathtub watching Argentinean programming in the middle of the night. With an intent focus on the television, I started to relax a little at a time. I said the Lord's Prayer over and over again, trying to focus on the words and their promise but couldn't submit to their meaning. My mind and body felt like they had been through a battle, and I even considered for a moment that something had been slipped into my drink at the tango show. I didn't know then, but I had experienced an intense panic and anxiety attack. In fact, it was the first one I had ever had, and it would lead to a series of more in the years to come.

That night in Buenos Aires, which left me feeling physically and emotionally paralyzed, was the beginning of something I never anticipated. What I didn't know at the time was the origin of those panic attacks. All I knew was that I never wanted to feel that way again, but I would soon have many other episodes that plagued me until I understood the core reason for the inner fight or flight feelings. What I hadn't trusted enough then was my reliance upon my faith to help me during those stressful times. Fear was creeping in, and I never saw it coming. Psalm 94:19 (NIV) says, "When anxiety was great within me, your consolation brought me joy," which reminds me that all I had to do was ask, and I would have received. I believe there is no greater way to fight fear than with faith.

The next morning was torture. With virtually little to no sleep in me and an unfortunate hangover mixed with the heavy, humid air of the city, we somehow made our way to the port for an early morning ferry to Montevideo. I felt like I had been hit over the head with a bat and could hardly move, yet I had to because this was the beginning of our fabulous trip. Besides, the week ahead meant lots of yoga, dance, and martial arts, so my energy already felt expended just thinking about it. Buenos Aires was beautiful, but my last memory was the sleepless, strange, and torturous night in the bathtub, and I was eager to leave.

Several hours on the ferry with some fresh air proved to be a tonic, and when we got to Uruguay, I felt more refreshed and hopeful that I was distanced from the events of the previous night. We met some of our friends who had already arrived from New York and checked into our accommodations, which had been arranged for the group by our fitness instructor and friend.

We were all staying in a modern boutique hotel, and seeing our friends there made me excited to be in a new environment, yet something inside of me felt a deep, growing terror. I was anticipating fear of the hotel room I was about to share again with Louise. We had traveled the world together and were more than compatible, but I felt enormous stress well up inside of me, thinking I could have another night like the one before. It was embarrassing, and the more I tried to keep my emotions in check, the more panic welled up inside of me. All I could think of when we went to lunch before we checked in was how nervous I was about how the room would make me feel.

It could have easily been blamed on the lack of sleep or the pounding of my head, but when the door opened to the hotel room, I had flashbacks to the night before and was literally in tears imagining what it would be like at night. It sounds silly now, but the confinement of a shared space with fresh memories of panic and anxiety from the night before was too much.

I went down to the lobby and asked for my own room. Louise was understanding as I told her I knew I was headed for another terrible night like the one before and didn't want to share space or the risk of being awake all night while trying to keep quiet. I also realized I needed to have access to a window, so the hotel gave me a room with a sliding glass door. I don't know why needing access to the outdoors or the sky was important, but it was.

Thankfully the night was without incident, but the physical feeling remained a possibility of coming back to me at any time. These feelings were new to me and created fear of what I needed to constantly anticipate next. It became an exhausting mental cycle of worrying about the next potentially uncomfortable environment that would cause me to feel unsafe. I felt controlled by something foreign outside of myself, and the internal battle was noticeable. My friends could tell I was not myself, and I tried harder to hide it, which made the feelings worse.

The next morning, our group loaded into two vans that drove north along the coastline past Punte del Este to José Ignacio, our final destination, which was a beautiful resort town that used to be a fishing village. The new scenery instantly distracted me in a positive way. It was impossible not to be awed by our accommodations at Estancia Vik, an open-air equestrian ranch-themed guest property that sat in the middle of vast green meadows not far from the ocean. The nearby, more modern sister property, Playa Vik, was just a bike ride away and was equally enticing and architecturally spectacular with its abstract angles pushing the limits of gravity. We spent the week enjoying our fitness schedule, which allowed us the use of the grounds at both hotels. It was one of the most beautiful places I have ever been, and I felt fortunate to be there.

During the week, I felt a welcome calm come over me, as I didn't have to navigate small dark spaces in anticipation of anxiety. It was an oasis and a gift to enjoy such incredible beauty with wonderful friends. The breathtaking surroundings, coupled with the challenging yet fun exercise schedule, were just enough to get my mind away from the memories of Buenos Aires and Montevideo.

Horseback riding in the meadows around Estancia helped me relax and commune with nature. Swimming at dusk after yoga in the dazzling dramatic infinity pool at Vik with the constellations shining through from the bottom was mesmerizing. It was easy to get lost in the beauty of it all. Sweeping ocean vistas, endless meadows, amazing local food, mind-blowing architecture with generously vaulted ceilings, powder room sinks, and art made of amethysts and large windows of our room allowed me to get far away from the fear I had felt in Buenos Aires.

However, once the large, heavy drapes of our bedroom were closed at night, I felt the reminder of lingering fear. I felt like a child asking Louise to keep them open just a crack so I could have some light. The darkness threatened to swallow me up and hijack my soul. The possibility of it felt threatening, and I prayed each night for sleep to rescue me.

The entire week in Uruguay was a relaxing once-in-a-lifetime experience, yet deep within me was a brewing internal struggle with a demon that seemed to have come along for the ride from Buenos Aires. It danced in my head, pushing me and enticing me to feel vulnerable and afraid. It wasn't until I was at the airport with our group having a last meal together before embarking on our trip home that I started to fear the flight and the confinement of the plane. One of the women in our group kindly talked me down and helped me through the anticipation of dread and fear that was gaining a grip on me. I had never felt so disconnected from my thoughts and body, but that night in Argentina was the beginning of something I would have to wrestle with and eventually learn how to manage.

Looking back, I can see now that the struggle was also one of searching for signs of light in the dark to anchor me. The constellations below me as I swam in the evening waters of Vik's dramatically angled pool, and the slivers of moonlight piercing through the blackout drapes felt like glimmers of hope and peace. Considering that, now I think of John 1:5 (ESV), "The light shines in the darkness, and the darkness has not overcome it." Light is the only thing that has the capacity to diminish the power of darkness, and I yearned for it. The light was my salvation, and it would take time for me to understand how important it was to spiritually stay in the light and not be swallowed up with fear. Seeds of my lifelong faith were eager to grow, and although I didn't realize it at the time, the beginning of spiritual warfare was also upon me.

I was a prisoner of the early foundation of my life that I didn't see yet. There was a system of invisible control that I was born into and raised with, and I didn't know about it until I broke free and decided to wrestle the enemy that was taunting me my entire life. It would be several years later, with the growing awareness of my dysfunctional immediate family system and the checks and imbalances that were ingrained in me, before I would realize why these episodes of panic and anxiety were happening. They became more and more apparent each time I would leave home, and especially when I would travel.

When I returned to New York, the attacks would begin the moment I contemplated driving, and once on the road, I would have to pull the car off to the shoulder to reclaim my focus. Movie theaters, subways, bridges, elevators, windowless rooms—all were invitations for the grip of darkness and paralysis to set into my mind and overtake me physically. Living in Manhattan definitely didn't help. Even though I loved my city, it became a labyrinth of possible pitfalls to losing control to anxiety. I started to anticipate my surroundings before I would arrive somewhere just to prepare my mind for battle, and it was exhausting.

On subsequent trips out of the country with my fitness group, I experienced similar isolated episodes of intense anxiety and panic. It seemed to happen when I would remove myself from my familiar home environment and view my life and family independently from a distance. I was normally a secure and confident traveler, but the experience in Buenos Aires tipped off a few years of these struggles. The emotional paralysis was at times embarrassing and confusing, as it was counter to the person I knew I was, who was usually very centered and strong. I had a similar agonizing night in a hotel room in Seville, Spain, that nearly forced me to pack my bag and fly home, but the kind support of my friends helped to ground me so that I could ultimately enjoy the trip.

Finally, I decided I'd had enough and wanted to find out why this was happening, solve it, and reclaim my life. I sought the help of a therapist in Manhattan who specialized in panic disorder, and we began a very comprehensive and incredibly helpful series of sessions so I could uncover the underlying reason for what I felt was controlling me. To this day, it was one of the most interesting and helpful things I've ever done to understand the psychology behind what triggers panic and anxiety.

My therapist encouraged my healing through the use of cognitive-behavioral therapy (CBT), which is essentially the management of emotions through talk therapy that focuses on how someone's attitudes, thoughts, and beliefs influence behavior and feelings. She wisely advised me not to address my issue through the use of medication because if I were to have a panic attack and not have access to my medication, it could become an additional stress. I am not opposed to those who do need medication for such things, but in my case, it was something that could have been an additional obstacle to overcome. Needless to say, I had some work to do, and I faced it head-on.

Years earlier, I noticed my father had started to avoid small spaces, large crowds, driving in big cities, and flying, unless absolutely necessary. I also observed that he stopped driving in unfamiliar places, especially at night. Once on a cross-country drive we had made together years earlier, he refused to drive through any big cities and preferred instead to stay in hotels alongside the interstate. It seemed strange to me, as he had always been comfortable traveling, but I noticed the changes over time and was now wondering if it was caused by panic and anxiety.

Once an avid flier, he instead began choosing to travel by train or car whenever possible. As I witnessed these changes, I saw his life appear more and more limited, and it made me realize what I didn't want to become: a prisoner of fear. I was determined to face the issue head-on and push through it and never let anything limit me again. CBT was the beginning of gaining some control at that time, and I was grateful for the help.

So, through careful and incredibly thorough processes, my therapist and I worked together, and slowly but steadily, I began to overcome the panic and anxiety that seemed destined to limit my day-to-day life. Perhaps the most defining moment of the work we did together was when she explained why this happens to people.

"Dena, the feeling of fight or flight you have during a panic or anxiety attack is your body's natural tendency to react to danger. We all have it, but those who suffer from panic attacks have the feeling, and it increases. Most often, it is rooted in a feeling of not being in control of some area of your life, so your body learns to react in a way that tells the brain you are in some sort of danger, so you experience feelings of fight or flight, to protect yourself." I falsely assumed my marriage was the underlying cause but later would realize that the core culprit was the dysfunctional patterns from my upbringing. It didn't become clear overnight, but I soon learned and believed that my deeply rooted patriarchal family system was stifling me and keeping me in a state of anticipating or experiencing panic.

What I learned later was how much of a prisoner I had become in my own mind and body from this complicated family of origin and how much I wanted out of feeling controlled. I loved my family deeply but didn't understand that my place and purpose among them was different than what I'd believed. The inner conflict was building, and all I could do was hold on and try to get a handle on it before it robbed me of my personal freedom.

Later I would learn that the dance of fear and anxiety was the enemy's way of trying to knock me down. First Peter 5:8 (NIV) warns us to "Be alert and of sober mind. Your enemy the devil prowls around like a roaring lion looking for someone to devour." The truth is I was not of sober mind while enjoying the night at the tango show. I was vulnerable being far from home, away from the familiar surroundings of my life, and perfect prey for the enemy to attack and try to destroy. He would soon find out that I was the wrong dance partner for such deception because I had God on my side.

The Temperature of Clarity

The waves of death swirled about me;
the torrents of destruction overwhelmed me.

2 Samuel 22:5 (NIV)

Clarity revealed itself the moment pain rushed in, like a rogue wave crashing to shore. Anything in its path would be wiped away only to expose those things that withstood the impact. After nearly fifty years of seeing my life through a lens I didn't realize was foggy, the sudden clarity burned my eyes, yet I could now see for miles, and almost overnight, the predictable landscape of life I once knew became rocky and hard to navigate. It was as though I could clearly see what was before me for the first time, and yet it appeared too steep and dangerous. I felt like a hiker who had embarked on a day excursion on what she believed to be familiar paths, only to have the weather change and take me suddenly off course and into the unchartered wilderness alone with few provisions. No longer was the trajectory of my life the one I thought it would be. My quest for independence was going to come at an enormous price.

A line was being drawn, and the shift was already happening. I was about to get a glimpse into the crevasse of my new and unpredictable life and see what was going to fall away and what would remain. The unusual behavior of my brother and parents was something that didn't make sense at the time. Looking back now, I can see that it was a rebirth and a sign from God that change was necessary. Hebrews 12:26-27 (NIV) says, "At that time his voice shook the earth, but now he has promised, 'Once more I will shake not only the earth but also the heavens.'" The words "once more" indicate the removing of what can be shaken—that is, created things—so that what cannot be shaken may remain."

***

I was on one of the highest floors of the building known as "Big Pink," a prominent luminous light pink glass skyscraper in downtown Portland. Ignoring a view I would have usually admired, with snowcapped Mt. Hood in the distance, I was all business sitting across from Michael Sutton, the lawyer I had found through the recommendation of a trusted friend in New York. I sought more understanding and answers to the operating agreement I had signed months earlier with my brother. It was a conversation I wish I'd been able to have with Alan Gartner, the lawyer who represented the LLC with whom an in-person meeting Gary had earlier discouraged.

On this trip, I had even reached out to Alan, who helped my brother craft the agreement, yet we were unable to establish a face-to-face meeting in my hometown of Eugene, where his office was located. When I finally got him on the phone, I asked him some questions, which he kindly answered, and then stopped short and told me that he could no longer help me and that I should seek my own counsel. What did that mean? He worked for the LLC for which I was half owner, and, suddenly, he was telling me he couldn't answer my questions and to go elsewhere for answers. I took his advice and sought my own counsel on my terms and decided to bill the LLC. After all, I was just trying to get some questions answered on an agreement I had signed as a partner.

More and more, I felt I had been played. Something was not right, and the fog was lifting. I wasn't focused on the picture-postcard view out the window but instead on the emerging clarity of my own jagged horizon. It wasn't anything I wished to ponder but had to. In only a few short months, the pain had thrust me into tackling new terrain by delving into things that would have previously not been allowed. But I was wiser now and knew I didn't need permission because I realized I had rights. I say "allowed" and "permission" because these were the untold boundaries I had blindly grown up with in my immediate patriarchal family system. It was all I knew, and although I felt respected at times, there appeared to be an invisible chain of command, and it usually made me feel I had to ask instead of state things.

I was about to grow up very fast. The blinders were coming off quickly, and all I wanted to know was whether the answers Gary provided to my questions prior to the signing were true. My unwavering trust in the men in my immediate family had clearly been too much. I felt at the time of the agreement signing when my whole world was turning upside down; he seemed to get me right where he wanted me: trusting him, believing him, and guided by him. I had never been so wrong.

The solid ground I thought we had shared started to immediately feel shaky as I remembered Gary had abruptly dropped Randy as trustee of his son's trust and quickly relinquished his role as the trustee on Randy's life insurance policy. All of these things would have happened in time, of course, but there wasn't huge animosity and fighting between Randy and me when we split. We knew we had responsibilities and kids to raise and our finances to manage together, and it was imperative that we remain a team. We knew that such changes would happen and that they would do so over time. Randy hadn't even moved out yet, and already Gary was in motion to change things.

Just after I had signed the agreement with my brother in November and right before Christmas, he dropped these bombshells on us, which cost us thousands of dollars of legal fees right before the holidays. We scrambled to place Randy's brother as the new trustee on his life insurance and struggled to face high legal costs for which we weren't prepared. It was the first Christmas I remember in all of our years together when we didn't even buy a tree, and it would be the last Christmas the four of us would celebrate together as a family.

When I think about the pain of our impending breakup and how important that last Christmas was, especially for the kids, and how my brother's actions seemed to literally wipe us out financially until the end of the year, I still can't help but feel resentment. There were few small presents laid out along the windowsill at our house in Connecticut near where the tree would usually be. It was a pitiful holiday.

Things were beginning to be so financially tight as Randy's industry was tanking with the sinking economy. He was a municipal bond trader and had had a very successful career up to that point, but the economy and his segment of the market was dramatically changing for almost everyone in his business. Suddenly, with our announcement of an imminent breakup on the horizon, the attitude of Gary and my parents felt unusually cold and impersonal. The more I needed the emotional support of my family, the more distant they became. Even with the growing divide in our marriage, Randy and I remained committed to being as peaceful as possible under the circumstances and always intended to put our kids first.

Despite our pain, we were intent on being responsible throughout the arduous process we knew was ahead. It, therefore, came as a surprise the way my family reacted. We had separated in the past on different terms, but this time it was me feeling like I wanted a break or, ultimately, out.

"You're ruining your life, Dena," my dad said. "You and Randy should live together for the next few years and make it work until Lily is out of school," was my mom's mantra. Why they felt it was their place to say these things perplexed me. It was our life, our marriage, and our decision. It was clear that they were not going to be emotionally supportive and that even though we were deciding to mediate and focus on the kid's well-being throughout the painful process, none of that seemed to matter.

Knowing I was facing a divorce, my brother had suddenly stirred up issues that immediately cost us money we didn't yet want or have to spend. It was as though someone had taken the steering wheel out of the hands of our lives and drove us into a different direction, with obstacles we weren't ready to tackle. We were focused on our kids being home, having Christmas, and somehow getting them through the knowledge that their dad and I were soon to be going our separate ways. Gary's actions, while a business transaction on behalf of estate planning, came at an awkward time and didn't give me the feeling he was as supportive as he had been in the months prior. Something inside of me wasn't settled, and I wanted to get answers, so they came to me loud and clear that day in Big Pink.

The meeting was nothing more than a review of the operating agreement and a more detailed legal explanation than my brother had given me of what I had signed. I was a fifty-percent shareholder of a valuable company and suddenly felt like a fool as the lawyer explained in layman's terms that the agreement I had signed was one that placed me in the role of a silent partner. I was told that the language was slightly unclear, even to him, in some areas, and I believe I had apparently been steered away from having a professional explain it to me for fear I would not sign it. Now I understood why Gary insisted on being the only one to answer my questions and claim that paying the lawyer to do so would be an expensive waste.

According to counsel, Gary had full control as laid out in the agreement, and by me signing it, I had relinquished my rights to make decisions or have a say on almost anything. We jointly owned commercial and residential properties in three different states, and I had never had a problem with him managing the LLC, nor did I ever intend to take away his power or his job. I signed with the understanding that I would have a voice in matters that concerned us both but with him at the full operational helm. I was shocked he would set it up this way because I had never given him reason to feel he wasn't in charge.

The irony suddenly wasn't lost on me that he demanded I sign around the same time a lot of changes were happening within the dynamics of our extended family. Looking back, I recall that my grandfather was ill, and our relatives, including my father, were worried about his hip surgery. My grandmother's dementia was worsening, and the relocation of my grandparents into a nursing home was on the horizon. Simultaneously, my husband and I were announcing our intended split, and that was upsetting and sad for everyone involved. Randy had been in my life since I was fifteen, and he was sixteen, and I knew then, as I know now, he was never someone to go after anything that wasn't his. We had our issues, but the apparent fear I see now that I believe my brother and likely my parents had was perhaps the reason for the sudden shift in what my parents always had proudly claimed to be an equal partnership and ownership between their two children. Being coerced into being a silent partner felt like one thing: control and fear on my brother's behalf of what my life might be like after my divorce. It made me feel sick to my stomach and actually drew me closer to the man I was planning to divorce because I knew his character but seemingly had miscalculated the lack of it in my brother.

My parents had mentioned to me many times in the past that Gary had often complained to them, saying I wasn't available to talk or wasn't interested in the business. Some of that was true, as I was 3000 miles away and not involved in the daily ins and outs of managing tenants in commercial properties or taking care of leases and other details he claimed as his full-time job. His calls to me always came around dinnertime on the east coast when my young kids were home or when we were getting ready to do homework. His complaints to our parents about how I wasn't interested became a broken record of theirs to me, and my many attempts to set up a weekly call that worked for both of our schedules fell flat. I believe his interest was never to sincerely partner with me at all; instead, I think he was seemingly motivated to run things himself and create a narrative that I was never available or interested in the company.

The truth was I was trying to keep my marriage together after a tough split some years earlier while managing many demands that raising kids in New York City and later out-of-state boarding school required of me. The few times I wanted to be involved in the business, I felt sidelined. My mother and brother took over a project on one of the residential properties I wished to manage, and after much pressing, I was finally brought in at the very end once most of the work was accomplished.

As an active member for decades in other family entities, a limited partner in the family business, and as a mother of two trying to keep my marriage and routine together, I was busy but not disinterested. Sometimes the most ridiculous comments by my parents would surface—that I lived too far away to be involved or that I wasn't available for proper communication. International corporations flourish in global markets with the use of modern technology, but somehow, our little LLC was something I lived too far from, in their eyes, to be a significant and effective partner. It was laughable, actually, especially in light of what I was managing successfully on my own as a New York City mother, without any family around to help.

I was deeply involved with my children's schools volunteering as co-chair of the Diversity Committee, the Book Fair, and the Communications Department as a writer for the school newsletter. I worked with the Development Office helping raise large funds by co-chairing two big annual auctions, one of them at the United Nations. I attended field trips, helped with bake sales while getting the kids to their tutors, music lessons, sports activities, and doctor appointments. It wasn't anything that other moms didn't do but learning to navigate some of that in and around Manhattan with taxis and strollers when the kids were little was a learned skill and a far cry from my upbringing in suburban Oregon. I was a busy New York City wife, mother, and volunteer and managed it well but certainly wasn't incapable of taking a properly scheduled call with my brother to discuss business matters.

Years later, it would become easy to see how I believe my brother seemed to know how to build trust and then find the weakest moment to present what he wanted, knowing how to persuade the outcome in his favor. It was a pattern I would come to recognize many times over in the years to follow, but at this moment, I was just barely seeing the crack in the façade.

I had been brought in during the summer of 2015 to learn more and partner with him on the ins and outs of the various deals and how things operated. Trust was being built, and he appeared to have a genuine interest in working with me. I knew the properties well as they had all been in the family for decades, and my brother made it clear to me before I signed the agreement by saying, "once we get mom and dad out of their last five percent, we can make our own decisions, Dena, and do what we want and call our own shots."

I was naïve to think he was referring to "we," meaning he and I were a team. But I suddenly learned that the document I read over several times carefully and trusted his answers had ambiguous language and details I thought I understood but didn't. It felt immediately evident why he didn't want to spend a few hundred dollars for me to meet with the attorney who drafted the agreement. I foolishly relinquished that right and couldn't believe my own brother would seemingly do such a thing. Now I was also starting to have clarity and an understanding as to why Alan Gartner told me to get my own counsel.

To make things worse, I learned that Gary and my sister-in-law, Micaela, had taken a large loan from the LLC years before to make a down payment on their home in the Bay Area. They borrowed a significant six-figures, and with some further research, I learned that shortly after Gary became general operating manager, he apparently changed the loan to a distribution without notifying anyone, thus never having to pay the loan back to the company. When I inquired with accounting about the transaction, I learned that my father was surprised when he received the financial statements to see that Gary had rolled the loan into the capital account, thus converting it to a tax-free distribution. It was then that my father asked at the office about what happened to the loan.

Regardless, it seemed my brother wasn't ever held accountable. Years later, my father would claim that he was in support of it, but that seemed counter to what I learned about his surprised reaction at the office when he first became aware of my brother's actions on the account. My observation over the last few years was that my dad seemed to easily change his narrative on past events, and this would be one of them.

A few years prior, Randy and I had found the apartment of our dreams in Williamsburg. Not only was it an amazing investment before the area became really popular, but it was a place we felt we could live forever. We could ultimately afford it, yet we were just shy by a few months on a part of the down payment. I told my father about the opportunity and the area and how we were trying to figure out a way to bridge the temporary gap on the five figures we were a few months shy of being able to fully put down. "I really wish I could find a way to help you, but I can't," he said. He never told me that I had the right to take the same sort of loan my brother did. What I didn't realize at the time was that the amount I was seeking to borrow for only a couple of months was barely six percent of the amount my brother and sister-in-law had borrowed from the LLC to make a much more significant down payment on a house.

It was years later when I found out that my brother's opportunity was not the same for me, even though we were equal but at the time much smaller shareholders in the company. I was never fully informed of the details of the loan, the conversion of the loan to a distribution, or the ability I had to have taken a larger loan myself to help my husband and me bridge the gap on something we would have easily paid back within some months.

The information I sought by traveling from New York to Portland was worse than expected. My mind was reeling, and I had to clear my thoughts as best as I could because I had scheduled another meeting with our investment broker a short time after that. The office had dealt with my family for generations, managing personal and business accounts. My kids had accounts there, and I had every right to visit the office, especially since I was facing a divorce. The purpose of the meeting was to have an overview of everything so I could understand exactly where things stood personally and professionally. I was taking the advice my dad always gave me, which was to call upon these investment professionals anytime for guidance and information. He always encouraged me to be connected with the investment team, and it was as good a time as any to visit with them as I had many times before.

They went over my accounts and those of my children, and I notified them of my marital split. I was told it was responsible for me to update them of such changes, and then I also said that I wanted to go over the investment portfolio for the LLC. I was brought up to speed on all and left the office feeling good about the meeting.

All I had done was come to Portland and meet face to face with people who could objectively give me the professional answers I needed and to have them update me on the current financial snapshot of my life. I decided to give Gary a call and tell him I had some new understanding of things and wanted to talk it through. It was time for transparency and clarity between us. He was alone in Hawaii for a shareholder meeting, and I decided it was as good a time as any to reach him so we could try to get on the same page. I felt empowered and calm as I picked up the phone to dial, and when I heard his voice on the other end, he said he was headed to his car, and I asked him to give me a moment before he started to drive. I wanted to be very clear and also give him a chance to respond thoughtfully to my questions.

"I am calling to let you know I'm in Portland and have had a few meetings to get a handle on my financials before the divorce and also better understand our operating agreement." There was a noticeable pause, and I took a deep breath and asked if he would accept my request for a distribution for which I was sorely overdue. The records reflected an enormous imbalance in our capital accounts by six figures due to his loan conversion, and I was asking for a tiny percentage of that, which wouldn't begin to scratch the surface on equalizing the obvious discrepancy. Immediately he listed everything that was not going well with the company and seemed to make excuses as to how financially stretched it was and skirted my request. He refused to answer my questions and said he would get back to me.

I knew I was acting well within my rights of the agreement and, as a partner, was requesting to be treated equally if not fairly. I also knew now that he was managing some of the investments much differently than I would have had I been in his position. Two days passed before he called me back. I sensed a power struggle brewing and firmly said that I would not leave Portland until my more than reasonable request would be honored. His anger appeared to build as I asked more questions about the new operating agreement and about the answers to my questions he had given me prior to signing. I made it clear that some of those answers were now very counter to what I had learned in an hour with an attorney of my choosing. The new questions I was raising were not being answered now, and a chill went up my spine as I felt fear take over.

There is a moment just before you decide to jump into a swimming pool, knowing it is cold, that you must brace yourself for that quick, sharp jolt of temperature difference between air and water. I knew I was committed to jumping in but didn't realize how long the sting between the two elements would last. It was at this moment I was about to find out.

Street Talk

Your word is a lamp to my feet
and a light to my path.

Psalm 119:105 (ESV)

"Your mother called me and asked for an appointment as she is worried about you," my therapist said to me on the phone. We never talked in between my weekly in-person appointments in Chelsea, so her outgoing call to me seemed important. I couldn't remember how my mother could have gotten the contact information for her, but it soon dawned on me. She had offered to help pay for a few sessions a month or so earlier when money was tight right after Randy moved out in January 2016. It must have been when she asked where to send the check that she kept the information and likely looked up the phone number. "Why does my mom want to talk to you?" I asked. "I thought our sessions were private." She explained that with the consent of the patient, it could sometimes be helpful to talk to an outside family member to understand more of what might be going on in a person's life that might not be coming up in session.

My father had messaged me days before on my birthday, saying, "I think your therapist is taking advantage of you." I don't recall how I answered him but didn't agree. His comment seemed counter to my mom's sudden interest in speaking to my therapist, and I wanted to believe she had good intentions. This all happened shortly after Randy and I separated, and my parents were reaching into corners of my life that I had foolishly assumed at the time were for my benefit.

My dad had taken the liberty to contact an insurance agent on a policy I had while reminding me about the money he knew I had in various dwindling accounts. It felt like a temperature reading on my life, and they were doing the parental thing by watching out for me, or so I assumed. "I wish you were feeling better on your birthday. Love, Dad." I don't remember feeling awful when he texted me, yet I am sure I wasn't jumping for joy on February 7, 2016, with all of the fractured parts of my life moving quickly around me while feeling unusually exposed.

My mom's concern at the time seemed normal, as the marriage of her daughter had fallen apart. I often spoke to my parents, brother, and a few trusted friends about the painful situations that were quickly unfolding. Any normal mother would be worried about her daughter and grandchildren, so a talk with my therapist, although unconventional, would maybe be okay after all. My mother said she was worried about me and wanted to check on how I was doing and offer any help she could. It seemed normal enough at the time. When I asked her why she went to my therapist instead of coming to me first, she said she was "concerned" and that I wasn't behaving normally. I'm not sure what "normal" is supposed to be when your whole world feels like it's falling apart at once, but she insisted that she "had a right" as my mother to be worried.

My vulnerability was that I also trusted my therapist explicitly. But isn't that what is supposed to happen between doctor and patient? I'd come to find our sessions extremely helpful as I navigated not only the anxiety but also the painful areas of my life. She was smart, forthright, and held me accountable for everything I brought into our sessions. I respected her professionalism, and trusted her so much, and knew I was safe. My belief was that my mom was putting us both in a hard position, and I didn't know what to do. I had the right to say no and wasn't pressured to accept the meeting between them, and I held hope that my mom's outreach was for the right reason.

Looking back, it's easy to see where I was failing to lean on God first. "I would feel most comfortable if you just listen to what my mom has to say but would appreciate my privacy being protected," I said as I cautiously consented to their meeting. "I don't know what you would need to offer that I couldn't myself." I thought I had a good relationship with my mom, but things between us were starting to change, and I didn't quite have an understanding of it yet. Because I greatly respected my therapist, I finally agreed that she could set up the call with my mother but with strict conditions, as there was something nagging at me that didn't feel totally right, yet I still consented.

January 2016, just a few months earlier, when the bottom had dropped out of my life, remains as one of the most emotionally searing and painful months I have ever lived through. Randy and I decided to part ways after nearly thirty years of marriage. We had been together since I met him in high school at the age of fifteen, and now I was alone. After years of working on the marriage, I felt a deep urge to break free, and it felt liberating and sickening all at

once. The panic attacks, empty nest, our increasingly divided interests, extended family pressure, job stress, and rumblings of a possible
move out of New York were all happening at the same time.

At the time, I primarily blamed my marriage for suffocating
me and believed that if I could just live by myself for a period of
time, even with a separation, that I could feel whole and get to know
myself or at least hear my own voice. I had been in the relationship
most of my life, so it was a yearning to be alone and figure out who I
was and to find my own calling.

Years before, Randy had moved into his own apartment as we
took a break from things, and now I felt like it was something I
needed as I was feeling lost. Instead, the space I sought for myself
came at a huge emotional price, as we finally discussed what I never
truly thought we would face: divorce. We had been through more
than most couples our age and were incredibly resilient but tired and
slowly drifting away from one another. Out of respect for the life we
have spent together and the children we share, I still can't believe this
is how it ended between us, but it did.

I foolishly believed that the panic attacks and lack of control I
felt over myself and who I was and wanted to be was because I was
swallowed up in the lives of my husband and kids. Initially, it was
easy to blame my marriage, but as time went on, I started to see
things very differently. I believe that as much as I felt controlled by
my dysfunctional family of origin, Randy likely did too, and I am
convinced that this challenging dynamic was also detrimental to our
marriage. Out of desperation to find myself and get the space I so
desperately craved, he moved out, and I found myself alone with
our two cats in a brand new three-bedroom two-bath apartment in
trendy Williamsburg, Brooklyn. I finally got my alone space, but I
hadn't dreamed it would be at such a personal price. When I look
back, I often say I was living in the right place at the wrong time.

I spent many evenings alone pounding the broken sidewalks,
lost in thoughts while exploring the old Polish neighborhood that
was beginning to gentrify. After eighteen years of living in uptown
Manhattan, Brooklyn was a welcome change. Instead of high-rise
apartment buildings with gloved doormen ushering nannies with

strollers, deliverymen, well-heeled uptowners, and their dogs through revolving doors to wide, smooth sidewalks with manicured patches of green space, I walked more carefully past my virtual doorman front door onto broken cobblestones and uneven concrete.

Williamsburg was cool, and I felt the streets spoke to me through all of the neighborhood graffiti. I quickly made peace with it, as it seemed to be everywhere, even in our garage. It soon became an obsession, as did the evolving street art for which the neighborhood was becoming internationally known. With music blasting in my headphones, I walked and walked and took photos of every bit of graffiti or street art that caught my eye. Taggers would cover something, and the next day the same wall could look different. I loved it, and between the music in my headphones, the uneven sidewalks, and my messy life, the streets numbed me from what I was beginning to face, yet not fully understanding all that was ahead. I felt a part of my story being expressed through the graffiti. What I saw was the pain, creative energy, and beauty in the messages, and I loved how the streets seemed to have a conversation with me. I was never alone because something was always being said from the streets.

One mural that was installed across the street from my apartment took on a special meaning. As I turned the corner from Bedford Avenue to North 10th Street one afternoon, I saw two people sketching the framework of a large image. Each day as I walked home from the L Train, I would round the corner and see the stages of what would soon become my new neighbor and friend. The gentle yet intense face of a young man with golden-brown skin, long dark hair, and deep eyes soon graced the side of the building next to the car repair garage. The artist had painted the complexion so realistically that up close, one could see the pores of the skin and the whiskers growing from his beard. It was as if a living, breathing human being was standing in front of me each time I gazed at the brilliant image.

Street artists often sign their murals with their Instagram address, and I soon became a loyal follower of @Jorit. I posted the evolving images on my Instagram page as a sort of visual diary without realizing it. Being able to express my emotions visually was a way to tell the story I didn't know was unfolding, but it became an outlet of expression. As alone as I felt, the people in the street art became silent friends who seemed to watch over me. What I didn't see then was that God was actually the real watchman, but I remained visually ensconced in what was evolving around the neighborhood.

Andy Warhol and Jean-Michel Basquiat, side by side in one of my all-time favorites on nearby North 9th Street, was colorfully painted by the Brazilian street artist widely known as @Kobrastreetart in his signature geometric design. I adored "my boys," as I called them, and stood in solidarity with the painted message on the mural "Fight For Street Art." Protect Yo Heart by @uncuttart was a message I found on the sidewalks every day, not only in Brooklyn but also in Manhattan. The messages came at me like ticker tape, and I felt not only the streets talking to me but suddenly God as well.

My emotions and routine were tangled, and life felt unpredictable, like the old streets I walked at night to clear my mind and filling it with new messages. "Loveless," "You Go Girl," "Love Breeds Love," "Love Is Love," "Follow Your <3," "Don't Fret," "Jesus Saves," "Love Wins," and "Too Many Humans Not Enough Souls," were words painted high and low. I soaked it up and took them as little signs that life would be okay. A favorite, which has since been painted over, said, *"You may paint over me, but I will still be here."* To this day, I still know exactly where that was painted on North 3rd Street, and I am glad to know it's still there under the layers. It reminds me that despite what or who covers you up in life, you still matter and exist.

Life as I had known it was burying me alive, yet now I was alone, unclear of my future and definitely naïve to the excruciating pain that was coming my way. That January, I lost myself in glasses of red wine at a favorite table at a Chinese restaurant on Bedford Avenue. I foolishly looked to the fortune cookie for more answers on my future. I was gazing into the abyss. One of our beloved cats had to be put down the same week Randy moved out. The awkward silence by some friends, my parents, and my brother becoming quieter magnified the feeling of loss all around me.

My place in the life I once knew was over. The awareness of this new reality was overwhelming. It was like the meals I was eating, too much, too rich, and too late. The fortunes from the cookies were empty, and I wasn't centered enough in seeking a higher place on a daily basis. Although I slept with a plaque hanging on the wall next to my bed that had the serenity prayer on it, I really wasn't living the message. The words were right, and over and over again, I accepted them yet wasn't putting them into practice. "God grant me the serenity to accept the things I cannot change, the courage to change the things I can, and the wisdom to know the difference." I got it, and I believed it, yet I wasn't fully living it. Something was missing.

Our kids were understandably hurting from the recent breakup of their parents, and I knew there was little I could do to help them and what made matters worse was they were away at school. I worried about them and knew they were concerned about their dad and me, especially with the unfolding stress of the extended family issues that were compounding our already painful circumstances with divorce. Sometimes I said too much to them out of my pain, and other times I said too little. There was no blueprint for what we would feel or face as a family or as individuals, but I knew we were each living with our own agony, and it added to the pile of regrets and resentments.

During this time, Lily reached out to me by sending a song that I will never forget as the lyrics seemed to say all that she couldn't. The gesture meant so much to me and also showed me her own strength in the storm. "Mom, I love you, and this song reminds me of you right now." I downloaded it and added it to my playlist, and as the song "Something Beautiful" by Tori Kelly unfolded, I felt my daughter's heart pour out to me through the lyrics, "In every teardrop there is something beautiful, Oh you are stronger than you know…"

The song was about fighting battles that felt unwinnable yet being strong despite the pain, and it kept playing over and over in my mind. I felt my daughter trying to reach me through the lyrics, telling me that I will get through this no matter what and that she was conveying to me through song that to her, I was strong and beautiful despite the battles. It made me feel as though my daughter was walking alongside me, and it gave me comfort.

One night after walking home from a restaurant, I was deeply lost in my thoughts with the wine and the music and the pain. I didn't realize it then, but the friendly girl who worked at the corner bodega saw me and said to me days later that she was worried when she noticed me walking and crying. She observed that I had headphones on and couldn't hear her, but she felt drawn to come after me and see if I was okay. My marriage and family were shattered, but the girl in the bodega cared. She seemed to see past the pain that was covering me up like the layers of paint over graffiti, trying to make me disappear. Her words made me realize some people still had compassion. I now just needed to learn how to care for myself and find true inner peace.

***

Tensions were running high between my parents and me, and heated conversations led me to finally seek advice from my therapist about how best to handle the mounting situation. The more I was learning about the new operating agreement I had signed with my brother, the more I was questioning my position (or lack thereof) in the LLC, which was intended by my parents to be an equal partnership. I felt that call to my brother in Hawaii was met with hostility and abruptness, and Gary said he would call me back, but it was some time before he did and his avoidance of me was both noticeable and concerning.

He finally did come through with the distribution I demanded while in Portland but made it clear that going forward, there would be no more. As he set the new rules, I was reminded of the enormous six-figure disparity between our capital accounts and felt it was not fair. I kept trying to open the door and gain clarity, but it was being closed again and again with inaccurate accusations of my motives. Reaching my parents on this issue became paramount, and my therapist advised me to sit down and write out the facts in a timeline and request a conference call with them from their winter home in Tucson.

The call lasted two hours with my parents on the line allowing me to tell my side of what I had learned with my meeting in Portland with the attorney who helped me understand the operating agreement I signed with my brother. My parents insisted they had not read the operating agreement, nor would they, as they claimed that they "didn't want to take sides." They made it clear that it was between my brother and me and they were no longer involved in any capacity. Nonetheless, they allowed me time to explain where I was coming from on the growing issue, and I was grateful.

My therapist reminded me to be factual and non-emotional and just explain what I had learned during my meeting. Following my prepared notes helped me keep order to what I was trying to express. I felt the conversation went well, and my father and I agreed that more communication with my brother was essential. Then suddenly, the mood shifted as soon as I shared my knowledge about my brother's loan from the LLC, which he converted to a distribution, thus creating an enormous imbalance in the members' capital accounts. I questioned whether they were aware of this six-figure discrepancy between my brother and me, to which my father became furious and started raising his voice and promptly exited the room. That abruptly ended the call, and I was suddenly left with more questions than answers in my attempt to close the loop with them and the growing divide between their two children.

It was soon thereafter that they started accusing me of suing my brother and wanting to use the business as a means to support me through my divorce, which was the furthest thing from the truth. I felt it was incredibly irresponsible for them to say that my meeting with a lawyer meant I was suing Gary. Just because someone seeks legal advice does not necessarily mean someone is suing another. My meeting with the attorney in Portland was nothing more than me trying to get much-needed objective legal advice on something I signed and was beginning to realize felt like a setup. I never imagined that seeking such advice would mean I would be accused of bringing a suit against my brother, but sadly, that is what became their narrative from that point forward.

I believed my parents were afraid because of their own experience with my mom's sister, who had gone through several divorces and often relied upon them for financial support. They couldn't have been more wrong about me, and yet I believe their fear is what put into motion their steadfast belief that I was just looking for handouts. It was evident my parents had no concept of matrimonial law or fair financial agreements in divorce, so I felt like their past experience with others who had fallen out of their marriages and received handouts from them were the assumptions they had put on me. My intent was to partner with my brother and become more involved in co-managing our assets while being a united team. It was becoming clear to me that the equal partnership they intended for their two children was really proving to be one-sided.

I was unsuccessful in reaching an understanding with my father in the conference call as his sudden departure from the heart of the conversation signaled that he was not going to discuss the subject anymore. For this reason, I believed it was important to try to at least reach my mother as she appeared to have what I thought to be some lasting compassion and willingness to hear my side. For some time, I had sensed that she felt more comfortable talking to me when my father wasn't around. I remember her communicating to me at times that she would call me as soon as he was out of the house.

Pressure was mounting daily. With little clarity on where my brother was with me in the partnership, as well as my unfolding divorce, everything around me felt like it was unwinding at once. I was pushed from every side and never felt so alone and misunderstood. I wasn't familiar with the term "gaslighting" then, but I believe it was exactly what was happening to me as my reality was being constantly questioned. Trying to be heard by my parents was an exercise in absolute frustration, and I had finally had enough and blew up at my mother. Perhaps I was impatient in my attempts to connect with her, having failed to do so with a call that later led to an angry written exchange between us in late February. Looking back now, I believe wholeheartedly that I was provoked into a rage that could be used against me later.

My father had an angry outburst toward me one summer when I was around the age of eighteen and working for him at his hotel in my hometown. The reasons for the disagreement were rooted in things that were happening behind the scenes at his business that I felt he didn't want to acknowledge. I came home speaking what I believed to be the truth, seeing things firsthand, and trying to get him to see what he was refusing to address. His reaction was to take the phone from our kitchen and rip it from the mounting on the wall and throw it through the glass backdoor window.

It's an incident I had forgotten about for years until this moment between my mother and I ensued. Instead of throwing something and breaking it, I said a lot of angry things and vented what felt like years of all of my pent-up frustration toward her expressing my extreme disappointment and utter hatred for her inability to listen or even show an effort to understand me. I used expletives and some words I can't take back, but I own it, and I am sorry. I recall being so pushed to my limit with frustration that I just used every ounce of anger and unfortunately put it into writing, foolishly assuming it was private and just between us.

Never did I think that my words would be saved and later taken out of context, much less kept in a file by my father and shown to people at the office or relatives, but they were, and I was told as much by those he approached. I felt it soon became the basis of my parents' claim that I was mentally ill and that they were likely trying to establish that as a means to discredit me. One extreme moment of stress, frustration, and shock over them not acting at all like what I believed loving and fair-minded parents should be sent me into a moment of overwhelming sadness and rage. I was facing divorce and was broke, scared, alone, and my words were being twisted, and the sudden awareness of what I perceived to be my mom and dad's unwillingness to consider my side of things with my brother was just more than I could take, so I got very angry. Honestly, I think anyone in my situation would react with some upset, but it became a point of reference for my parents, which they wouldn't let go.

I had forgotten about my dad and the window he broke years ago with the house phone, but as I was blamed over and over for having such a vile temper in that one moment, I started to recall vividly some of the outbursts my father used to have during my upbringing and the phone incident was a big one. To be fair, years later, he mustered up an apology to me that appeared to cause him pain, but he did say he wished he had listened to me and that I had been right. I remember so well how anguished he was to admit he was wrong, and his eighteen-year-old daughter had brought things to his attention he wished he had acknowledged, but at the time, he just got mad. Apology accepted, and we moved on, but it wasn't until I had an outburst that I remembered the kitchen door and the three solid weeks of silence in which he refused to speak to me. Somehow, we moved on and never spoke about it again. But the file with copies of what I thought to be a private exchange between my mother and me, something he tried to show others, felt like an attempt to undermine me and prove what my parents claimed was my mental illness.

Around the same time my mother wanted to speak to my therapist, I found out that I required a complicated surgical biopsy to rule out breast cancer. I had faced the same situation years before, and it was coming at me again, but this time I was facing it alone. My kids were away at school, Randy had moved out, my parents weren't available, and most of my friends felt distant in light of our recent divorce rumblings. It was an awkward time.

I took a cab to the hospital in Manhattan, unsure how I would get home to Brooklyn after the surgery, knowing they wouldn't likely dismiss me unless I had someone waiting. I was scared even though I knew I was in good hands with the surgeon who had performed the same surgery years before at Sloan Kettering. I still felt very alone. I'd hoped my mother would at least call and ask how I was, but there was silence. Her interest in seeking a meeting with my therapist in Chelsea seemed to take precedence over my surgery at the Dubin Breast Center of the Tisch Cancer Institute at Mount Sinai Hospital on the Upper East Side.

The environment at the cancer center felt serious and scary as I sat alone, waiting to change into my hospital gown. I prayed and asked God to be with me and knew I would try to lean on my faith but the feelings of wanting my mother were overwhelming. Once in the dressing room, I started to make the change into the blue gown and funny hospital socks. I had flashbacks to when I was changing for my planned cesareans at both Santa Monica Hospital, where Jaylen was born, and later at Lenox Hill in Manhattan, where Lily was delivered. Both times my parents were eagerly awaiting the birth of their grandchildren in the waiting rooms and being supportive as parents are in such moments. This time I was facing another possible cancer scare, and no one was waiting for me on the outside. At least I didn't believe so.

As I folded my clothes and stepped outside the curtain, my dearest friend, Donatella, stood there with her arms outstretched and said, "I'm right here, my sister; you aren't alone. I don't want you to go through this all by yourself." I started to cry. She had driven to Manhattan from Long Island, and as clear as an answered prayer, she stood there and promised she would be waiting for me to make sure I got home safely.

By the grace of God, the results of my biopsy came back negative a few weeks later, but the call I expected from my parents to check on me and see about the outcome never came.

Strong Currents

We're all equal before a wave.

Laird Hamilton

I trusted him. Although I was nervous, I mostly felt excited. Paddling out, I carefully followed him past the comfort of the reef and the shallower areas I knew well to new depths I had only seen from shore or from the safety of a boat. He said we didn't need an instructor, and I didn't question his judgment.

I was probably about thirteen years old at the time, and I always felt safe with my dad. We were closer than any father and daughter I knew, and I often had friends say how lucky I was to have him in my life the way I did. I considered our bond to be special, and I loved my dad immensely. His word meant everything to me, and I looked up to him and often told people he was my hero. We loved to ski and hike together, and surfing felt like a natural new thing to try. We both enjoyed being active in the outdoors, and this was no exception.

He guided me toward the horizon as the water turned from blue to black. Suddenly when I glanced over my shoulder, the distance to shore appeared to be the length of a football field or more, and I felt he was my lifeline to getting back. Our approach seemed to come only from spending years watching surfers from the shore, and suddenly we were seeking waves of our own on rented boards and claiming territory with the locals.

Even though these Hawaiian waters were as familiar as the swing set in my own backyard back in Oregon, I felt like an imposter for a moment venturing into areas of which we were not at all worthy. A few sets went by, and before I knew it, my dad was up and calling out to me that he had caught a wave. "Hey, I'm up! I'm up," he yelled out as he cruised by before falling back into the water. I was so excited and remember trying and trying, but soon my efforts came to a screeching halt when the stinging on my ankle made me call out in pain. I looked back and saw nothing, but the pain came like the waves that were washing over me again and again. I was crying and hurting, so we paddled back to shore. It was then that I had my first run-in with a jellyfish and my last encounter with a surfboard until later in life when my purpose for riding was much different.

Although it was only a sting from a jellyfish, the pain was intense and kept coming in waves. My ankle was swollen with welts, and the thrill of being out on the surfboards with my dad became secondary to the throbbing that wouldn't stop.

Many years later, I would learn that I didn't have to be led by anyone into unknown territory where I felt vulnerable. It would take a long time before I actually questioned following the leader of the family into unchartered waters. Unfortunately, by the time I learned that lesson, the deep waters I was in were infested with sharks.

***

My parents were each the eldest of three and came from families who bore them the same year in different states. My mother was born in Sherman, Texas, and my father in Santa Monica, California. They ultimately each ended up being raised in the small logging town of Cottage Grove, Oregon, twenty miles south of my hometown of Eugene. Both of them came from families tied to the timber industry, which was a major economic force in the region when they were growing up. My maternal grandfather had a degree in forestry and owned a sawmill in the next county before it was burned to the ground by an arsonist. He tried to rebuild but found it impossible to recover, so he later spent many successful years as a timber cruiser for Bohemia Mining Company, one of the big lumber companies in the area.

My paternal grandfather was heir to a lumber baron who had a third-grade education with a fierce drive for success. People called my great-grandfather "Giant" because his dreams were so big, and he set out to achieve them and more. His were huge shoes to fill, and my grandfather did well trying to learn and ultimately taking over the successful family business while creating some new ventures of his own.

My father always said he felt like the kid who came from the "rich family who had the big white house on the hill" in the small town, and he often told me he despised it. Despite how philanthropic and truly committed his family was to the community in so many good ways, my father seemed to dislike the spotlight. I remember being told as a child that after he spent some time trying to find work out of state, he finally settled back in Oregon, worked for the family, and ultimately created his own successful company. I believe his family of origin felt like a mixed blessing to him.

My parents met in high school and dated into college until they finally married and had me before graduation. My father graduated with an economics degree from the University of Oregon, and my mother always wished she had just finished "those last few credits" for her art degree, but she never did. My younger brother came along a few years later, and my parents were busy raising us in Cottage Grove for the early years before buying a house in the university area of Eugene. My brother and I went to the public schools that were all within walking distance from our home.

A stay-at-home mother, my mom was unusually busy taking care of not only us but also some of our "latch key" friends as well as neighbors or relatives who would drop by from time to time for a lengthy chat, coffee, and sometimes stay for dinner. If my mom wasn't outside washing the car, tending her garden, or mowing the lawn, she was inside cooking, hosting, and caring for others. I often said I lived in a "glass house" as I always felt everyone could look at our life through the doors that were open to all.

My bedroom was my sanctuary and a space I loved. Somehow, I ended up with the largest room in the house, and my parents often joked about how they chose the wrong room. My brother and I shared the top floor with one bathroom at the landing of the stairs that separated our bedrooms. When I was a teen and often ran up the stairs and closed my door, Gary and his best friend took the door off of my room as a prank. They waited for me to run upstairs and grab for my door to shut the world out, and I suddenly realized the joke was on me. When I think back on it now, it strikes me as funny, but at the time, I was furious.

For the most part, Gary and I were close, as siblings go. We had our usual squabbles over silly things like whose turn it was to carry the clean laundry up from the basement or whose turn it was to clean the birdcage or feed the dog. We each had our own circle of friends and moved in different crowds at school. I tended to have a wide range of friends, and he stayed close to two or three good buddies. We usually had the same reaction when we would come home together after school and see people parked outside whom we knew would likely be there well into the dinner hour. It often felt as if there were few boundaries to our home, and I believed some people knew they could take advantage of it whenever they wanted.

Like my parents, Gary and I had very different personalities. My mom and I were the outgoing, social butterflies, and my dad and brother were more reserved and comfortably chose to be quieter in the background. In high school, we played in the same concert band and had a shared deep love of Motown music, in which our father heavily influenced us.

I remember feeling protective of Gary during his very first day of nursery school. We attended a Montessori school that was operating out of the local Presbyterian Church. Like our bedrooms, a bathroom separated the two classrooms. My teacher asked if I wanted to see my brother during his first day, and I said yes. As I entered his classroom, he was walking with a cup of dry beans from an area of class that had cups and measures. All at once, the cup dropped, and at least a hundred beans or more scattered all over the floor. I quickly tried to help him, and in true Montessori teaching style, his teacher reminded me that Gary needed to learn how to clean up his own mess. I remember to this day feeling worried about him and wanting him to be okay on his first day of school.

Both sides of my parent's families lived in both Cottage Grove and Eugene. Holidays were big happy occasions; we were all close, and tradition was strong. Christmas Eve was spent with my mother's parents, who had deep roots in their faith and always reminded us of what the holiday was really about. My grandfather would read the Christmas Story from the book of Mark or Luke, and it became a beloved tradition for years.

My maternal grandparents lived simply and were the salt of the earth. My grandfather was the son of a German Presbyterian minister from the Midwest, and my grandmother a native of a small town north of Dallas and the daughter of a nurse and farmer. They were both raised with strong Christian family values devoted to church, family, and community. They met and got married in her hometown of Sherman during the Second World War, just weeks before he was sent overseas as a paratrooper pilot in Europe. My mother was born later that year at nearby Perrin Airforce Base while he was abroad.

"It was love at first sight," he used to say with a twinkle in his eye as their love for one another was undeniable. I recall going to their home and always feeling a sense of security and peace. My grandmother had a slight southern accent from her Texas upbringing. Every little thing she did, from making a cup of coffee, doing a crossword puzzle, cooking bacon just right, or making her simple salad in the familiar little wooden bowls, was all done carefully and with pleasure. The way they approached life has made an even greater impression on me as I've gotten older. They were the epitome of strength, love, and integrity.

Unlike my mother, who was brimming with energy like her father, my Grandma Margaret, was steady and calm. I often think of what it felt like to sit at her kitchen table as a child and talk about the day ahead. Little things we did together, like ironing handkerchiefs for my grandfather or polishing her silver tea set, were all done with mindfulness and joy. I remember the serenity and safety of being in her kitchen and talking and feeling unconditionally loved, as it has given me great comfort all these years after she has passed away. Every time I go to my hometown, I make a trip up Willamette Street to their gravesite and sit with them and remember what good people they were and how much I loved them, and how I need them now more than ever.

My father's parents spent years creating and operating their local family business, extending philanthropic efforts throughout their beloved community, being active in their church, and enjoyed extensive travel. They were extremely loyal to the humble roots of the small town from which my grandfather came and his parents, my great-grandparents, loved. They were heartfelt and generous in all ways and adored family more than anything. They met when they were both attending USC. My grandmother fell madly in love, she used to say, when she saw my grandfather in uniform sitting at a restaurant counter eating a slice of pie. Shortly after graduation, my grandmother, who was raised in Santa Monica, happily followed the love of her life to the small logging town in the southern part of the Willamette Valley, where they made their home.

My grandmother, Joy, got her degree in fine arts and, as a talented artist, carried that flair into everything she did. I remember sitting at her art easel with her as a young girl watching the brushes being carefully dipped into the oil paint and enjoying the colors unfold through her eye and hand. She had a quick sense of humor and was fun and every inch a lady. She treated me like a daughter she never had and even named me when I was born. It wasn't until she died and my relationship with my mother had deteriorated that I realized so much more about my grandmother and how deeply loved I was by her.

I have fond memories of my childhood and look back on so much of it as though it was a fairytale. Everything was beautiful, and traditions were strong, experiences were plenty, and there seemed to be so much care and love between all. To this day, I believe much of it to still be true, but the lingering darker moments in my own family of origin started to rise as my own adult life started to move down a new path. By the time Randy and I split up in January 2016, my maternal grandparents had both passed away. They loved Randy dearly, and I was always glad they never had to see us part ways.

My father's parents were just a year or two into assisted retirement living and then nursing care when we separated. They also didn't ever really know about our split or the changes that were taking place in my life. I remember trying to talk to my grandmother about some of the pain but saw that it confused and hurt her too, so I didn't go there and kept my last years with her light and full of love. I needed her more than ever but was aware of her limitations, being elderly and living in the past.

What I didn't know then was that some things were taking place behind the scenes, as the matriarch and patriarch on my father's side were aging and becoming more vulnerable. It wouldn't be long before I returned to the familiar waters in Hawaii, the same ones I once paddled through with my dad to catch waves as a teen but would do so this time with very different intent as an adult and do so alone.

Imposters

I'm not crying because of you; you're not worth it. I'm crying because my delusion of who you were was shattered by the truth of who you are.

Steve Maraboli

Her habit of avoiding conflict with her husband at all costs was as damaging to her daughter's health and their family dynamic as were his domineering behaviors. They were partners in making control—not empathetic connection, not unconditional love—the language of the family.[1]

Dr. Edith Eva Eger, *The Choice*

As promised, my therapist just listened to my mother and didn't offer any of my personal information. I really didn't have anything to hide, but I was not feeling comfortable with how my mother took liberty without my permission or prior knowledge to go to my personal therapist to insist she wanted to help me. At the same time, she would talk to me and claim she was trying to help if only I accepted her version of what was unfolding between us all in the family. Years later, I would be even more glad about the insistence of my side remaining silent because what I learned later was that it appeared my mother was on a mission to seek some sort of false diagnosis of me.

Friends and family were starting to approach me, saying that my mom or my dad were openly communicating that I was mentally ill, including claims of me being either bipolar or manic-depressive, among other things. It felt slanderous and irresponsible, and when my kids learned what was happening, it was very hurtful to them as well. Overall, their message seemed to be that I was not well and needed medical attention. My dad even said as much to me by writing in an exchange with me that I will be better when I treat my "illness." It seemed like gaslighting to a major degree and felt like they were hoping to pin me with some diagnosis to explain why they believed I had changed and why I was so defiant, as they would insist. Pain, separation, gaslighting, blame, loss, and grief over my broken marriage and now misunderstandings with my brother all added to how I felt, but to say I was "mentally ill" felt slanderous. Had I not been so provoked and constantly dismissed over my feelings by my parents, I doubt my anger would have risen to the ugly level that it had, but it did, and they seemed to want to make a spectacle out of it to others.

No less than two weeks after my outburst, my mother had already shared our "private" exchange with my therapist in what felt to me like a betrayal. Her outreach to my therapist, under the apparent guise of wanting to help me, seemed to become a chance for her to share unfortunate rage and venting that I had put in writing. Sadly, it sounded to me like it was all about her instead of wanting to be there for her daughter, who was facing an enormous life change

I needed my mother; I was going through a divorce. My kids needed her. All that was happening was a standoff about how she felt mistreated and how mentally ill she claimed I was. It was the beginning of years of my one extremely angry moment being taken completely out of context and peddled around to anyone who would listen. It appeared to give my parents the perfect platform to claim they were being abused and that I was crazy.

Texts from my dad asking if I was getting the help I needed, or my mom inquiring whether I was in menopause and then my dad just flat out saying to me that I was "hormonal," "menopausal," and an "angry old woman" were some of the things I really didn't expect from them when I was already hurting and needing parents who were supportive. This was the opposite of what anyone wants from their own family when they are newly separated and scared. The painful words kept coming, and I stopped trying to defend myself as it seemed to me that they were trying to just shove me down as I was actually starting to rise and become my own person. I kept holding some secret hope that I could reach them and be heard on what was happening in my life and how their unconditional love was what I yearned for the most.

Despite the growing rift between my parents and me, they surprised me by allowing me to move from the apartment in Williamsburg to their prewar studio on Manhattan's Upper West Side. It felt like they were trying to be helpful, and, wanting to believe as much, I accepted their offer. It was a lifeline as I really couldn't afford much yet and needed to remain a New York resident until my divorce was finalized. It was a chance to keep a foothold in New York while I figured out my growing partnership issues in Oregon. Our lease was up in Brooklyn, and the three-bedroom, two-bath apartment was too expensive to keep. I had found their well-located, efficient 350-square-foot studio for them decades earlier and managed it for them. I was grateful to still have a little place in the city where my daughter could visit on her weekends away from boarding school.

I was immersed in great personal transition and also felt the deep desire to head to Oregon and try to establish myself in the partnership with my brother. I needed to create a life of my own, and I felt if I could spend time in Oregon and learn more about the business and give the time I now had, that it might mend the misconceptions between us. I loved New York, but it also reminded me of pain and my marriage, and I yearned for some distance, so I put my furniture in storage, moved some clothes and personal things into the studio, and rented an affordable apartment in Portland. I was hopeful that one year there with a foot still in Manhattan would allow me time to transition into a new life, repair the broken relationship between my brother and me, and give me some space while my divorce finalized. It was also an opportunity to spend some time with my son, who was attending college in Portland.

April 2016, I left the last marital home I had shared with Randy and closed the door on decades of one of many homes I had created for my family. My emotions were all over the place and ranged from relief to deep sadness. Seeing the empty places Randy used to have his things in the dresser or closets or some of the things he had left behind brought tears and heartache of a life that once was between us. The movers had come to pack things for storage, and I called an Uber to pick me up along with my boxes, amp, and bass guitar. As the van left the neighborhood, I said goodbye to the familiar street art images painted on the walls and buildings that slowly disappeared from my sight. Crossing the Queensboro Bridge into Manhattan, my heart felt heavy as I saw memories of my married life on each side of the river. I was headed back to the Upper West Side, which had initially been a happy place and then followed by some very hard dark years.

Bittersweet doesn't begin to describe the feeling of familiarity and disdain for my arrival at the studio. When I got to the apartment building, Anthony, the superintendent, met me at the curb. I had known him for years, and he felt like a trusted friend. He looked squarely at me while grabbing my largest suitcase out of the trunk and calmly said, "Everything is going to be okay." As he helped me unload my belongings from the van into the studio, I was so grateful and at a loss for words. I thanked him profusely but really wanted to say, "It's not the divorce that is feeling hard right now; it's what my parents and brother are doing to me that is killing my soul." I didn't want to involve him in any of it and thanked him for the help while wiping away tears that kept burning my eyes. That night I slept on the hide-a-bed that would be my permanent bed for longer than I imagined. My parents' belongings were packed tightly in each closet with no room to spare, so I lived out of a suitcase until I managed to create space with rolling racks and stacking things under the bed. It wasn't the elegant sprawling classic seven-room prewar I'd lived in on Central Park West a few blocks away with my husband and children just years before, but it was a place to lay my head, and I was grateful in that moment for what I had.

Stirrings of my faith were within me, but I wasn't drawing close to it on a daily basis. My emotions were controlling me, and I would eventually realize how fleeting and exhausting that would become. Boxes were packed and unpacked, and my life was separated into the east coast, west coast, storage, and the suitcase from which I was living. From May 2016 to May 2017, I lived in what I now call "the triangle," which spanned from New York, Honolulu, and Portland. I recognize that all three places are very nice, and I was always grateful to land in one of them and try to settle for a while before having to move on, but it was definitely challenging as the baggage I carried from place to place was a lot more than a suitcase.

As family problems grew, I felt less and less as though I belonged to anyone or any place. I became an observer to life in each place I landed and tried to connect with people and places before it was time to move on. I yearned to find grounding beneath my feet, yet nothing felt solid or safe, so I did what I could to move forward with the work before me and kept it all in a small roller suitcase, which I called "my office." That suitcase became my carry-on and my carry-all for whatever I was working on at the moment.

The Honolulu apartment was one that had been in the family for years and was now owned by the LLC for which my brother and I were partners. It was one of the last places that felt like home, and I was grateful to spend time there. My dad had even messaged me on one of my trips, thoughtfully saying, "You should spend time there as you need to contemplate the rest of your life, and it's a good place to rest and do some thinking about what is next." I still believed that he was a caring father watching out for his firstborn and only daughter. I held onto his words at that moment and felt he was trying to understand the enormous transition that was before me, but his benevolence was fleeting, and I began to form emotional boundaries for myself to shield my heart from the growing pain.

Upon my arrival to Portland, I reached out to my brother and asked if we could meet face to face. He often drove to Oregon from the Bay Area and was in town several times a month, so I felt we could easily meet and try to resolve our growing issues. My meeting with the lawyer in Portland over the operating agreement had just been to get clarity on the documents, and I was eager to try to find common ground with Gary and see if we could change a few things so our working relationship could be more fairly defined. I wasn't interested in taking over, nor was I asking for a paying position; I only wanted transparency, inclusiveness on decisions, and more equality in how things were run. For years my father and brother had asked me to become more involved, and now I was able to fully commit the time and concentration. I was finally in Oregon, ready to be included, but immediately started to feel sidelined.

At once, my request to have my legal bill covered by the LLC for clarity on the operating agreement was questioned by Gary and later paid not as a partner expense to the LLC but rather as a payment against my capital account. He also made it clear that any future legal invoices on my behalf of my inquiries into the operating agreement and partnership would be denied. My requests for meetings with my brother were ignored and finally declined, and my father even chimed in from time to time, saying things like "your brother is afraid of you," and he "doesn't want to partner with you." I replied by reminding him that my brother had nothing to be afraid of since he had created a document that put him fully in charge of our joint assets. If anyone was to be afraid, it was me.

My mother kept falsely claiming that since I was set on suing my brother, he was going to keep a distance. I felt she was adding extra drama to my visit with the lawyer, and it seemed to become her platform to tell me and others that I was suing Gary, which was not true and very irresponsible in my opinion. I was baffled by what I was hearing, as it was simply shocking. My parent's narrative seemed to become their warped truth, and it was exhausting to keep defending myself. The more educated I was on the partnership, the more distant my brother, the General Operating Manager, became. I felt powerless, and I believe it was exactly what he had wanted when I signed that agreement. His silence with me in our so-called "equal partnership," as intended by our parents, solidified my beliefs.

My meeting with the lawyer to go over my agreement with my brother was never an attempt at a lawsuit. I was an equal partner seeking clarity and answers I wasn't getting from the LLC's manager, who appeared to be living solely off our joint assets. My brother drove a Mercedes company car, had used company funds to purchase a boat owned by the LLC, and he often used the residential properties to entertain his friends.

True, I had also used the residential properties for personal use, as had been the custom for decades with the different generations. We always shared access and were accommodating to one another, but things were starting to change. Suddenly the family calendar that was kept in the office for reservations on the residential properties in Central Oregon, Hawaii, and San Francisco stopped being available and was no longer used. Communication on simple things like who was going to use the condo for the Fourth of July or Thanksgiving became a mystery. It was ridiculous, and even writing about it feels so, but these became what I believe to be calculated steps to create a greater divide with each day over something that was supposed to be my father's "legacy" as he called it, and his "life's work." Baby steps toward division were becoming the norm, and it seemed to me that my parents were in constant contact with my brother on the situation.

It wasn't long after I got settled in Portland that I realized moving there was a mistake. I had been hopeful of at least spending several days a week in the office to educate myself more on the inner workings of the business. Calls to arrange face-to-face meetings with my brother fell on deaf ears, and when I inquired with the office about his schedule or whereabouts, I was told that he had given instructions for my calls to be ignored and go straight to voicemail and not to be returned. His comings and goings were becoming a mystery. The person who was in charge of our joint assets seemed to do all he could to avoid any contact with me and apparently from others. Family members would tell me that Gary would show up unannounced in the office or at different family business properties. His lack of communication was something felt by friends and family. It became a real-life "Where's Waldo" game of cat and mouse, and all it did was confirm my belief more and more that there was an ulterior motive. This wasn't partnering, nor was it the intent he had said months before, which was, "As soon as we get mom and dad out of this, we can do whatever we want." I believed that I was also someone to be gotten rid of, but the only way was to apparently trick me into a silent partnership. The behaviors were foreign to me as my brother and I had always been close. Suddenly I felt shut out on every level.

My fruitless attempts to connect with him became almost laughable, but it was mostly maddening. Finally, about a month or so after I had arrived in Portland, a surprise email invitation suddenly came from him. He wanted me to meet him in Salem at the office of our CPA. I put the date on my calendar and looked forward to it as I thought it might be a chance to forge some common ground on how my time in Oregon could be spent partnering with him and learn about the daily workings of the company.

The meeting was uncomfortably formal between my brother and me, and I kept trying to find the purpose in it as the CPA kept asking me if I had any questions, and they seemed to be questions I had tried asking my brother for months with no answer. "I am curious why one partner has been allowed to take a substantial loan and convert it to a distribution without the knowledge of the other partner, which goes directly counter to what the operating agreement states. I am here today to get some of those questions answered." I don't remember getting a definitive answer and left feeling less informed and more confused as to the purpose of the meeting but later realized it was nothing more than something I felt my brother had to do to appear as though I had been included. It felt like an attempt to prove he had met with me so he could then check off a box that this had been completed.

We awkwardly walked out to the parking lot together. An earlier invitation by him to follow up the meeting with lunch had been mentioned, but the growing tension between us was evidence that a meal wouldn't be shared. He asked about Jaylen and Lily and whether our kids might have some time together. "I know mine would like that very much," I said, "but they are in boarding school and college, and I can't speak for their schedules. It's best to ask them directly." I remember seeing the pain in his eyes at the mention of our kids, and it was clear that this tension was likely affecting his son, who I suspected was only hearing one side of things.

My heart hurt thinking about it, but I also knew that I had tried to extend myself many times to no avail. To me, the meeting in Salem was nothing more than a formality to simply check off what needed to be done. We stood for an awkward silence and then said a stiff and empty goodbye. I left feeling more confused than ever about my relationship with him and what his intentions were. I really didn't want to believe what was becoming more obvious by the day, but the divide was growing.

My intent was nothing more than to become a more involved partner, learn the ropes and take charge of my life as I shifted from being married to single. Randy was providing the maintenance I was legally allowed, and I was starting to earn a little extra money on the side as a new consultant with an international online skincare company. I was interested in gaining my independence, but the narrative from my family was that I was seeking support to live off of them and the business. It seemed clear to me that the intentions of my parents to pass the company equally to their two children was likely more in theory than in reality.

By July, I was asking my father if he had any part in the new operating agreement between Gary and me or if he had read it. His short response came back as "no to both questions." My father started to become angrier in his exchanges with me while at the same time they were preparing to move from Oregon, where they had spent their whole lives. Their apparent paranoia toward me seemed to grow, and I felt more and more misunderstood. I asked questions and tried to get "my side" out to them and was met with comments from my dad like, "there you go, stupid; you spend all your time being a brat and not educating yourself." He sometimes chose other more demeaning words to call me that are unrepeatable yet unforgettable from a father to his daughter. This was not the father I knew and loved, and his cutting comments often caused me to respond defensively. His words stung in waves reminiscent of the jellyfish attacking my ankle but now it was my heart that was stinging.

That August, Jaylen received a note from my mother saying, "There are always two sides to things," which felt very confusing in light of their storyline being one-sided and my attempt at a conversation to find common ground constantly ignored. It wouldn't be until a few years later that Psalm 27:10 (NLT) would become a pillar of strength for me as I felt I was losing my parents. "Even if my father and mother abandon me, the Lord will hold me close." As promised, God was there, but my parents were slipping away, and I watched the foundation of my family crumble into what felt to me like an impossible avalanche of lies, fear, and deception.

My mother said I had changed and was different, and the truth is I was different. I had grown, and I was beginning to see behind the curtain that had shielded me from the reality of what I thought was unconditional love and what I believed my family to be. I once had a therapist say to me that as soon as I broke free from my codependence, those who are closest to me may not ultimately be happy with my growth. At the time, his advice meant very little, but now I was beginning to understand that my personal quest for independence and respect was something that felt threatening and foreign. It was the beginning of a very deeply painful time, but a necessary one to break free from the chains I believe I had been born into.

It felt more and more to me that my parents were apparently now more interested in money than family. Maybe it had always been the case and something I hadn't noticed before, but the newfound clarity I felt was evident. Suddenly I was realizing what I believed motivated them, and it was shocking. I knew they took pride in what they had and were conservative investors. My father was always reading and talking about the economy and investing and the ups and downs of the market. Being married to a bond trader for decades,

I had learned a different view of looking at some of it, and when I would bring up bonds, my dad would sometimes kiddingly say, as his father used to, "that's what you use to get out of jail." The focus on money was more evident than ever because what I was feeling was their fixation on it over relationships, which I believed were priceless. Matthew 6:24 (NIV) says, "No one can serve two masters. Either you will hate the one and love the other, or you will be devoted to the one and despise the other. You cannot serve both God and money." I knew what I was starting to see, and I didn't like it.

The doors to my family's homes were now closed to me, and invitations for holidays ceased. My father continued to insist that he had no involvement whatsoever in the LLC and that it was now between my brother and me. However, while Gary was on a lengthy holiday vacation to New Zealand with his family, the signatures of my dad were on all of the business checks being generated by the partnership. I was wholly unaware from my brother that he would be overseas and had put my father in charge of financial transactions. It wasn't until I requested account statements from the bank that I noticed my father was listed on the new LLC account and thus appearing to be handling operations in my brother's absence. It was suddenly very hard to believe my father's repeated claims of being totally uninvolved when the evidence clearly showed otherwise.

I was reminded of my brother's earlier insistence in 2015 that I sign the new operating agreement so that my parents could be taken off the partnership agreement as well as the former bank account. I remember the new bank account being the main argument for me signing the documents before the end of the year so that a new account with only our names could be established. The signatures on the checks and my father taking over the transactions while my brother vacationed abroad certainly said a lot to me.

At the break of dawn on Christmas morning, 2016, I got into a cab, which cut through the empty streets of Manhattan, down through the center of Times Square where two and three-story neon lights flashed throughout the usually vibrant area now void of people who were most likely enjoying the holiday morning at home. I felt extreme loneliness but focused instead on my destination.

My kids were at the house in Connecticut with their father, and it was our first Christmas apart, so I had planned to get out of town. I flew eleven hours alone nonstop to Honolulu on a packed plane. Once I arrived at the condo I planned to get settled while waiting for my children to join me a few days later. I had a meeting in late January as a shareholder of the property and believed it was as good a time as any to go where I felt I belonged. It was also here that I could experience the last vestige of familiarity in a place I had always called home.

Hawaii was a place I would visit a few more times in the coming years, and I was grateful to connect with longtime friends and make new ones, who all instantly made me feel like ohana. As my old life seemed to slip away, I look back now and see the blessings of new relationships made during this time which helped fill the fractured places in my heart. Always with welcome arms to dance and have fun in community events was a group of kama'āina dancers who immediately treated me like their own. Invitations from old friends to paddle at sunset with an outrigger team, invites to lunches and dinners by others all warmed my heart and made me feel included. This was the spirit of aloha that resonated strongly and always called me back to the 'āina.

When I walked in the door, I exhaled and said a prayer. It was one of the only places left in my life that felt safe and welcoming. I sat by the window that Christmas and watched the colors of the sky change from day into night as the evening lights of Honolulu emerged. As I witnessed the sunset over the Pacific, I knew that magnificent sight was the most beautiful and meaningful Christmas gift I could hope for, and I was thankful.

Aloha 'Oe

Ola I Ka Makana Ma Ke Akua
"Life is a gift from God."

~ Hawaiian Proverb

On the evening of January 13, 2017, while I was in Honolulu, my grandfather passed away in Oregon. Lily had just left the Islands to return to school, and Jaylen was still with me. We had all enjoyed bringing in the New Year in Hawaii, and I was grateful for our time together in the familiar family island hale. A day earlier, I had managed a short conversation with my grandfather, which was mostly one-sided with me telling him I loved him, thanking him for all he had done for me and for all of the wonderful memories. My family in Oregon told me that he was very pleased that he got to hear my voice, and I was so thankful for that final moment between us.

The news of his passing came to me in a text message from an extended family member. I stood in the living room he and my grandmother enjoyed every winter and looked out the window to see the magnificent sunset that was unfolding on the horizon. The vast view from the 29th floor of the apartment stretched from Waikiki Beach across Ala Wai Yacht Harbor to Ala Moana Beach Park and beyond to the airport, where my grandfather loved to watch the airplanes fly in and out. This was a view he had seen thousands of times, and I took it in with a heavy heart and new eyes.

He had served in the military on Oahu and was to be deployed to Japan during the war. The mission never happened as Truman dropped the atomic bomb on Hiroshima and Japan surrendered before my grandfather's platoon left Hawaii. Nonetheless, my grandfather remained stationed at Pearl Harbor. Soon after, my father was born in Santa Monica and was brought to Oahu as a newborn to meet his father for the first time. The flight from Los Angeles to Honolulu by prop plane took fifteen hours in those days, and my grandmother always talked about how terrifying it was to fly so long and low over the Pacific.

A photographer for the Honolulu Star-Advertiser captured my grandparents in a photo as wives were reunited with their military husbands at the Aloha Tower adjacent to downtown. The photo made the cover of the paper and in my grandmother's arms was my infant father, being seen for the first time by his father upon their reunion in Honolulu. The photo looked as if they were walking in a hurry, and years later, my grandmother told me it was because their car was parked in an expired meter, and they were trying to avoid a ticket. They managed to get their photo in the local paper but may have risked getting a ticket for the delay. It's meaningless, but I wish I knew the outcome of that part of the story. It has always been a favorite photo of my grandparents, so young, happy, and carrying my father to their military home on Oahu. They were obviously elated to be together after all that was going on in the world.

Hawaii was special to my grandfather, and it was because of him that the Islands became part of my life. When we were young, my brother and I would spend spring break in Honolulu with my grandparents, and they would take us to their favorite places. Seeing it all now through the window over the ocean and searching my mind for the places and the memories was priceless.

My first Christmas at ten months of age was spent in Honolulu with my great-grandparents, grandparents, and uncles on my father's side. We stayed at the Halekulani, a historic hotel comprised then of bungalows along the shores of Waikiki and a special gathering place for Sunday brunch under the giant banyan tree. The hotel is still there but is now a much more modern and elegant version of its early, simpler years. I have always had a sense of pride, knowing it was the first hotel I ever stayed in and that my first plane ride was to Oahu to spend my first Christmas with family. Hawaii has always been very dear to me as it was to my grandfather.

There were years when the family rented a small neighborhood home in Poipu, Kauai, long before the location became a visitor's hotspot filled with expensive hotels. My grandparents and parents would bring in the New Year at a local restaurant, and the next day, my brother and I would play with the party hats and whistles they would bring home. We would buy puka shell necklaces from roadside kama'āina, who had strung them together by hand. To this day, I still own one of those coveted real shell necklaces, which are machine-made now. Looking back, I remembered all of the little things that suddenly were very big in my mind: the drives on Kamehameha Highway through the sugar cane fields to the pineapple cannery where my grandparents loved to get fresh pineapple; the long drive to Hale'iwa just to visit some of the local painters whose art my grandmother loved. Those were different times and places on Oahu, which today are major tourist destinations. I also recall dining at Kemo'o Farms, a restaurant and a staple of island base military life in the '40s, and a favorite place they would go with other military couples stationed near Schofield Barracks.

I remembered the drive to Pearl Harbor with my brother and me in the back seat of the car, wishing we were at the beach while instead, we were on a tour down memory lane with my grandfather at the wheel and my grandmother telling us about my dad as a baby playing on a blanket in the front yard of their barrack home on the base. My father never enjoyed being in the sun, so I always found this image of him funny, especially when my grandmother would say he was so tan the first year of his life.

Holidays were spent with generations in the islands on Oahu or Kauai and big family dinners at the Oahu Country Club where they were members. My grandmother had a closet full of Hawaiian muumuus, and my grandfather usually had an equally colorful shirt to match. They loved Hawaii, and my grandmother later became a member of the Watercolor Society of Hawaii. She would take me to the art walk on Sundays along the fence near the Honolulu Zoo. It was a place where local amateur artists showed their work, and some later ended up in the popular galleries and shops along Kalakaua Avenue. They loved the beach, and I have so many memories of my grandmother using her tube of Bain de Soleil sun lotion, probably devoid of any sunscreen but orange in color and giving off that bronze glow she loved. They always took a radio with them to the beach and two little folding chairs, which still hung in the closet that night as the tears streamed down my cheeks, remembering him and thinking of her now without the love of her life.

My father was in the hotel business and in the 1970s became a minority owner in a high-rise hotel project in Waikiki. I remember him making over a hundred round trips between Oregon and Hawaii during this time as he oversaw the venture. The office where he worked was just one block away from the Aloha Tower, where his father had first seen him as a baby. I also remember my parents telling me that they were seriously considering enrolling my brother and me in school in Honolulu and moving our family there permanently. They finally decided to remain in Oregon, but it was around this time that I recall my father finding the family condo where I had spent most of my life. With my divorce and now my parents closing off my access to their homes, I had little that felt familiar. Honolulu was home, and as I watched the sun go down, I felt the memories of my grandfather wash over me. It was ironic that I was in his beloved place while hearing that he had just passed away. The thought of it made me feel even more connected to him as he passed from this world to heaven. I looked out across the ocean that was so familiar to me, and the beaches at the water's edge feeling so much like my own backyard. I knew there was one way and one way only to honor my grandfather while I was here, and I fell asleep that night thinking over my plan.

Neither my parents nor my brother contacted me to tell me my grandfather had died. When I heard the news, I reached out to my father in a text and told him how sorry I was that his dad had passed away. He seemed grateful and emotional to receive my message, and I could tell he was hurting. I chose my words carefully and with sincerity. I never heard any details from my parents on my grandfather's final moments, and it was clear they were not going to be the ones to go to for information.

Months later, when an informal gathering of close family spread his ashes in a stream outside of his hometown, I was also not invited or informed. When I finally heard about it, later I asked my mother how it went, and she seemed to brush it off like it wasn't important. I was the first grandchild, and my grandfather had always been good to me. I was very close to his mother, my great-grandmother, as well as my father's mother, who was now a widow and suddenly the matriarch of the family. If not for the texts and calls of a few caring relatives, I would not have known about my grandfather dying that day. The chill in the air was growing, and I had no idea how much colder it could get, but it would.

The next morning, I set out to find a fresh flower lei, something that used to be so easy to find on the street being sold by kama'āina, who would sell them to tourists. The small floral shop in the nearby hotel still sold them, and I headed there with my swimsuit on under my clothes. Once at the beach, I sat in the same place I used to with my brother and grandparents. Their favorite spot was in front of the Hilton Hawaiian Village just near the lagoon by the famous rainbow tower.

In the 1970s, when no one paid attention to the dangers of sun damage, the beach was lined with heavily tanned retirees whose leathery skin was almost a badge of honor. No umbrellas or any sunscreen over SPF 8 was ever in sight. I spent years in that spot with the tourists and the locals, enjoying the small waves and watching my grandfather set out to snorkel in the nearby reef. For as long as I go there, I still see my grandmother swimming just enough not to get her hair wet and my grandfather making his snorkeling pilgrimage to the reef and back before he settled in their foldout seats with the transistor radio they carried with them. This was where I knew I would say goodbye. I sat down, and put the lei in the sand and made the shape of a heart. I prayed to God and thanked Him for giving me such a wonderful grandfather who was such a big part of my life. I was thankful for the connection I felt to him through his roots in Oregon as well as here, and I hoped somehow, he would know from heaven that I already missed him.

When I was ready, I put the lei around my neck and swam out to the reef in his memory and said a final prayer and took the lei and tossed it as far as I could, sending him and my memories into the place he loved most. It was also a place I loved as much, and I felt connected to him through the water and the tears and waves. Aloha 'Oe—until we meet again. "Rest in peace, my dear grandfather, Carlton, I love you," I said as I watched the lei float further and further out to the waters I once tried to surf with my father. When I couldn't see it anymore, I turned back and swam to shore, my tears mixing with the ocean but feeling thankful that I was there and could give a final farewell to his beloved island.

Evil Forebodings

If your brother sins against you, go and tell him his fault, between you and him alone. If he listens to you, you have gained your brother. But if he does not listen, take one or two others along with you, that every charge may be established by the evidence of two or three witnesses. If he refuses to listen to them, tell it to the church. And if he refuses to listen even to the church, let him be to you as a Gentile and a tax collector.

Matthew 18:15-17 (ESV)

Unreturned calls and emails for requests to meet face to face with my brother continued to be ignored or denied when I was in Oregon. I'd hoped that my move there would at least allow me to be involved in a small part of the business. Gary lived in California, and surely with me now in the state of Oregon, it could be helpful to him and to us both for me to spend time in the office or help with our commercial tenants. I was finally seeing the pattern that was emerging with my business partner and the general operating manager of the company we shared equally, except since signing the agreement, I believed I was now clearly relegated to a position of being someone who was only on a "need to know basis only." It was a term I had heard Gary use for years when dealing (or not dealing) with certain people, and I believe he sort of relished the idea of not having to answer to things unless others really needed information. I had been silenced, allowing my brother to make all decisions on our joint assets, and I didn't like it.

Gone were the inviting conversations about partnering we had had for months leading up to the announcement of my divorce. Then I had felt included as a partner and involved in the future of what we shared equally, but I had suddenly become nothing more than someone who would owe taxes on my share and watch him live fully off our company. I no longer had a say in anything that was always something we were to share equally, even if he was the general operating manager, which up to this point hadn't been an issue with me. Doors were closing, and conversations weren't happening, and I felt I had no choice but to try to find a way to meet him face to face. This time I intended to do so as his sister, not as a business partner.

I took a chance that he might be in Eugene, so I rented a car and drove from Portland to my parent's apartment. They had sold their nearby home along the Willamette River after the announcement of my impending move to Portland and quickly made Arizona their permanent residence. The apartment in Eugene seemed to serve as a holding place while my dad still had his office in town and his mother living at the nursing home just steps away from their rental.

I sat in the parking lot, not knowing if Gary was there or not, but since I didn't see his car, I thought I would wait to see if he would drive up. I waited for about forty-five minutes and then decided to drive around. I was so tired and afraid of falling asleep in the parking lot, so I drove up and down some of the nearby streets, and when I returned, I finally saw his car parked in the lot, assuming he may have come in from dinner. I took a deep breath and decided to face him, and although I had never been inside the apartment, I knew its location as my mother had mentioned it to me when they moved.

I got to the apartment door and said a prayer in my mind, trying to stay calm. My heart was beating out of my chest as I knocked. It was met with silence, so I knocked several more times until I finally said, "Gary, it's your sister, and I know you are there. Would you please let me in so we can talk?" Suddenly the door flung open, and my brother stood there looking at me with no expression as he flatly said, "Why don't you come in and take what you want?"

I was stunned. "I don't want anything other than to talk to you." I looked around the apartment, and it was stacked with boxes and familiar belongings from my parent's house. It was clearly a place in transition but easy enough to move around. Months earlier, I had asked my mother if I could stay there when I came to Eugene if they didn't mind. She declined, saying, "We just moved and have too many things around, and it's just not a good time to have anyone stay there." They had always given Gary and me keys to their homes, and I still had the one to their Tucson home and recently sold Eugene home on my keychain. It was totally out of character for them to shut me out, but they did. When I reminded her that I was her daughter, also in transition and moving, and would just be grateful for a place to stay when I came to my hometown, it didn't seem to matter. I asked why Gary was allowed to stay but not me. "Your brother comes to Eugene and works and needs a place to stay. Because he is working, he isn't in the place much when he does come to town." I found it interesting and sad how she seemed to qualify one of her kids over the other as to how they were allowed access to one of their homes, now apparently based on employment status.

It was the one and only time I was inside that apartment and the feeling of being surrounded by familiar things I had grown up with suddenly felt odd. It was like seeing my whole life in broken fragments, which mirrored my emotions. I decided to focus on my face-to-face opportunity with him as we carefully sat down across the room from each other, which felt very awkward. It was clear he had been caught off guard, so I apologized but also said I was frustrated being constantly ignored.

"I am here to see you and try to find some starting point of a conversation. I would also like to see if we can find some common ground and rework that operating agreement, which I signed and now feel was unfair." He carefully chose his words and offered no opening that felt friendly, much less inviting to discuss much. The greatest rise in his voice came when he said that I should buy him out and that I had signed the agreement, and basically, that was that. If I wanted out, I could buy him out, period. It was a cold exchange, and as I exited, the new familiar chill in the air was ugly, and I realized I didn't know this person anymore. I felt his eyes on my back as I turned to leave, and when the door closed behind me, I knew it might be the last time I was ever in a place belonging to my parents. The divide felt clear to me. He was still in the family, and I was not.

I was still spinning over and over in my mind, my mother allowing one of her children access to their apartment while keeping the other out. To me, it seemed unnecessarily cruel and selective based on the argument that one was working in town and the other was not. Having two kids of my own, I could never imagine setting such obvious and ridiculous boundaries for one and not the other. When I brought it up with her again, she said, "It's a very complicated security system to use, and you need a key fob, and, well, we just don't have access for any more people other than who is on the list, so you'll have to make other arrangements to stay elsewhere when you come to town." I saw it as a very flimsy excuse to just say no.

She suggested I stay with my in-laws, who also lived in the same town and were always welcoming. Even so, I reminded her that I was getting a divorce and that the timing might be awkward. Not that my in-laws wouldn't have had me, but for her to turn me away as her daughter and expect my in-laws to take me in should I want to come to my hometown to stay a night was really beyond my comprehension. The behaviors of my immediate family were foreign, and I kept trying to find a way to connect, to let them know I still cared about them even though Randy and I were parting. I loved them, and I needed my family, and they were simply not going to be available to me as one would believe parents should be when their child is going through a divorce or, for that matter, any hard time.

Family is family, and, suddenly, mine wasn't feeling like it, and I was becoming increasingly frustrated and hurt. I felt trapped, unheard, misunderstood, and punished for seeking a divorce and my rightful place in a company for which I was half-owner. The repercussion of that was the growing awareness that I would lose my parents and my brother. My father told me that I was ruining my life. Really? I didn't see it that way at all, and they knew my marriage had had some rough years, and I had worked hard to remain in it, and then at one point, my mother said, "I have a lot of regrets not supporting you years ago when you were thinking about getting a divorce. I should have been listening to what you needed." Well, here I was at round two on that, and they were shutting the door in my face for reasons I didn't understand.

When I thought back to the earlier years when my marriage was in a bad place, Randy had moved out, and I was emotionally devastated and left home alone with two young children. My mother told me then that she and my father wouldn't be coming to New York to be with the kids or me as they didn't want to appear to be taking sides. She said it would send a bad message to Randy, so instead, my brother was sent to New York, and although he was supportive in many ways, his ultimate goal seemed to be to get me in front of an estate planning attorney they had found in Midtown to sign papers to protect my then barely five percent share of the LLC in case there was a divorce.

At the time, my parents were majority shareholders, and my brother and I were in the minority. I was so numb and in shock over the state of my marriage that I just dutifully followed what my brother and parents wanted. In retrospect, I see now that it was a time when my young children and I really needed family around us, but family business matters seemed to trump everything, and my parents stayed away. My housekeeper and babysitter at the time were of more emotional support to me than my mother, as I look back now with a heavy heart, seeing this with new eyes.

I needed to know my rights, but my attempts to find common ground with them were no longer their goal. I realized I was going to be alone in my quest for justice on the matter. I wanted out of that agreement, and I wanted clarity and some answers.

***

One night when Jaylen was at my apartment in Portland, I became very emotional over the recent events. It was unfair to shoulder my burdens on him, but I was fragile and feeling hopeless. I tried and failed to hide how I was feeling, but my broken heart became impossible to deal with, and my emotions poured out as I lay on my bed feeling deep despair. I was embarrassed but also tired of being strong, and the moment caused me great vulnerability when what I really wanted was to be a pillar of strength for my son, who I knew as also dealing with so much in his own world.

In between my pathetic sobs, he sat on the edge of the bed and said a prayer over me, which made me catch my breath. I looked up at him through my tears as he lovingly said, "Mom, I'm doing what you tell us to do in times like these." It was a beautiful moment borne out of sorrow and pain that proved to me that God is still in control and that, thankfully, my son knew where to turn not only for me but maybe for himself. I was so proud of his strength and sensitivity, knowing that he chose prayer in such a difficult time.

Around this time, my Guardian Angel arrived. It was someone I believe God put in my path at this moment to help guide me through the mess that was becoming more and more tangled. My Guardian Angel helped me so that I was suddenly allowed to reconnect with the lawyer in Big Pink and do so with solid footing, knowing someone had my back. I was unable to do it alone as I didn't have access to my own assets to seek the answers I felt I deserved. Suddenly a door opened, and I felt a glimmer of hope.

When it had become clear that working with my brother was off-limits to me whether I lived in Oregon or not, I made plans to return to New York permanently. My daughter also needed me, and although when I left for Portland initially, she was fine with it as she said, "Mom, I will be in boarding school and busy, so it's really okay. I'm good." Her comments had suddenly turned into "I miss you, and I wish you were here." She needed me, and the changes that were taking place in the relationship with her father and me made me realize how much my being closer to home would help her and me as well. Moving to Oregon for the year had initially felt right, but returning to New York was now more important, and I saw she wasn't as ready as she thought for me to be living far away, and frankly, neither was I.

I had made many trips back and forth in the year I was in Portland, but New York was home, and I felt it was time to come back and to do so on my terms. Randy and I had moved there during the early years of our marriage just after Jaylen was born, and we did so solely for his career. This was now my turn to come to New York on my terms, and this time, I really wanted it. I missed my daughter, I missed the city, and I missed my friends.

The year in Portland had been good in other ways, as I had forged relationships with old friends and got to spend some time with my son, which was wonderful. I became involved in an online marketing business and also found a local dance studio that welcomed me into their community. The few hours a week I had to lose myself in the music and choreography gave me a valuable outlet. My dance friends brought me a lot of joy and something to look forward to when my days were otherwise filled with numbing frustration and pain dealing with an unfolding divorce and splintering partnership with Gary. Along with making new friends, I enjoyed the closer proximity to extended family and my in-laws, who all treated me lovingly and well. I love Oregon, but New York was calling me back, and this time, I couldn't wait to get there. The only challenge was that my only place to stay until I could secure my own apartment was at my parents' studio, and doing so created an increasingly awkward existence between them and me.

The irony of being allowed in their New York studio but not their Oregon apartment was also confusing. It seemed more and more clear that they didn't want me in Oregon and that my physical distance by being in New York, or even Hawaii, was optimal for some unknown reason. My mom sent a text saying, "More opportunities for you in NY. We will still pay for a yoga class or a business class or any other class you want to take…"

Months earlier, I had wanted to take a business finance and accounting course so I could be more helpful as a partner with the LLC. Since my brother had hired a business coach for several years at the expense of the company, I thought I might get some courses under my belt, but the opportunity for this at company expense was not granted to me by my brother. My parents instead offered to pay to get me certified as a yoga teacher (something I had briefly expressed an interest in but didn't pursue) as well as a business course, but I didn't want or accept their offer. I wasn't looking for handouts; instead, I was looking for equality as a rightful partner.

The irony that my brother benefitted in so many more different ways from our joint assets than I was blatant. I was actually embarrassed for him. He seemed kept, and yet my parents continued to put the blame on me for wanting to live off the company. I still held onto the belief that I was part of the family and that I belonged, but the closed doors in Oregon were evident and strange. It left me with a growing sense of uneasiness about what was really going on, and I found myself constantly stressed as I anticipated the next unwelcome surprise.

Before I left for New York, I was invited to an extended family dinner celebrating the birthday of a relative. While at the dinner table, someone in the family turned to me and asked what I got. I thought the question was in reference to what I had ordered for my meal, but after a few laughs, the question was reposed and more specific, "What pieces of jewelry did you receive when your grandparents opened their safe deposit box to give items away to the women in the family?" I sat dumbfounded. I didn't know anything about this, and when I asked for more details, I was told that it had taken place in 2011 and that each son had been given jewelry of my grandmother's to disperse at once to their wives and daughters.

I was the eldest granddaughter, and this relative was stunned when I said I knew nothing and had received nothing at the time they were making such gestures. My grandmother had personally given me a beautiful diamond necklace many years earlier, but this event was entirely different and appeared to involve all of the women in the family. That night I pored over the past in my head, trying to recall that event. I then remembered my parents taking me to a new safe the size of a refrigerator they had installed inside their garage to show me some jewelry they had just acquired that had belonged to my grandmother, who, at that time, was still alive. I admired it, recognized some of the pieces, and said how nice they were while they carefully put them back and said they would be kept in the family.

What I didn't know was that I had come to understand that my father and his siblings had been given instructions by their parents to give carefully selected pieces to all the women in the family, including me, but for me, that never happened. The divide between us over the LLC issues started to take place in 2016, and it hurt to think this had happened years before. Why? What was the motivation to lie and to keep something like that from me? My residence was 3000 miles away, and my lack of daily contact with the other women in the family was proving to be an advantage for such situations. I tried not to let it get to me, but it was, and that's when the nightmares started to wake me up at night. It was when greed started to become a very evident dark force in my family of origin, and I felt the spiritual warfare building.

I would find myself in a cold sweat waking up from a dream where I was calling out. I felt my throat tighten as the danger coming at me felt like it would threaten me physically. I was struggling with my emotions, and my dreams were becoming nightmares. Suddenly the lies and the deception and my place in my family as a daughter and sister were confusing and unclear.

I left Portland for New York with a pit in my stomach over many things that felt unfinished but was glad to be in familiar surroundings again and clung to my one happy hour of the day, which was dance or yoga at the gym. It was the only place I felt I could disappear into myself and be free and be with my community of friends who meant the world to me. But when the vinyasa flow or the choreography stopped and the music went silent, my head would begin to fill with endless thoughts and fears. Living full-time in the studio was the turning point of many things, most importantly, my faith.

Six Feet Under

She weeps bitterly in the night and her tears are (constantly) on her cheeks…

Lamentations 1:2 (AMP)

Wide awake while the world is sound asleepin'
Too afraid of what might show up while you're
dreamin'
    KING & COUNTRY—"God Only Knows"

During the breakdown of the company partnership with my brother, we were expected to communicate from time to time as fellow board members of a different family entity for which he was both president and treasurer. During the spring of 2016, when I was transitioning to New York full-time from Portland, I was put on the spot during a meeting and nominated to chair the fall meeting that would be held in Arizona. It was presented by my brother as a chance for him to take a "much-needed break" as well as a "learning experience" for each board member to take over the reins from the president and create the agenda, select a meeting venue, and arrange all details associated with the two-day meeting. I had been given full authority to be the first one to take on this new responsibility and was expected to create my own agenda, in addition to the usual business that the board needed to address. The entire next meeting was in my hands, and I was to plan everything from beginning to end, which included travel, accommodations, meals, meeting materials, and the full agenda for the board. I was offered the assistance of the board's admin but was given full authority over the planning, content, and execution of the meeting. The one thing I wasn't able to change was the date, which was set for the same weekend as Lily's parents' weekend activities at her boarding school. I already felt greatly conflicted and in a quandary.

Under normal circumstances, I would have been happy to take this on, but I believe the timing of the assignment was suspicious. I felt like I was expected to accept the challenge and not waver. As if my plate wasn't full enough, I didn't feel like I could decline, as the undercurrent of the nomination felt as though it was a test. I feared my argument against it would have come off as though I wasn't interested in the work of the board, which was the furthest thing from the truth. So I swallowed my many excuses, including divorce, another cross-country move, parents' weekend, financial instability, housing issues, and of course the most obvious, which was the mounting pressure between my brother and me over our strained business partnership, and accepted the assignment.

It definitely felt like a setup, yet I took on the responsibility and decided I would use it as a means to be positive for the group.

There had been a growing uneasiness surrounding leadership and a breakdown of effective internal communication. My brother's close friend had been hired as a financial advisor to the board, among other things. I just felt like the best thing to do was to consider it an opportunity to do good and to show that I was a professional even under fire.

The rest of the board was aware of the mounting tensions between brother and sister, and I committed myself to never bringing a word of it or a hint of tension between us into the board room. I was all business and took the appointment seriously but knew it felt like a deterrent to the growing issues between partners. At the same time, we were forcing a friendly front to everyone on the outside. But my emails and written demands for a face-to-face, as well as clarity on wanting our operating agreement to be rewritten, fell on deaf ears. He finally flat-out refused to meet with me under any circumstances yet expected me to do his job for the meeting while he got paid in his role. The entire situation made me feel like an indentured servant, and in a failed attempt to reach my father on the situation, his words back to me cut like a knife: "I love you but can't stand you and don't like you."

This demeanor was so unlike the father I knew. It felt like it came from a deep, dark place, and it was so foreign to me. I kept asking myself what could possibly create this kind of behavior from a father toward his daughter. If the tables were turned and one of his siblings was not being a fair and transparent business partner, I doubted my father would have sat by without seeking some professional advice on how best to handle the situation. I wasn't far enough along in my walk of faith to understand or even call upon the scripture that reminds us who the true enemy is when we are met with hostility or hatred by another. Ephesians 6:12 (NIV) says that "For our struggle is not against flesh and blood, but against the rulers, against the authorities, against the powers of this dark world and against the spiritual forces of evil in the heavenly realms." My hurt and anger were focused on my father when he would say things that disparaged me, and it would take time before I was able to understand it on a higher level and accept that he was actually a prisoner of the enemy and that my anger toward him was misplaced.

It was under this mounting pressure that I took up full-time residence at the studio. My parents sent many mixed messages that ranged from "We are never there. Please, use the place as we are glad to help you," to "We aren't in the business of supporting you, and that should be up to your husband, please let us know when you might be moving." If my son or daughter had found themselves in the situation I was in, I can tell you without a doubt I would have been there unconditionally on every level, which is what I believe good parents do for their kids, especially one who was facing such a major life change after nearly thirty years of marriage. The studio wasn't even their main residence and sat empty most of the year, so their mixed messages about me using it temporarily made no sense and felt cruel.

I wasn't asking for their financial support, rather a place to lay my head while I gained some grounding in my evolving circumstances. On the one hand, I felt like they were adding to my stress by seemingly siding with my brother while pushing me out. I had never experienced this behavior from my parents. On the contrary, for years, I had seen my mother tirelessly be there for her sister or some of her friends, even one from my early childhood who had spent eight years in the California Women's Penitentiary!

My mother had sent money, written letters, and offered endless emotional and financial support to this woman for years. She was my age and had even stolen from our family and me when I was young. My mom bent over backward to be a mother figure to her for as long as I can remember, even after she was a convicted felon, and here I was her daughter, going through a divorce, facing a legal entanglement with my brother and trying to figure out the next steps of life and I felt pushed away and dismissed by my parents. I took particular offense to it in light of the supportive person my mother had enjoyed being over the years for others.

Suddenly I felt as though I was being treated very differently and likely only because I was a partner in a family company. While I was trying to make progress, I kept feeling like shovels of dirt were being dropped on me, making me sink even further. The assignment to organize the meeting and all the details certainly was some of that, and at a later date, I believe my dad slipped by saying, "Your brother wasn't fair, as he set you up." It would be months before he said that, but indeed it did at the time feel like what he later called it: a setup.

Around this time, Randy and I were both told by the office manager that our direct communication with the family business office was no longer allowed by my brother and that all contact had to go through the lawyers. It seemed especially unfair to me that Gary could still have contact with the office, but I could not. As Randy and I worked on our divorce, this became a hardship as the office held files on financials belonging to our kids and to my partnership with the LLC.

It was even more of an obstacle as many of the files I also needed to access to plan the upcoming family business meeting were held in that office. It felt like another major roadblock to me and one I felt was likely borne out of spite. Finally, I was given a key from a thoughtful family member and allowed into the office to do research for the meeting, but my brother only allowed it when I was accompanied by another board member or the office manager.

I also learned that Gary had tried to put restrictions on me accessing any information on the LLC's investment portfolio, which didn't seem right in light of the fact that I was a fifty percent owner of the company. My solo meeting in Portland with the lawyer at Big Pink and later with the financial advisor had apparently created what I believed to be a false sense of fear by my brother that I might eventually position myself for a suit against him. My notes to my counsel on the matters at the time included me saying that "I have had no notification from Gary why he has set things up with such intense secrecy."

It was an impossible time, and my emotions ran up and down like a roller coaster. I was glad to be in New York, to be among my friends and back with my dance and yoga community, and near my business partners in the skincare company. I attended social and business events and tried to build my clientele while managing the stress of divorce and being a bi-coastal mother and the growing issues with my brother. My only outlet was the gym, often followed by a large plate of pasta and a glass of red wine or two. I gained 20 pounds that year in a terrible cycle of overeating and feeling trapped in my thoughts, as well as the confining 350-square foot studio.

I was not myself, and my emotional stress became confusing as I would call my mom but not always get the unconditional love I was seeking. I feared going to sleep at night because I knew I would wake up and start the emotional cycle of worrying all over again. I felt deeply alone, scared, frustrated, and trapped. My daughter also seemed to feel my stress, and I could tell her visits to me were uncomfortable seeing me living in such tight quarters sleeping on a hide-a-bed that was propped up with my many boxes and belongings stored underneath. On top of it all, the pre-war studio walls were starting to show cracks in a wall between the kitchen and bathroom, as it appeared that a water leak might be brewing deep within the old plaster.

Over the Fourth of July, I accepted the gracious invitation of a close friend who let Lily and me stay at her place in the East Village while repairs were being attempted on the leak in the studio. I felt thankful beyond words but also ashamed because my world felt so unstable. My parents were telling me that I might have to move out just as I had gotten settled since the water leak could take months. It was a very uncertain time, and sometimes I was able to retreat to our house in Connecticut, but that felt awkward as my personal belongings had been relocated by Randy into the basement, and I noticed photos of me were taken down. The whole energy in the house didn't feel the same, but it was still ours, and I had the right to be there, and it gave me moments to exhale and take stock of our lives.

Every inch of the house had been a work of love over the years between Randy and me. When we found the house, we were especially pleased to discover that the beautiful exposed beams throughout the home had small markings on them from Roseburg Lumber, which was from the town in Oregon where he was born. We had so many good times in the house, and it reminded us so much of our upbringing in Oregon, as the house was surrounded by the woods. Every room and item collected had a story of our long history together, and it was mostly a good feeling to be there even though we both had moved on with our lives.

I knew the house was becoming something of my past, but going back on occasion was nice and also a reminder of how many good times we did have and how much love I believe we would always have between us even though we were parting ways. A lifetime of history between two people who met as teens is impossible to erase, and I don't believe either of us has, but we have had to learn to move forward, and in doing so, I am always grateful for what a wonderful father he is to our kids and the peace between us that exists and is priceless and a testimony to the kind of people I believe we have always been.

As my family issues mounted, Randy and his family proved to be more of a family to me than ever, and the irony was that we were divorcing. His family was treating me the way I wished my parents would. The words of my father both to me, and at times to Randy, were just out of left field. Likely, coming from a false narrative about my motives, all I could think was how blind I had been before that day in Portland when the lawyer finally gave me the truth. My seeking legal and financial advice had seemed to create an angry tangle of unnecessary misunderstandings resulting in my ultimate isolation.

My life felt transient. I lived from the suitcases and boxes that held my clothes but had nowhere to be unpacked in the tiny studio. Money was so tight I remember struggling at times to pay for groceries, a weekly metro card, or personal necessities. My assets were tied up with a partner who made me feel I was held hostage and unable to help myself even though I should have been allowed to under the circumstances. What little I could do to help myself, I did. I was trying to build my online business as it offered me the flexibility I needed and supplemented some of what I was getting in maintenance for the time being.

The majority of my time was now being spent on legal matters as I worked with my lawyer in Portland to somehow navigate my way out of the impossible operating agreement, which felt like a noose around my neck. I was also spending a huge part of my time now planning and organizing the family business meeting that would take place that fall. It felt clear to me that the amount of extra work my brother had handed me likely came for a reason. I resented that he still got a paycheck for his work, yet I was doing his job for free. If I complained about it, I feared I would be giving him reason to attempt to oust me from the board. It was a terrible position to be in, on the one hand trying to fight my way out of the entanglements, and on another, trying to prove myself. The densely packed studio was both a safe haven and a cave of perpetual stress.

Papers were stacked around me, and finding a sliver of workable desk space in the studio was challenging. I wanted to prove to my father and brother that I was a professional and would do an outstanding job preparing the agenda for the upcoming meeting, yet it felt like a cruel joke to put on me as they knew I was navigating my divorce, my kids trying to finish school and our stressful financial situation. I really needed to put my time into looking for a full-time job, but the excess work and responsibilities and the crushing commitment to the legal issues were taking an enormous number of hours each week.

At one point, my mother decided to become a skincare client, and I was happy to help her with items she needed as it benefitted us both. I needed the business, and she was happy with the beauty products. I felt like it was an olive branch, and I happily took it and appreciated that it gave us something to talk about that wasn't family dynamics. Who knew that a skincare regimen could bring such a reprieve? Well, it did for a time, and it made me happy.

My days were spent juggling so many things coast to coast and continually feeling like I was getting nowhere. I spent hours researching details and solidifying plans for the meeting, my business, the legal issues between my brother and me, and the mounting forensics that were taking place in the accounting of the LLC. Then, there was my divorce, what the kids needed, how to handle our house and who would get what, touring colleges with Lily, and trying to help her feel grounded while I struggled with it myself. I was constantly busy and felt so much kept heaping on top of me that it was hard to catch my breath sometimes. My trust in my parents wavered as their interest in my using the studio also walked a line of them wanting me out.

The hardest thing was that I couldn't access my own resources to get myself into my own apartment. New York was expensive, and the struggle was real.

August and September of 2017 were two months of extreme confusion as most of August, my parents were distancing from me again. My dad would text me questions about my intentions around how long I would be in the studio, and my mother would send another text saying, "You're going to have to find another place soon as it's not our responsibility to take care of you. That is something your husband needs to do." The meeting I was planning for the board was in October, and by September, my dad was telling me to stay in the studio and "Don't worry about paying us anything; we are happy to help you right now as things are challenging." I held my breath, then I exhaled, then I wanted to believe, and then I didn't.

On the one hand, my mother was incredulously saying, "My doctor has advised me against spending time with you because it's harmful to my health as I have what they call 'broken heart syndrome.'" Then in a text a few days later, I was getting "I love you, please come to Tucson for Christmas" from my father. Their messages seemed jumbled, confused, and conditional. All I knew is that I didn't know what I could trust, and somehow, so much of what they seemed to be saying felt like blame. I knew one thing for sure: my own heart was breaking. But never would I allow that to be the reason I would tell my mother not to have a relationship with me.

What was clear was that things were *not* clear, and the cycle of going to bed, waking up, and going through my day became agonizing. Consciousness hurt. The moment my eyes opened in the morning, and I took in my surroundings, I felt six feet underground even though I was living on the fifth floor of the building. The flood of awareness over my situation upon waking each day was unbearable. My mind would start racing, and the voice in my head would remind me: I'm getting a divorce, my parents don't love me, my brother hates me, I miss my kids, I miss my house, I am broke, I have a legal call today from Portland, I have a divorce meeting in New York, I have to plan this family business meeting when "family" feels fractured, I need my own place, I don't know how I'm going to pay my credit card bill this month, do I have enough money for groceries? It was an endless loop of negative narrative that caused me enormous stress that wouldn't stop rolling over in my mind until about noon every day.

I remember feeling like I could start to exhale around lunchtime and stop catastrophizing everything in my mind once I sifted through the morning emails and mounting expectations. I would become stabilized for a part of the day until it got closer to bedtime, and then the cycle would begin again, and I would worry and cry and have bad dreams until the moment I would wake up and feel buried again. This often caused me to drink wine every night with a carb-loaded dinner until I could fall into bed without feeling so much pain. I knew so much of this was not healthy, yet the emotional pain was tearing at my soul.

Fear of sleep and nightmares and then waking up feeling buried in a grave with walls of emotions, boxes, stacks of papers and rolling racks of clothes and suitcases and knowing every inch of the crown moldings from staring endlessly at the ceiling and every sound coming from the apartments on each side of me became a vicious cycle. I would wake up in tears, crying for my mother, my kids, my freedom, crying to be heard, and feeling like my side of things wasn't validated. I felt attacked, smothered, and silenced. The world was going on without me, and I felt I was left to dig myself out of the grave that seemed to get deeper and darker every day.

The only time I felt free was when I was out of the studio walking the streets of Manhattan. Eating, sleeping, and working in the small, cramped studio surrounded by the remnants of my life while trying to escape the bondage I felt from the legal process was suffocating. The walls were thin, and I felt like everyone on the floor who knew my parents had likely been told by them who I was and why I was there. My mother always got to know everyone wherever they went, and I sometimes had questions from residents if we were related, while some actually thought I was her.

It felt like the house without boundaries I grew up in as a child, and I could almost hear the whispers as I stepped onto the elevator to go to the laundry room in the basement or outside to get fresh air.

To them, I felt like I had been portrayed as that mentally ill woman with Asperger's, bipolar or manic depression who was going through a divorce while living in their studio because I was broke and had treated my poor brother disrespectfully and was ruining the entire family. Some of the looks I got suggested to me enough of what I believed was happening. I felt vulnerable and paranoid at times because my life seemed like an open book to anyone who would listen to the false narrative I believe was being passed out like candy at a parade.

My electric bass and amp sadly sat in the corner collecting dust. I had been an avid player for a few years leading up to the separation, but when Randy and I went our different ways, the music continued for him but stopped for me. Part of the reason was that my desire to play had waned, but mostly because the noise would likely call more attention to me than I wanted from the thin walls of the small studio. My appetite for music was therefore satisfied through my playlists on my headphones or in dance class.

The music echoed so much of what I was experiencing, whether it was heartbreak or feeling misunderstood. Some songs were just too painful to listen to as they reminded me of my many decades with Randy, but what was resonating most were strong female voices talking about overcoming hardship. I clearly remember walking from the 86th street subway one night with tears streaming down my face as I got closer to the studio, which felt like I was going back into my cell. Alicia Keys was pouring her heart out in "Pawn It All," a song that resonated deeply within me as it was about surviving in New York despite loss and hardship. "See, I learned the hard way," she cried, "now I'm doing it in my way..." played over and over as I made the turn on Columbus Avenue just a block from the studio.

The music mirrored my heavy emotions as I felt cheated and wronged. Abandoned by the ones I loved when I needed them most, I knew I would fight to stand strong even while my assets were at stake and the gifts from my grandmother had seemingly been intercepted, and my character had been attacked. I was not without my guts and integrity. I wanted to break free and start over. They could take my material possessions and tell embellished stories about me, but my character of who I was and would be was strong within my soul.

Even with moments of inner strength, there were more days than I want to admit where I fell to my knees in tears missing my grandma, my parents, wanting them to hear me whether here on earth or from heaven. I cried and cried, and my eyes were swollen, and sometimes my eyelids were bruised purple from pushing out so many painful tears. As silly as it sounds now, I remember taking photos of those bruises on my eyelids because I hardly believed it myself. The pain was deeper than I could bear at times, and I often made mental notes to myself to never ever forget that agony, as I vowed if I ever rise out of it, I would try to help someone else who was in a deep state of grief.

A beautiful leather-bound Bible which had been given to me a few years earlier by Donatella suddenly appeared among the stacks of my belongings. I found myself slowly turning to its pages seeking answers and understanding as often as my pain grew. The seeds of my faith were being replanted in that small studio as the painful moments of being alone faintly reminded me of the hopelessness I'd felt years before over Lily and her kidney problem. I was trying to fix things I couldn't, and I was sinking under the pressure, and those loved ones I so desperately needed I felt instead were working against me. I wanted so much to be heard and to understand why they appeared unwilling to hear my side instead of adopting their own narrative.

The "I love you" text from my dad around this time, out of the blue, fell totally flat as I sensed something insincere behind his words. Gone were the days when he would call me by my silly yet familiar nickname, "Tweety." The usual terms of endearment had noticeably ceased, and I knew that when I was addressed now by my birth name, the formality of the growing rift was more than noticeable. It felt scary. Our relationship was becoming unrecognizable to me.

I deeply missed having a mother. I needed my mom so much, and I looked at the framed photo of her with her own mother sitting on the top of the dresser in the studio. They were arm in arm, both smiling, and I yearned to have that easy, loving relationship with my mom. There were photos of my kids and my parents and some of the happy years we all had when they first bought the studio and came often to New York.

It was a life that didn't exist anymore, and I felt it was an unnecessarily cruel way to be punished for wanting a divorce and to exercise my right to manage my own life. I never wanted to hurt anyone. I just wanted to be happy and to feel a sense of myself for the first time in my life. The price of that desire was enormous, and the emptiness over my mom not being in my world like the smiling photo of her with her own mother caused me to double over in anguish time and time again.

I finally put the photo face down as I could no longer be reminded of what I didn't have and felt I deserved from my mother. If I brought up how much I missed her and needed her, she told me that I had pushed them away. It often got back to me from others that my parents were claiming as much and that they longed to be with me but that I had simply shoved them away and that their hearts were "broken." Yet, I knew otherwise. There were emails and texts from my father to me and my kids that said things like, "We are done with the McCoys," or "We wish you well, but we are moving on." The martyrdom of how they felt pushed away was almost laughable but mostly pathetic as it was quite simply the farthest thing from the truth, and it all got back to me over time.

My sense of reality was wavering as my own truth felt negated and rewritten. Echoes of their perceived sadness over me not being in their life found their way back to me from family, friends, and relatives, yet their interactions with me were so vastly different than what people were hearing. I was not free. I wanted people on the outside to hear me and to hear my truth. My mind kept turning over John 8:32 (NIV), "Then you will know the truth, and the truth will set you free."

The television on top of the dresser was my only window into the outside world, in addition to the small western-facing windows off the studio, which faced West 85th street. If I wasn't looking at the tops of trees and cars, I was watching TV to try to get my mind off the mounting issues, yet I felt disconnected from what was happening in the world. The news was too much, and I couldn't connect to anything that brought me more pain as my own life had enough of that to supply an entire TV series. I waffled between watching *American Pickers* and episodes of *M*A*S*H* to keep things light and relatively predictable.

Through the deep yearnings for a maternal voice, I found "Enjoying Everyday Life" with Joyce Meyer, a midwest mother of four who had risen from her own dysfunctional family of origin to create a worldwide ministry. Her messages about overcoming unspeakable sexual abuse from her father were nothing like what I was going through with my own, but I deeply resonated with her feelings of disappointment with her own mother, who she said was unable to stand up to her father to protect her. Her only brother had a lifetime of ups and downs, and I felt her message of survival come from a place in her heart that spoke directly to mine.

I heard the Word of God reach me in a new way through her sermons and her no-nonsense messages of staying strong in the storm. When I couldn't sleep, I found having YouTube videos of her handy to just listen and find peace, which helped me immeasurably. The more I could hear the positive, hopeful words of God, the more my negative self-talk diminished. I didn't realize it then, but I was learning to fight the enemy. As Joyce often said, "The mind is the battleground." It also made me feel less alone, and it brought a maternal voice I needed so much during that time. Most importantly, it connected me in a new way to hearing the Word of God through a messenger who reached me in a way I needed, and I was grateful.

Her sermons inspired me to make a daily routine of looking in my Bible for scripture and seeking the Word of God on all matters. It wasn't an overnight transformation, but it was a small step into trying to climb out of the grave I felt destined to face every morning when my eyes would open to the first light of day. It was a humble beginning of remembering not to lean on my own understanding and to seek the Word first. I was realizing it was time to start climbing out of the pit.

***

September was a rush as it always was to get kids back to school and settled into a new routine, except my kids were grown, with Jaylen in college and now living in an apartment off-campus in Portland and Lily starting her senior year in an upstate boarding school near our house in Connecticut. We were touring colleges coast to coast with Lily and trying to help our kids feel secure and settled while our family was unraveling. Randy and I always did a good job of making sure we were covering what was needed with our kids, and the irony was still not lost on me that we were in the midst of divorcing while working well together to make sure our kids came first.

It was a stark contrast to how I was feeling about my own life and being a daughter to my parents and how complicated their relationship was with me. It was more and more evident that my father and brother were very close, and as my quest to get out of the punishing operating agreement forged on, the absurdity of what was supposedly being said about me kept circling back. My father kept insisting that he was no longer involved in anything with the LLC and that it was all up to my brother and me. The irony, of course, was that Gary had hired our father's personal attorney to represent him in our quest to divide our business partnership. Whether my dad was involved in that or not, I do not know, but it felt too close for comfort and extremely one-sided. To make matters worse, my brother was allowed to use company funds to pay himself back for his legal matters, while I had to pay for my own. In a sense, I felt I was ultimately paying one and half times since the assets we shared were also taking a financial hit from this arrangement. Surely an hour with the attorney for the LLC, when I had requested it upon signing the agreement, would have been less costly than the mess we were in now to split the company.

It was clear that the relationships I always counted on in my family felt different. My father had always been my hero. I had always spoken highly of him to friends and family. I worshipped my dad and loved him so much and missed feeling like I could go to him for advice and unconditional love as I always had. My mother seemed compliant and distant, and her intentions with me felt confusing. The closeness I once had with my only sibling was gone. It was as though I was related to strangers, and of course, I wasn't perfect and had had my normal ups and downs living so far from my family, raising kids without relatives close by and trying to navigate the stress of living in New York City, which was entirely foreign to the way Randy and I had been raised in Oregon. New York had brought out the best in us and the worst at times, and it strengthened us and weakened us as well. Our first few years in Manhattan found us rooted in weekly visits to church and trying to establish ourselves in the community there as we had enjoyed with a much smaller church in Los Angeles. The thread of faith was always with us, but the routine and the commitment had eroded.

What remained strong was our commitment to our children. Despite all that was happening in the family and in our marriage, we were bonded as parents and always wanted the best for the kids. As Randy and I worked closely to make sure our kids were getting ready to start a new school year, we made it a point they knew they were loved, cared for, supported, and put first. I have so much respect for our little family; even in the worst of times, while each of us was going our separate ways, we did our best, and I believe our kids felt our efforts. As for the absence of my own parents, both for myself and my kids, I was embarrassed and confused. Sadly, I believe the kids felt that too.

There seemed to be a continued effort on my parents' part to convince people that I was mentally ill, as friends and family would tell me that they were told how sick and unwell I was and how my parents believed I had damaged the family. It was tiresome and hurtful. At one point, I even received a message from my father telling me that Asperger's was a "malady that ran in our family." What? This talk was completely out of left field and absolutely unfounded. I was tired, alone, grieving, and stressed, but definitely not mentally ill! On the contrary, I was busy and focused on doing a lot coast to coast, managing an impossible array of things with little to no support, and actually doing quite well, considering. Our family business meeting was weeks away, and somehow, the pressure seemed to mount, and it wasn't long before the agenda I had painstakingly created was upended and halted.

My father, brother, and even my mother (who wasn't on the board, but whom I had invited as a special guest to the meeting and which she declined) made it clear they did not welcome my decisions to have an invited guest speaker make a presentation on effective communication, workplace ethics, and good business practice. My mother messaged me, almost sounding offended and accusatory, asking me why I would bring up such subjects to the board. I told her that I welcomed her presence so she could learn more. I had been introduced to the author of a nationally acclaimed book on the subject and an expert in small and large business dynamics. I felt I had found someone who could make an outstanding and meaningful presentation to help us forge a more cohesive board and do so constructively. Months of planning, transparency, professionalism, vetting the right speaker, and working the message of inclusiveness into the agenda alongside our regularly scheduled business came to a screeching halt.

A battle of a new kind arose that became even more ridiculous, and it was more and more evident that, in fact, what my father had said to me about being "set up" was starting to feel more like a reality. After a wholehearted effort to embark on what I had been promised and to do so with the utmost professionalism, I decided to step aside and just let the situation be what it was: an unfortunate unfolding of events that, in my opinion, short-changed everyone.

Weeks of emails flying back and forth over their insistence that I should not have a speaker of any kind was counter to the instructions I'd been given to run the meeting exactly as I wanted to and organize an agenda of my choosing. The irony was not lost on me when a few weeks after the meeting, my father wrote an email to the board saying how much he wished we could all find better ways of working together and getting along. It went right into the face of what I had worked so hard for months to bring to the table, and I took the opportunity to respectfully remind him. He also accused me in an email to the board of bringing my personal issues into the agenda, which I vehemently denied. When I reached out to him for explanation and proof, he ignored me.

That October, after both kids were back in school, I attended a convention in Massachusetts with my team from the skincare company. It felt like a welcome reprieve to focus on something I was doing outside of the family and learn how to cultivate my own side business. It was an inspiring and wonderful group of dynamic men and women who were incredibly inclusive and supportive. As much as I tried to put my entire focus into that meeting, I was side-tracked with the thoughts of the legal issues, mounting bills, and upcoming meetings I was running the following week in Arizona.

The holidays were looming and text messages about everything from Christmas to Grandparent's Day at the schools and what plans seemed on again and off again kept coming in from my dad. It was clear there was a lot of confusion going on, and I just tried to focus on the present moment, although it was extremely hard. I managed to keep my tears and pain inside as much as I could and rise to the occasion of attending the convention and enjoying the attendees, but it was challenging as I knew more was coming, but I didn't know what it would look like.

When I arrived in Arizona to chair the meeting, it had been twenty-two months since I had seen my brother face to face for anything business-related between us. My requests for an in-person meeting had continued to be turned down or ignored. We suddenly found ourselves in the board room where we had to work together for a different purpose, and, to be fair, we did the best we could. The unspoken tension was evident, and my brother's close friend, Jeff, the financial advisor, sat next to him. His presence brought up extremely uncomfortable issues with me from the past, which I had to overlook in this environment, yet still, they lingered. The climate in the room was noticeably tense. Everyone knew we were engaged in a legal rift over trying to sort out our partnership issues, and the elephant in the room couldn't have been any bigger.

I had planned the morning breakfast in the board room to the smallest detail. Everyone was invited to arrive thirty minutes before the meeting to enjoy a private buffet breakfast and some small talk as we usually did. I left the seating arrangement to everyone to find what felt comfortable and had even downloaded a playlist of some of my dad's favorite music (which I knew happened to be my brother's and mine as well since our father influenced us with Motown, R & B, and soul).

The music played low in the background for thirty minutes for us to try to set a friendly tone before I called the meeting to order. Right in the middle of Stevie Wonder's "Don't You Worry 'Bout a Thing," my dad, seemingly agitated, said, "Turn the music off. It's too much!" It was so ridiculous that I nearly laughed at the irony of it all and was convinced that he didn't even hear the song, which I knew he loved. It appeared that he showed up already deciding to be tense, so I shut it off and let go of some of my attempts to create a lighter pre-meeting environment. That was out of the question, it seemed, so I threw my shoulders back, opened the meeting, and continued the best I could with what was expected of me.

To make matters worse, those two days of meetings were even more awkward as my mother claimed she was too sick to come as a guest to the meeting. She was also too sick to come to the planned family dinner that evening, yet she managed to have lunch the next day with another relative who told me later that my mother arrived bearing a psychology book apparently to explain my "condition."

As a mother myself, I couldn't imagine hurting my own children when they are down. I was definitely down, and yet I was expected to show up, be organized, have my act together, and produce. My marriage was over, and I needed the unconditional love of my parents instead of the constant feeling they were adding to the pain. To this day, I will never understand this approach, as my maternal instinct is to be supportive and helpful even if I may not agree with the choices my kids make at times. Unconditional love started to take on a whole new meaning as never before.

The only thing that made some sense was a line that Joyce often referred to when others hurt you, and you can't understand why.

"Hurting people hurt people," she would say, and it would be a while before I really embraced and accepted that because I was still in a place of trying to understand the "why" and feeling like the treatment I was receiving was totally unacceptable. My flaw was that I kept looking for the loophole from which to be heard, and it was an endless quest to nowhere. Leaning on my own understanding instead of stepping aside to let God take over was far from my reach. Submission had suddenly become a distant memory, and the price for not seeking it continued to create heaviness in my soul.

When I returned to New York from Arizona, I felt the walls of the studio closing in more than ever. Being in the sunny southwest and having a hotel room of my own with a closet and dresser that had room for my belongings felt like a long-lost luxury. As soon as I got to the studio, I saw everything facing me at once: boxes, papers, an increasing water leak that was going to require a major repair, and an eventual move on my part. I sat at the little desk, which was piled high with books and papers that reminded me of the mounting legal process that was growing by the day. The family business meeting was over, but now I had to finalize the minutes of the two-day meeting and wrap up the months of work that had taken time away from divorce and growing issues surrounding the operating agreement I had signed.

It became obvious that I needed to start looking for a place of my own. I didn't have money to put down on a deposit as everything I had was going toward legal bills, but I needed to find a way. I felt the holidays upon me, and the mixed messages from my parents and the long New York winter months approaching, and I knew I had to do something, so I started to pray about how I could get my own place.

Angels appear when you least expect them, and another one showed up around this time and insisted that I accept her invitation to temporarily use her mother's studio in her nearby apartment building. I believed that I needed to make a real move to a place of my own, but she persisted until I finally accepted her generous offer. The spacious studio was on the top floor of a pre-war apartment building where she and her family also lived. Her mother lived on the west coast and was traveling to New York less frequently, and the beautiful studio apartment with a fireplace and an outdoor terrace sat empty.

Angelica, whom I had known since we were sorority sisters at UC Berkeley, was so kind and sincere with her offer that I thanked her and found myself working in my parent's studio by day and then walking seven blocks to West 78th Street in the evening to sleep in the beautiful studio with large windows and vaulted ceilings which allowed my mind to escape the cave I was in on West 85th Street.

As much as I didn't want to accept her offer since I was already living so close by, I realized what a gift it was to wake up and not feel physically buried as I had in the studio. My emotions were still heavy and a constant struggle, but the stacks of boxes and clothes around me weren't there to suffocate me upon waking. I often grabbed my cup of coffee and sat in the morning sun on the terrace. I had never been so grateful to have the sky above me and a little break from the overstuffed quarters I was in just a few blocks away.

The time I spent at her mother's studio was a reminder of how blessed I was to have good people in my life and how grateful I was for such kindness. I don't know if Angelica knew how much those nights and mornings in her mother's studio helped me catch my breath again, but they did, and I will never forget the feeling it gave me to break out of the environment, which should have been a safe place but instead was strangling me.

Rest Easy

Be strong and courageous. Do not be afraid or terrified because of them, for the Lord your God goes with you; he will never leave you or forsake you.

Deuteronomy 31:6 (NIV)

During the last half of October, I found myself spending a few days finalizing the minutes from the meeting so I could sign off from my assignment. It was endless as emails kept coming from my brother, father, and, at times, Jeff, as to how they thought they should be done. I was capable and had done this before and didn't understand all of the added direction.

It became almost like a silly power struggle over me finishing a task that I had no problem completing. At one point, it was nearly demanded of me to let my brother do the minutes, but I refused, as it was my meeting, and I wanted to make sure I completed the task from beginning to end. I became more stubborn the more they pushed to do it themselves, as I felt it was something they wanted to control. I dug in and stood my ground on the exhausting issue. Their emails were relentless as I plodded through the thankless task and finally submitted the final minutes to the President himself, my brother. When I pushed send on the email, it finally closed the nearly six months of responsibility my brother had handed to me, for which they finally (at the urging of Jeff on the last day of our board meeting) agreed to pay me a tiny stipend. I remember my father throwing out an offensively smaller number before the board closed the meeting, to which Jeff came back and gave a slightly more respectable number. My dad questioned his suggestion, which laid more offense on me, but I said nothing. Regardless, I did my best and was relieved to finally be free from the "special assignment."

At the same time this was going on, my efforts to break free from the operating agreement with the help of my lawyer was escalating as forensic accounting was in full swing. By the end of October, my counsel formally requested that my brother no longer use company funds to pay himself back for his legal bills. A demand for him to cease buying or selling company assets was also formally communicated. These were "requests" which ultimately did not stop him from continuing some business as usual. My intention was to peacefully resolve the issues between us and find a solution to part ways fairly without filing a lawsuit. Since it was impossible to get him to agree to amend or change our operating agreement, the process was exhausting and challenging.

I knew the only thing to do was to try to get out of the agreement and the partnership, which may have been equal in shares but was clearly unequal in benefit. The tax burden alone was something I wanted off my back. Receiving little to no communication from the person in charge of my largest asset was unacceptable. I was locked in and had zero say over anything except the glaring issue over the large six-figure imbalance in the capital account. The fact that records showed he had admittedly taken a loan to purchase a house and later converted it to a distribution while I couldn't even get a few thousand dollars together during a severe hardship so I could establish a rental apartment of my own in New York to be close to my daughter felt extremely unfair. The growing awareness that my parents seemed to turn a blind eye to this glaring issue was beyond comprehension.

Tensions surrounding details of my divorce and our jointly owned house were rising at the same time, and Randy and I worked together to try to find solutions to the mounting housing issues I was having. It amazed me, as always, that we were splitting up yet able to conduct ourselves as adults, while Gary and I were not able to sit down as brother and sister and work out our issues. Randy and I could be at odds yet always found a solution to keep moving forward. Unfortunately, this was not my experience with Gary.

It was clear that the leak in the studio was becoming a mounting problem, and it wasn't long before the water had to be shut off in the kitchen, so I was only able to use a pedestal sink and the bathtub for all water needs, including bathing and cooking. My parents were pressing me almost daily to move out, and I prayed for something to give. The holidays were coming, and I couldn't fathom how I was going to get through it all. Each day I rose, I read a devotional and tried to take the extra moment to open the leather-bound Bible to read the accompanying scriptures. It was these little moments upon waking that gave me pause and focus away from the six-foot grave from which I awoke. Hope came in tiny steps and then tears, followed by the flood of emails that would tell me which direction the day would go legally. I saw no end in sight, yet I knew I needed to focus on the way to ultimately get out of the studio.

Calls from my best friend Georgia in Portland were always a welcome reprieve at the end of long days. With her upbeat personality and positive outlook on everything I was going through, she often had me laughing when we would refer to my family issues as episodes of the popular '80s' shows, Dallas or Falcon Crest. Sometimes she would send me images from scenes in those shows, which would make me burst out laughing. She always helped me try to find humor in the unfortunate family dynamics that were brewing. Even with my plate overflowing, she and I found moments to collaborate on a small business concept.

Developing the name and the logo were tiny signs of new possibilities springing forth from the ashes, and then a fire would start again with the legal issues and pull me away to try to put it out. It was hard to put all of my energy into things that could create work and a new life as I was trying desperately to break from the ties of my old one. It was like swimming and drowning all at the same time, and the effort was emotionally draining, but she was always there to help me find some laughter in it all.

My mother had stopped speaking with me except to email me orders for skincare products, so our relationship had formalized as one of consultant and client. Lily was starring in the school musical, and Randy and I made time to see her performances, and Jaylen had even flown out from Portland to see his sister on stage. I thought about the special moments my parents were missing in their grandchildren's lives, and it made me sad. They were invited to many things but seemed to find many excuses as to why they couldn't attend.

As the relationship with my mother eroded, I focused on my own daughter and the time I could have with her on weekends in Connecticut or when she came to the city. Even though we were no longer living the way we once did in a sprawling apartment a few blocks north of the studio along Central Park West, we were just happy to be together, even having to share the hide-a-bed surrounded by boxes.

I was so proud of her and knew the situation with the divorce, and my family unraveling was so hard on both of my kids, yet they remained strong. The relationship I had with my children was one

I yearned for with my parents, and the closer I was to my son and daughter, the more heartbroken I was feeling over their favoritism of my brother over me. It was something I couldn't imagine with my own kids. I loved them unconditionally and equally, as did Randy. My mind churned over these thoughts, and they constantly exhausted me. I would tearfully cry out to God morning and night and ask Him to guide me.

In November, I learned from Lily and Jaylen that my mother had gone overseas on a trip to Israel by herself. She never mentioned it to me but sent small token gifts to my kids. My dad circulated photos of her smiling in the streets of Jerusalem, which he even later emailed to me. I was surprised she was traveling as we had been told from time to time by my father how she was continually struggling with health issues and could therefore not be at various family events, yet here she was beaming and looking happy, healthy, and strong. I wrote back to him and thanked him for sharing the photos and told him I was glad she was well enough to take a trip. My answer was admittedly passive-aggressive, but I wanted him to be aware that her trip appeared to be the exception to what we had been told about her lack of ability to travel. I knew she was in a place she loved as her father's side of the family lived there long ago when it was Palestine, then under Turkish rule. I recall seeing many photos of her father and aunt as teens, living and being educated there as their father had been.

The area spoke to my mother. She had only been there once before in the 1970s, so I knew this was a big event for her. Why would she not share it with me? I saw her happy and enjoying herself in the photos and wondered what it would have been like for us if things had been different.

It could have been an amazing, life-changing trip for us and one where we could have visited areas together that were meaningful to her: places I had always heard her talk about from her father's childhood, and stories of her great uncle, who was a spy against the British back when the Suez Canal was opened. I knew fragments of the stories and had seen the photo she loved so much of this relative in Arab clothing riding a camel with two men flanking his side. It was an important piece of history to her as her own grandfather, a Presbyterian minister of German descent, had at one time also lived in Alexandria, Egypt, with his wife running an import and export business there before moving to the United States.

I knew bits and pieces of the history and always dreamed of my mother and me traveling there together so I could understand more. I had been baptized with water from the Jordan River collected in a bottle by my great-grandmother in the late 1960s and kept until long after I was born. My mother stored the water in the same bottle wrapped in paper stashed on a bookshelf in my childhood home. Whenever I took it out to look at it, I was always reminded of a far-away exotic and ancient place I'd only heard about in books or from my mother. Now she was back in the place where the Jordan River flowed, and I wished I could be there with her.

In 2010 I had been fortunate to visit Egypt with my fitness group right before the Arab Spring erupted. Just as Israel was so important to my mother, Egypt was to me. I had hoped that one day that we could travel to both places again and do so together, yet there she was, carefree, smiling and living life to the fullest in the photos while I was struggling to make ends meet, dealing with a divorce, helping my children and freeing myself from the legal entanglements with my brother which sucked the life out of me. We couldn't have been coming from more different places at the same time.

My days were still being spent working in my parent's studio and then sleeping at night at the apartment of Angelica's mother. My parent's place had WiFi and held all of the necessary files I needed to access during the lengthy legal processes, so I found using it as an office was most helpful. On the rare occasion I would work late and be too tired to switch locations, I would take my chances and sleep in the small space that haunted me at night and smothered me in the morning. It was one of these mornings that I will never forget as it changed my life.

Sunday, November 19, 2017, at 7:11 a.m. I woke up in the studio surrounded as I always was by the rolling racks of my clothes and boxes and stacks of files and papers around me, except this time, I was not alone. At the bottom right-hand side of the hide-a-bed was a rolling rack of clothes that were all too familiar as they hung there, partially blocking the light from the nearby window. I felt a peaceful presence in the room and wasn't scared but wondered for a split second why, and then I saw Him.

His face was shrouded in the long sheer scarf that hung at the end of the rolling rack. His eyes gazed upward, and his face was framed with a full beard. The pattern on the scarf was the same as it had always been, but it was now appearing as a three-dimensional vision with an unquestionable presence that was close to me. I noticed an unfamiliar calm come over me, and I was aware of my breath being steady. My half-asleep brain was now fully alert as my eyes fixated on the Presence. I felt a message so strongly from Him, not in words but fully by the space he occupied. His Presence made me realize that I was not alone and that he was very close and had always been and always would be. I reached for my phone to take a photo as I very slowly felt the Presence starting to leave. The pattern on the scarf remained the same, but its three-dimensional form slowly morphed into one. I snapped the photo before the scarf became flat once again.

I knew what I saw was a miracle, and yet it felt so normal and calm that I had to ask myself if I realized what had just happened. Isaiah 41:10 (NIV) says, "So do not fear, for I am with you; do not be dismayed, for I am your God. I will strengthen you and help you; I will uphold you with my righteous hand." It was made clear to me that morning that although I felt as alone as I ever had in my life that Jesus was with me, watching over and protecting me. My family seemed not to want to hear me, but God was listening and validating my existence and acknowledging my struggle. His presence was unquestionable.

***

My parents invited Randy and our kids to their home for Christmas, which they declined, under the circumstances. That invitation said so much to me that my parents were likely trying, yet confused, and possibly angry with me, or not knowing how to approach me, so they instead invited my soon-to-be ex-husband and our children to their home under stressful times. Their messages continued to feel like a lot of doubletalk, as we were still often told they were "done with the McCoys," and yet soon thereafter, an invitation like this one would be extended. It felt like gaslighting, which creates a void in a relationship that causes you to question your own reality. Their absence of an invitation to me felt intentional and mean-spirited. How could my kids feel comfortable going to the home of their mother's parents with their father when their mother was seemingly ignored? It felt like a constant game, and thankfully, Randy and the kids didn't want any part of it either. There was no need to question my own reality as I knew who I was. I was a child of God, and I knew that I was trying to break free from a family system that felt intent on punishing me for wanting to live my own life.

I ultimately accepted a gracious invitation from Donatella to spend Thanksgiving with her family at their home on Long Island while Lily was with Randy in Connecticut, and Jaylen chose to be with his girlfriend and her family in Orange County.

A month later, Christmas was a memorable, bittersweet week with Lily and me at our home in Connecticut as we baked, cooked, and cut a tree down together at a nearby tree farm. We brought every decoration out of the basement storage to make the house festive, if even for the two of us. It was a beautiful Christmas with my daughter that I will never forget.

My mother told Lily and Jaylen that she and my father had finally decided to spend Christmas apart. She claimed that my dad had work in Oregon to tend to and that she wanted to stay home in Arizona. Regardless of their reasons, I wondered if they had had a disagreement that had ended up with them spending the holiday season so far apart. Since they weren't communicating with me, I had no way of knowing for sure, but deep down, I had a feeling there was more to the story than what they had told my kids and perhaps others. I was very hopeful that the New Year would present a new path for peace on earth and goodwill toward men. If it could start within my broken family, it would surely be an answered prayer.

Gimme Shelter

In God is a shelter in the time of a storm.
Dr. David Jeremiah

You have not given me into the hands of the enemy but have set my feet in a spacious place.

Psalm 31:8 (NIV)

Strong, steady bursts of heat pushed through the metal grill of the floor heater near the window, which I had propped open to equalize the temperature during the day as I huddled over the nearby desk. Older buildings in New York often felt overheated in the winter months as the boilers were set for the entire season. I struggled to keep my mind focused on the tasks before me. These were the tiresome hours and efforts to legally disentangle myself from the unfair operating agreement, fractured partnership with my brother, and the divorce. This was not the full-time job I had envisioned, but the time commitment was the same, if not more. My thoughts kept wandering to my desire to move and to start the new year in my own apartment.

My mother was suddenly sending me texts in the new year inquiring about when I might move, and her interest seemed fixated on me vacating the studio as soon as possible. Money, my life, and my divorce were topics I didn't want to discuss with my parents anymore, and yet as long as I was living in their studio, which sat empty most of each of the nearly twenty years they had owned it, seemed to be a prime issue for them, so my greatest desire was to get out as soon as I could.

It's true that they needed to have a major repair done on a leak within the studio walls that was becoming a problem. I knew it was a matter of time that real work needed to be done, which was understandable. However, the greater matter to me was my parent's preoccupation with making sure I was out and that they were not helping to house me during a challenging personal time. They kept reiterating how that was up to Randy to deal with me, which made me feel like a child. Why did anyone have to deal with me? I wasn't asking for handouts. I was asking for a divorce and to co-manage my shared assets in the LLC as an active participating partner. At the very least, I wanted a say as to how those assets were managed. The irony wasn't lost on me that the operating agreement I signed and my brother's total unwillingness to partner with me under the new agreement was something I believed prevented me from helping myself. I felt the company was nothing more than a liability and tax burden for me while my brother enjoyed all the benefits. My life felt controlled by what seemed to me to be unfair circumstances, and they were quickly eroding my self-esteem.

I was trying to come up with a deposit and first and last month's rent and all that it would take to move, which at the time was a great hardship, yet for my emotional well-being, I knew I needed to move so I could start to find some peace. The mixed messages from my parents were frequent as they would often say, "We are doing so much to help you, and after all, you're living in our place" or "When do you think you will be leaving?" It had become a tiring game I no longer wanted to play. I didn't feel I had parents who were concerned about their daughter, who found herself in a transitional stage of life, and who might need some compassion and understanding. Instead, I felt like a burden and a constant source of their badgering, and I wanted out.

Around this time, I got a text message from a relative in Oregon who asked me if I had received a check from my grandmother. Apparently, my paternal grandmother had done some gifting to two generations of the family for tax purposes, and I was to have received a check for $15,000 from her. "No, I haven't received anything and haven't heard anything about it," I said. Another relative asked me the same question a few days later, and my answer was the same.

The money was unexpected and would have been an enormous help to immediately get me out of the studio and stabilized so that I could move forward, but I didn't know anything about it, and it felt strange to ask my father whether I was to have received a check from his mother. I finally made some calls to several relatives and learned that everyone from the two eldest generations received the same amount and that mine should have been received weeks ago. I knew nothing about it, so after much more inquiry with relatives and the bank, I learned that the check intended for me was written instead to the order of the LLC and deposited directly into the company account. It was a matter I quickly brought up with my father as I learned he was the one who had executed the checks for the entire family on behalf of my grandmother.

"You have a loan that you and Randy took from the LLC, and the check was issued to the company to go against that debt," he told me. The debt was for tuition for one of our kids that I had taken when we had hit a very hard spot and needed a small loan. We had every intention of paying it back and had signed papers with the LLC to do so, and in light of the enormous six-figure loan converted to a tax-free distribution by my brother, I felt my loan, significantly smaller, by comparison, was something we would have no problem paying. I had also not been allowed to roll it over into a tax-free distribution, as Gary had done with his six-figure loan. Our smaller loan was a constant reminder both by my brother and father that we owed the company that money.

He then added that my brother was tired of paying legal bills and didn't want me to use the money for more legal efforts against him. I almost laughed out loud at the irony of his comments since my brother was receiving personal reimbursement for his legal costs through our company and I was not. Once I heard my father say that I believed it was the most likely reason of all for not giving me the money from my grandmother. Little did they probably realize I truly needed it for housing.

In light of our divorce, legal bills, and the recent unexpected expenses caused by my brother's untimely exit on Randy's life insurance over the holidays, we were undoubtedly more stretched than usual but had not intended to skirt our responsibilities. Regardless, my father took it upon himself to issue my gift check from my grandmother (at the time, he knew I was struggling to stand on my own and find my own housing) and arranged to have it deposited into the company account without telling me. I was never told she had directed checks to two generations, nor had I been told I would be a recipient. She was elderly and likely didn't know the details, as her power of attorney was in charge of managing her affairs as far as I knew. It became a matter I immediately brought up with my lawyers.

In the meantime, I had finally found an apartment and wanted to move. I now had to fight to get money that was intended for me that would have been an enormous help during a very challenging and painful time. I considered going to Hawaii and starting my life there as I co-owned the condo in Honolulu and had friends and connections. It was a place where I was extremely happy, and I knew

I could live for a while and perhaps get settled at least legally with things before being able to stabilize myself before making a bigger step. I would have to keep my residency in New York and go for three to six months until I could figure out the situation, which seemed to get messier by the day.

No sooner had I started to consider this as a temporary fall-back option to my housing crisis, I was notified that my parents had rented the condo in Hawaii from the LLC through my brother. A sweetheart deal seemed to have been made, especially since the building association rules didn't allow short-term rentals, and the rent they would pay would go directly to the company, from which I was never receiving income anyway. My brother was allowed to do this as the general operating manager, and since the agreement he had drawn up prevented me from having any say about his actions, I was forced to accept it. I believed it was a way to keep me from accessing the jointly owned property at a time I was contemplating a move, if even a temporary one.

Doors were closing all around me. I was becoming deeply depressed and frustrated and felt extremely alone. All I wanted was to lead my own life and use what I had to help me get grounded so I could stabilize myself, work, and become a self-sustaining person. But everywhere I turned, I felt sabotaged. I had so much to work with, yet it was all tied up, and in order to gain access to what was rightfully mine, I had to fight for it legally in a battle I didn't want in the first place. To walk away meant I was still obligated to the liability and tax responsibility of my brother's business decisions.

The quick decision for my parents to suddenly rent Hawaii and take up occupancy there for the next few weeks or months for the season without considering any discussion with me, a part-owner of the property, felt calculated and cruel. I was embarking on a divorce, my kids were trying to focus on school, and my brother and dad appeared to be working very closely together. Even though my father constantly denied it, his name was still on the bank account at the LLC. The seeming lies were evident everywhere.

One night I finally fell apart at the seams. I cried nearly every day, but it had all become too much, and I let it all out. The disbelief over what was happening became overwhelming. All I wanted was to be able to have a conversation with my mother without feeling like it would be used against me. I needed her as a daughter would want her mother when her life was changing and her marriage was over. I yearned for her care and advice as mothers should do when their children need them, no matter how old. I missed having a mom, as the one I used to know was gone. Conversations and texts were laden with loaded questions and what felt like traps. It was a feeling I had not known between us, and it made me extremely sad.

The accusations and putdowns by my father were inconceivable. He questioned my intelligence, my decisions, and my desire to be an independent woman. The words he chose and the way he spoke at times shocked me and showed me this was coming from a deeper, darker place than I could understand. I now believed that I was the focus of all of his anger. Gone was the dad who would call me excitedly over a trip he was planning or an idea he had. The books and articles he would share with me stopped. His tone was flat, disengaged, and felt accusatory. As far as he was concerned, I had ruined the entire family, and there was no changing his mind.

My brother was another story. He had all but disappeared and was making access to my rightful knowledge of the partnership and its operations nearly impossible. Everything between us and the business had become an enormous struggle, and why? Because I had chosen to get a divorce? Did that threaten the family system so much that they truly didn't want me to be my own person and exercise the rights I had and finally give time as a partner in the company, which was equally mine? I wanted to learn, not take over. I wanted to claim myself and my life in ways I never had before, and I also was taking the advice my father had given me for years, which was to become involved. Here I was, trying hard to do that, and I was being shut out.

"How can you treat me this way?" I cried out alone and in disbelief over the way my parents seemed to forsake me. I started to feel a deep anguish and hopelessness that scared me. I felt misunderstood and starkly alone and knew I needed to talk to someone who would listen. I decided to reach out to a life-long friend in San Diego whom

I trusted and knew would be there for me. She knew my family and some of the new dynamics and was a good listener. My pain was so evident, and my feelings of confusion concerned her greatly, especially since she was across the country and knew I was hurting and alone.

After a long talk, we hung up the phone, and I felt even more alone than usual and lay on the small strip of wood floor between the bathroom and the foot of the hide-a-bed and cried until I couldn't breathe. It was a pathetic moment, as my spirit was crushed, and I lay there gasping for air, unable to make sense of anything or how I got to this place of feeling so discarded and mistreated. I watched my tears make a puddle on the wood floor and felt like I would drown in the ocean of my own sorrow. I don't know how long I laid there, it could have been hours, but I finally picked myself up and fell onto the hide-a-bed fully clothed. My hair was a tangled mess, and my face was swollen from my endless sobbing. My hopeless despair turned into a slow exhale as I lay on the bed, trying to let go of the gripping pain in my soul. The eerie echo of familiar Rolling Stones lyrics rolled over in my mind, "Ooh, a storm is threatening my very life today, If I don't get some shelter Ooh yea…" The song mirrored my feelings as I felt I was about to fade away into nothingness. I slowly closed my swollen eyes and fell into oblivious exhaustion.

Sleep was shortly interrupted by a knock at the door. I glanced at the clock on the desk, and it was close to 2:30 in the morning. Looking through the peephole, I saw Anthony, the super, who apparently had come up to check on me in the middle of the night. I opened the door, and he stood there in his pajamas, clearly exhausted but worried about me.

"Your mother called from Hawaii and wanted me to check on you." It would have been about 8:30 p.m. in Honolulu, and I had no idea how she had suddenly become worried about me, but here was Anthony in the middle of the night telling me that he was sorry about my divorce and that I was going to get through it. I apologized for the late-night interruption and told him it actually had nothing to do with my divorce and more to do with family issues, and I was so sorry he had been asked to check on me. He was so kind, and I thanked him profusely and told him not to worry, that I was fine.

Apparently, the friend whom I had confided in contacted a relative of mine, who then reached out to my mother out of concern for me. I was embarrassed but also realized that my dark mood had been scary and that it must have concerned those who cared about me enough to want to make sure I was okay. I went to my phone and saw it had run out of battery while I was sleeping. Once I charged it, I checked to see if I had slept through a call or a text from my mother, but there was none.

Anthony had been sent to check on me, but why wouldn't my own mother call me directly first? As a mother myself, my instinct would be to reach out to my child before I reached out to anyone else, but my mom decided to reach out to the superintendent of the building in the middle of the night instead of trying to contact her daughter first.

To this day, the incident was never brought up by my parents, nor did they ever check in with me to see if I was okay or ask if I needed help or whether I was in crisis. Weeks and months later, I heard from friends and family who told me my parents were talking openly about how I was suicidal and how mentally disturbed I was. Wouldn't a concerned parent check in with their child if that is what they believed? What right did they have to assume their own narrative without checking the facts before talking so openly to people? Did they ever think how this might affect their grandkids, who were also hurt by the stories they were hearing? Not once did they ever reach out to see how I was or to verify if what they were saying was even true. I felt more anguish by the slanderous stories they seemed to be telling people, which added to my pain. It became a vicious cycle of evil and hurt.

The truth is, as I look back now, I acknowledge that I was deeply depressed that night. But if someone had contacted me about my daughter or son in that situation, I not only would have reached out to the nearest person to get to them, I would have also made a call at once to my child. To me, that is what a loving, concerned parent would do. I could have been in the hospital, and I don't believe my parents would have contacted me to see if I was okay or needed anything. The entire incident seemed to bolster their narrative that I was crazy and mentally ill. I was none of those. I was hurting and alone, and their neglect added to the pain. It was time to get out of the studio. Living in the space they owned felt like they owned me too, and I wanted out as soon as possible.

It would be several years before I became aware of the scripture in 2 Corinthians 4:8-9 (NIV), which says, "We are hard-pressed on every side, but not crushed; perplexed, but not in despair; persecuted, but not abandoned; struck down, but not destroyed." At the time of my lowest moment in the studio, I literally felt pressed on every side, persecuted and struck down, but the truth was, as much as I felt crushed and destroyed, I was not. I was extremely tired and in deep emotional pain, but I knew God had a plan for me. While my bank account was constantly on the verge of being overdrawn and I could barely meet some of my basic needs, God was making constant deposits of priceless unconditional love, strength, clarity, and awareness into my soul. The seeds of that spiritual wealth were starting to grow from deep pain, and in time would serve me well.

It wasn't long before God sent a second guardian angel to lift me out of that dark pit and place my feet upon solid ground through a dear friend whom I had met only several years before. As I was fighting legally to get the money that was mine and was being kept from putting it to good use to help bridge my existence from my former life to my new one, this second angel presented a generous offer to loan me the money needed to help me move out of the studio at once. She arranged a deal with Randy that helped put a plan into motion to get me out of my parent's place once and for all and out from under the barrage of emails and texts constantly asking me when I would vacate. Finally, with the generous help of this angel, a plan was made to get me into a place of my own and one that allowed me proper space for Lily to have her own room. I wanted my daughter to have a place with me so she could come home and not have the stress of her grandparents lording over me or us anymore in the miserable studio quarters, which at one time I had loved but now equated to a prison cell.

The incredible kindness of my beautiful guardian angel imparted a desire for me to help others should I ever be in a position to do so. I have never had someone go out on a limb for me as this dear friend did, and I was and will be forever grateful to her for helping me move onto the next phase of my life. Randy was extremely helpful in this effort too, and I remain thankful to him for standing by me in order to get to a better place away from that which was suffocating and hurting me.

It took me six months of legal wrangling to finally extricate the gift check out of the LLC and back into my hands. Half of its value went to the lawyers who helped me right the wrong. My father had allegedly violated a co-trustee law in the state of Oregon by not telling his siblings about taking the gift check intended for me from my grandmother and depositing it into the bank account of the LLC. Once he and my brother were notified by my lawyers of the law that had seemingly been broken, the check was immediately reissued to me, and the matter was closed, but the pain of his intentions was not forgotten.

After some forensic accounting on the issue of the missing gift check from my grandmother, it was also discovered that part of the fourth generation of the family had each received the same $15,000 issued from the account of my grandmother. Apparently, my father had also made sure that when he oversaw the issuance of these checks, that each of his three grandchildren also received money. Jaylen and Lily got emails from my father, who claimed that he had funded each of their trusts that January in the amount of $15,000. There was no mention that the funds originated from the account of their great-grandmother, and the original intended gifting to the second and third generations had spilled over to the fourth and gone over budget by $45,000. It was something I raised with the family as a questionable issue, as it wasn't the original intention of my grandmother, nor did I feel it was fair to others in the fourth generation who didn't receive the same. The situation was discussed but not pursued with my father and quietly dropped.

On February 6th, the day before my birthday, my mother texted me, sounding like a landlord. She was notifying me that I had to be out of the studio by February 25th. I thought of them vacationing in Hawaii, enjoying the apartment, while I was facing another birthday alone, struggling to keep my bills paid and get my growing legal matters in order.

The next day the text from my mother had a different tone, albeit one that sounded more obligatory given that it was my birthday. It was acknowledged like a checkmark on a list, and I felt it lacked sincerity. Her birthday was six days after mine, and already I was asking myself how I should address it, given my feelings, but I knew I would rise to the occasion and be authentic. I was determined to keep taking a higher road than they, and I was starting to feel better in my soul because of that decision. So, on February 13th, I sent a bouquet of flowers to my mother for her birthday with a sincere note to mark the occasion and just felt in my heart at that moment that it was the right thing to do.

A few weeks later, I managed to rent a small storage space near the location of my new apartment and started moving my belongings in preparation for my move. I was almost more excited about the storage space than the new apartment! I laughed to myself at how just that new sliver of storage space could have been the new digs I was looking for all along. There was a noticeable and immediate shift of positivity I felt with each box I managed to carry out of the 350-square foot prison. I delayed my move-in date to pro-rate the month and save a little money and used the storage space as a bridge to get myself moving forward. Randy had given me the idea, and it was a great one as it gave me hope. I never knew such a small place where I could lock my belongings away would give me immediate peace, but it did.

The day before my move, I took a vial of essential oil to the new apartment and made the sign of the cross over every doorway and said a blessing. I took no chances as I wanted the space blessed and cleared for me to move in and to feel safe. My faith had grown, and I was coming from a place of gratitude as I said prayers in each room and made sure the doorways were all touched. It may sound crazy, but I truly believed that I was leaving a very negative space and didn't want to bring a hint of that energy with me into my new home.

On the day I left the studio, I had a moving company bring the furniture that had been stored in the Bronx since we left our Williamsburg apartment. All of the things Randy left for me were moved into my new place, and it felt bittersweet as the beautiful curve of the glass coffee table we once shared reminded me of living on the Upper East Side and the artwork we had on our walls brought back memories. He gave me the sofa, and I let him have the matching end chair which he wanted. We peacefully and respectfully emptied the storage unit we shared, and it all started to feel okay.

On the first morning, when I stood in my new kitchen and looked out the window across the river toward the city, I noticed two skyscrapers connected by an elevated bridge, which gave the illusion of an enormous cross. Every morning, when the sun reflects off the water onto the beautiful skyline, that cross is a constant reminder that I am in the place where God wants me. My faith is front and center in the view of my daily life, and because of it, every morning, I am filled with enormous gratitude.

Rockin' Down
The Highway

Listening for the happy sounds
And I got to let them fly…
  The Doobie Brothers—"Listen to the Music"

Fridays after school, my brother and I would pile into the backseat of my parent's station wagon that was loaded up for our weekend getaways to the mountains. A cooler was packed, bikes were strapped to the bike rack, and the eight tracks were stacked in the front seat waiting to be played. Our first stop was the grocery store on the edge of town where my mom would pick up last-minute odds and ends, and my brother and I were allowed to get candy and comic books for the two-hour drive. My dad's mood was light, and he was happy to make sure we were pacified on the short road trip. The two-lane highway led east past orchards and Christmas tree farms through tiny towns named Cedar Flats, Walterville, Rainbow, and Nimrod. Once in a while, we would stop at a filbert farm and load up on salted and smoked nuts grown and packaged by the locals living just over the Goodpasture Bridge along the scenic McKenzie River.

It was the early 1970s, and my dad played a rotation of The Doobie Brothers, Creedence Clearwater Revival, The Spinners, The Isley Brothers, The Doors, Stones, all the good stuff, and his choice of music left a lifelong impression on my brother and me, as we still share the same love of the music of the era. Gary and I would get along for most of the car ride and then start to get anxious after sitting for so long, as most young kids do while in the back seat. The Cascade Mountains unfolded before us as we climbed higher in elevation. Soon Three-Fingered Jack, Mt. Washington, Mt. Jefferson, and The Three Sisters were visible. Once at the summit, we could see the valley in the distance, which was confirmation that we were close to our destination. The Resort could be spotted through the Ponderosas along the highway, and we quickly shifted our minds from the confines of the backseat to the anticipation of jumping on our bikes and roaming freely.

These were happy days, and the music never skipped a beat as the eight-tracks and vinyl constantly played from the living room stereo and turntable. Speakers were sometimes brought outside on the deck, and the volume was always turned up. Free and easy times in a place we loved created cohesiveness in my family of four, and the good memories still linger today. The family home at Wild Creek Resort was enjoyed for a long time year-round, as we hiked and swam in the summer and hit the ski slopes in the winter. My parents were great about getting my brother and me out into the wilderness for camping trips, hikes, and outdoor adventures.

There were endless good times with friends, playing board games, enjoying fondue dinners, and a constant stream of great music. It was an emotionally rich time even when things weren't perfect on cold winter nights when the power would go out at the resort, and we would group together in sleeping bags near the fireplace to keep warm, yet we made the best of the bumps in the road. I look back on those memories with extreme fondness, and the songs still bring back so much nostalgia of what my family was about and the closeness we once had. We were family as a family should be.

I can still hear my dad loving the heavy bassline and singing "The Rubberband Man" by The Spinners: "You're bound to lose control when the rubberband starts to jam…" I'm convinced that these special years and my dad's influence in his love of soul music were why I started learning how to play the bass guitar later in life.

Music bonded us as a family. We danced, we sang, we played favorite songs over and over. My dad was happiest when he was away from home. A heavy cloud lifted from him whenever we were on vacation, even if it was for the weekend just two hours from home. These were memorable times, and I remember feeling comfortable and confident and on even footing with my brother and parents. We were happiest when we were out of town and active in outdoor sports, sharing meals together or with friends, building a fire in the fireplace, and blasting music that made us want to dance.

I would run to my room, whether at home or at Wild Creek and grab a long '70s' style peasant skirt and run out into the living room and spin and spin around and around to Proud Mary. My dad would sing and watch me enjoy the music: "You don't have to worry 'cause you have no money, people on the river are happy to give…" We would sing "Rollin, rollin" loudly together, and I remember feeling happily lost in the songs.

I remember the volume up, sliding glass doors open, sun shining, mom sunbathing on the deck, and dad huddled over the stereo blasting the driving guitar opener to China Grove, singing "When the

sun comes up on a sleepy little town, down around San Antone..."
Every time I hear that song by the Doobie Brothers, I'm transported
to those blissful days in the '70s that felt simple and happy.

Years later, when I had a family of my own, I would take my
kids along the same road from Eugene to Wild Creek, often listening
to the same music creating many of the similar feelings those early
days impressed upon me. I've since dubbed them the Wild Creek
tracks in my playlist, and when I feel nostalgic about my childhood, I
hear the lyrics and songs which remind me of such happy, easy times.

The language of music remained strong between my brother
and me, and my dad often kept up with our evolving taste. When
I was in high school, he would drive me twice a week to Portland,
another two-hour trip this time north of my hometown, for classes
I was taking at a popular modeling school. We would listen to The
Police, Madonna, Devo, Prince, and other early '80s' favorites I was
into at the time. I was so impressed that my dad loved what I was
listening to and how he seemed to actually like the new sounds of the
electric drums and synthesizers. He was so cool and fun, and I carried
cassettes for the drive, and he often had some of his own. I remember
him listening to Madonna singing "Holiday" and seeing him come
alive at the new genre of music. He absolutely loved it, and I enjoyed
watching the music make him happy.

When my mom would make the same trips with me to Portland,
the music would switch to country, and we listened to a lot of Willie
Nelson and Kenny Rogers, who were her favorites. I have so many
memories of the thousands of miles my parents drove me back and
forth between the two cities that "On the Road Again" could have
been our theme song. These were joyful times as we listened to music
and lyrics together, and I felt my parents cared for my interests which,
twice a week, took a lot of time from our routine at home. It never
occurred to me that my brother may have been jealous over the time
we had and the commitments I was making to learn and grow, but
looking back now, I see where that was possible.

I still have such good memories of those days, and the music
carries my mind to the far corners of the songs, the miles, the mood,
and the emotions I was feeling like an early teen evolving into my

own life with my own interests and desires to reach beyond the corners of my backyard or my county. I was following my dreams and my parents were beside me, steering wheel in hand, music non-stop on the stereo, and engaged in conversation or just singing the lyrics with me. It all was so meaningful, and I felt unconditionally loved. I treasure those days, their love, and the endless melodies and rhythms that bonded us and carried us along the stretches of highway that broadened my horizons as a young girl growing out of her comfort zone and into new and exciting arenas.

Many years later, when my brother and I were in Las Vegas attending a family business meeting, he pulled me aside and said, "Don't fly home; let's drive together and enjoy the trip." When the last of the extended family checked out of their hotel rooms, we loaded our suitcases into his car and headed for Los Angeles. He seemed to look forward to our time together, and on the long drive, all of his favorite music from those early days came out as we reminisced about our childhood.

We talked and talked about the influence our dad had on us and the music choices that carried us well into adulthood, often keeping us in a past genre that we savored and understood as only we could from our childhood. The music continued to connect us, and he brought forth new songs from the same era that he loved, and we laughed and sang together. It felt as though he was the only person in the world who really got that part of me as we loved the early Motown, soul, funk, and R & B from a bygone era.

I look back so fondly on that road trip even now. Despite all that has transpired between us, I am grateful for those happy memories sailing down the highway with rich music from our childhood blasting on the speakers and laughing at our past and the fun we used to have. We had moved from the back seat to the front seat, and he was in charge of our destination, and I was happy to be invited along for the ride.

Cognac

If a house is divided against itself, that house cannot stand.

Mark 3:25 (NIV)

Just a couple of weeks after I moved into the new apartment, I was invited to house-sit in California for a dear friend whose family was traveling to Africa on safari. Initially, I felt a bit torn, as I was so happy to finally have my own space and was eager to get settled, yet I needed the job and also wanted to help her as I was honored that she would entrust me with such a big responsibility. She lived in the hills just east of Malibu atop a bluff overlooking their horse stables, vineyard, and winding creek. It was a gorgeous setting. I was excited to see them and spend some time with the family before they left on their big adventure.

I boarded the flight to Los Angeles, leaving unpacked boxes stacked high in Lily's new room and many odds and ends to my life that had been separated and stored awaiting rediscovery. By now, I was used to the suitcase life and looked at this as an adventure and vacation, even though I knew I had a lot of work ahead of me. I was headed to a beautiful ranch home with horses, chickens, four rescue dogs, reptiles, and a mule. It was a happy zoo, and I always loved going to California as I had lived there for twelve years, and it always felt welcoming. In so many ways, I felt like I was going home as these friends were like family, they had a godly home, and I always felt enormously thankful and blessed to be in their presence. Even with them soon to be leaving halfway around the world on vacation, I felt their unconditional love and trust of their beautiful home and animals, and it filled me with enormous gratitude and joy.

After spending a few days with the family to take notes on all of the care and feeding instructions for all the animals, it was time for them to be on their way. When their Uber came to load them up for the trip to the airport, I knew I needed to be extremely organized and focused to take on the responsibilities ahead of me, but I also did so knowing it was a tremendous gift to have time in a home and with so many loving animals.

The irony wasn't lost on me that my parents had spent time over the course of the past year closing the doors to their homes to me. The apartment in Eugene, their home in Tucson, and before I left New York, they asked me for the keys back to the Manhattan studio. I had taken care of that property for them since I found it just before the birth of Lily and helped them get an interior decorator and later a housekeeper. I was the eyes and ears of that place, but as soon as I moved out at their urging, they wanted the key back. At my friend's home in California, I had been entrusted with the keys to all the cars, the sprawling home, the animals, the barn, and the credit card to run errands and order food and needed supplies for the livestock and dogs while my own parents were taking back keys and making excuses as to why I was no longer able to visit or stay in their places should I be in my hometown.

Each morning I awoke to the four dogs who wanted to be fed or to go outside, and once I got them settled, I moved onto the barn, which was down the hill from the main home. The ride in the golf cart to the stables was refreshing, and I loved the smell of the nearby ocean air with the sun warming the ground. Visiting the "girls," as I called them as I'd enter the henhouse, was a chance to laugh at the frantic "ladies" running around waiting for their dried treats of worms as I refilled their water and feed. Gathering fresh eggs each morning was an enormous gift and a reminder of my childhood when my mother had banty hens in our own backyard when I was young. I loved dragging the long garden hose out of its coil to water the plants alongside the fence and up along the hill where the family had planted the beginnings of the season's garden. The feeling of cold water rushing from the hose to the ground while taking a few sips here and there from the flow took me back to my simple days in Cottage Grove when my mom had her own garden, and we tended animals and flowers.

One evening after I had finished feeding and watering the horses, I draped my arms over the fence of the riding arena and closed my eyes just as the sun was starting to dip below the tree line. Tears streamed down my cheeks, and I prayed to God, thanking Him for this precious time and for the magnificent surroundings. My heart was so full of gratitude, yet aching and fragile. I looked up to the palms, and as the sun started its amber descent into the horizon, I saw Cognac, the bay quarter horse enjoying his last few strides outside of his stable. I had let him out into the arena for some time to stretch and walk before it was time to put him in for the night with the other horses.

He slowly made his way over to me and pushed his muzzle into my chest. I wrapped my arms around his neck and talked to him as he seemed to pick up on my emotions. I knew from the family that he had been rescued from an abusive situation and therefore seemed to have a gentleness about him that resonated with me greatly. I felt he knew my heart as I did his at that moment, and it was magic. I have been around horses my whole life but had never felt a connection as I did in that experience with Cognac. His gentle yet strong presence anchored me as the tears kept falling. I knew I would lock that memory away forever as I felt God speaking to me through nature and my ability to recognize it as it was happening. Without a doubt, it was the beginning of a deeper walk with my faith.

During my stay, I became aware of each animal having a similar moment with me. We bonded in times I was feeling enormous emotion, and the dog kisses and even the shy mule would give me pause as if to say, "I love you, and thank you for being here." I believe animals have a special way of always trying to connect with us, and when we open our own hearts and become vulnerable in new ways, either through pain or joy, they respond. The funny thing is that even Waffles, the African Sulcata Tortoise, gave me a few smiles! It became a happy game of hide-and-seek, trying to find her along the side yard to give her fresh lettuce and tomatoes each morning. I have a photo of her smiling at me through the dewy morning grass, clearly happy because she knew I was about to feed her, but just knowing she felt my presence was such a gift. Believe me when I say that tortoises can smile!

While at the house, I found time to slow down, take in my surroundings, and enjoy the connection I was feeling to the land and the animals who were all in my care. What became more and more evident was how much I was also in theirs. I felt God placed me there to remind me that unconditional love came in many forms. I was in so much pain over the loss of my family and marriage that all I was seeking to replace it was often lost in the pursuit of being heard or being understood by those who were no longer in my life. The legal struggle with my brother was becoming intense and was a constant backdrop of my existence no matter where I was, but the love I felt from the animals was a welcome change. I thought of the dark and lonely months living in the studio and how focused I was on getting out and feeling free. This was a beautiful start to experience that newfound freedom, even with the family chaos and pain growing by the day.

My college roommate, Luz, who had become a soulmate for life, told me she had a strong feeling I was at the house in California for a reason. She told me she sensed a deeper purpose in my alone time with the animals and the responsibilities that surrounded me. She encouraged me to read the Book of Job during my stay, so each day, I sat down at a favorite place in the house to slowly read from the Bible about Job and his struggles. It was a story about why good people suffer and why others prosper. The timing of reading this story was uncanny as God reminded Job about how despite the world's dangers, it also has beauty and order. Job's deep anguish over his losses nearly destroyed him, and it was something that resonated so much with me as I read about his impossible challenges. His list of complaints and frustrations was long as he poured out his burdens to his friends and to God himself.

Again, I was reminded of the turmoil I was in with my brother and parents and how misunderstood I felt. As soon as I had moved out of the studio, their focus shifted to trying to find out where I was. My list of grievances was long, and my tears were endless, but I was filled with a glimmer of hope surrounded by nature and away from anything that could harm me. I kept my whereabouts quiet except to close, trusted people who knew what I was going through. It wasn't enough that I had vacated the studio and was fighting in the short term to recover what my grandmother had left me, but I was also fighting to be free of the ties that bound tightly around the circumference of my life as I was trying to gain my own footing.

God's advice to Job was, "Then adorn yourself with glory and splendor and clothe yourself in honor and majesty. Unleash the fury of your wrath, look at all who are proud and bring them low, look at all who are proud and humble them, crush the wicked where they stand" (Job 40:10-12, NIV). Job learned to put his trust in God and was humbled by His greatness, saying, "I know that you can do all things, no purpose of yours can be thwarted" (Job 42:2, NIV).

My own house was divided. I sat in a godly home whose owners were halfway around the world, and yet, I powerfully felt their love and the love inside the walls. I felt the love they had for their rescued pets and the love and trust they had bestowed upon me with the honor to care for it all while they were so far away. My family had failed to keep itself together, and the foundation of who we once were or perhaps never were, kept eroding, and yet the strength and promise of God's Word was growing inside of my soul, and my desire to lean more on Him rather than on my own understanding was beginning to take hold.

This became even more important in the months to come as I learned that greed would eventually attack my children. Gary had been the trustee of Jaylen and Lily's trusts, for which my father was the trustor. He had generously set up trusts for his three grandchildren, and my brother managed my children's trusts, and Randy managed the trust of our nephew. After some discovery, we found out that after many years of Jaylen's investment being mostly in the hands of my brother that the trust had little to no growth. As parents, Randy and I were never privy to the financial statements, but our belief over the years was that our children's uncle was doing what was right by them. Sadly, we soon believed we were wrong.

Jaylen, who was the eldest of the three grandchildren, had a trust that had been charged the maximum in fees by my brother, which was not illegal, but we believed morally and ethically wrong. Randy never charged fees to manage our nephew's trust. My father's goodwill investment to grow a nest egg for his eldest grandson literally had seen very little growth over the years, and once Jaylen was old enough to manage his own affairs, he gladly took over the reins. When my father found out about the disparity, he paid back some of the money to Jaylen that had been taken out in fees by my brother. To me it seemed like another instance where my brother wasn't held accountable and my father stepped in to make up for the loss.

It was a time where even my children were learning the importance of grace over greed at a young age. My father chose to stand by my brother and his decisions even though I knew my father to be a much better investment manager than his son. To say we were disappointed was a severe understatement. True colors were showing loud and clear.

As God asked Job to humble those who had done wrong against him, it was quickly becoming a lesson I was trying to apply in my own impossible and painful journey. Our multi-generational family, which I believed we all honored and loved, felt forever and disappointingly divided beyond repair. As I flew back to New York from California, I knew it was time to start creating my new home while strengthening my reliance upon God in all things.

Searching for My Father

There could never be a father
Love his daughter more than I love you
Paul Simon—"Father and Daughter"

And I will be a father to you, and you shall be sons and daughters to me, says the Lord Almighty.

2 Corinthians 6:18 (ESV)

It wasn't long after I returned to New York from California that I had to go to Oregon for a family business meeting. Getting fully settled in my new apartment still had to wait as I found myself packing yet another suitcase to head west again. There wouldn't be a smiling tortoise or a loving horse to greet me during this trip, as my responsibilities would be different and challenging in ways for which I felt both calm and nervous.

The legal situation with my brother was increasingly complicated as we seemed to move painstakingly slowly toward any resolution. The family business meeting I would attend would cause us to have to face one another and work in an unrelated capacity and for very different goals. Our unfortunate issues were between the two of us, yet the ever-present shadow of my father in the background always felt evident and foreboding.

My dad texted me for weeks leading up to the meeting, asking where I was now living and whether I was taking antidepressants. The random questions felt totally inappropriate and probing. He also reached out to my kids, trying to plan time with them at the family house at Wild Creek, which my brother and I now co-owned. I was reminded that my legal team had requested in the previous fall that both parties not use the residential properties in Hawaii or Central Oregon while we were in the midst of our legal process. It was a demand I believed from a distance often went ignored, and now my dad was trying to plan a trip with the grandkids at a property I co-owned without including me in the communication. To be fair, he may not have been clear on the details of the demand not to use the properties, but I felt sure he knew from my brother. I also remember telling my parents at one point that we had drawn a line on the use of the properties by me through my lawyers as we tried to sort out our partnership differences.

He reached out to Randy, which felt awkward since he knew we were in the middle of figuring out our divorce. If they were having conversations about football or mutual interests, I wouldn't have cared, but my dad always liked to talk about money, and since I believed he was still very aligned with my brother and we were in the midst of so much legally, I felt it was very inappropriate for my father to contact Randy. I started to notice that once I moved from the studio, his outreach to connect with those closest to me appeared to increase.

My dad was working with Gary to help explain the trust issues that had arisen with Jaylen's knowledge of the state of his investments. I had questions of my own for my father about this and other issues but decided to wait until I saw him in person to inquire further. I felt an undercurrent of uneasiness brewing and couldn't put my finger on it, but it was evident.

The meeting was tense as my brother, as President and Treasurer, led most of the meeting with the help of Jeff, who was soon being replaced by a new financial advisor due to an unfortunate terminal illness we had learned about at the previous meeting. The replacement was a younger financial colleague and friend of Jeff's who had come to the meeting from his home in the Bay Area to be in the mix and get to know those of us in attendance. I had decided from the moment the wheels touched down at the airport that I would do all I could to remain calm. It was an enormous struggle as I had so many questions for my father, but I also knew, given the legal situation with my brother, that we had to remain all business.

My father was another story, however. On a break during our day-long meeting, I approached him in the hallway while he was talking to two other relatives. After much thought, I had decided this was my opportunity to speak to him face to face about the issue of the gifts my grandmother had selected for each of the women in the family and had distributed through her three children. My father had been instructed, as were his siblings, to give her carefully selected pieces of jewelry to each woman in the family, which in this case included me as her eldest granddaughter. I asked him in the presence of two others, who knew the situation well, as I felt it would be a good time to just get to the bottom of something I never knew about when it happened years before.

I was careful and respectful with my words, sticking to what I had been told but also asking for clarity, which I felt I deserved. I believed I had been kept from the truth long enough, and it was time to ask him face to face. My father was understandably caught off guard and flustered but tried to keep his cool, especially in the presence of others who I knew were aware of the truth. His answer felt defensive, and I believed, factually questionable. He said a few terse words, including that the necklace I had been given decades earlier by my grandmother "would suffice." His comment shocked me as my inquiry was about the fulfillment of my grandmother's intentions with her belongings, not what he believed would fulfill an obligation. It really wasn't up to him, but his comment appeared to solidify my belief that he had likely made a choice that fit *his* desires and not one that fulfilled his mother's wishes. He stammered some more on the issue before we all went our separate ways for the duration of the break before reentering the board room. I wasn't satisfied with the outcome but was relieved to finally have a chance to start an honest dialogue about something that I believed had been kept a secret from me by him for too long.

As people came in and out of the room, his temper noticeably flared as I entered and took my seat. I stayed calm even though I could feel my upper lip twitching and was sure he could see it. My eyes looked carefully at him as I forced myself to remain steadfast. "God, please be with me and keep things peaceful and protect me from strife. Help me stay in your presence, Lord," I prayed quietly in my mind. I reminded myself not to give in to fear but to remain in faith. The wheels touching down on the tarmac and the promise to myself to stay calm ran through my mind with my prayers.

I saw his anger churn under the surface and realized this was not the father I once knew and loved. There was a darkness inside him that I recognized as the enemy. He grumbled something about how he couldn't stand to be in the same room with me, and I noticed some of my relatives look at each of us in disbelief. Spiritual warfare felt like it was upon me, and my resolve to stay peaceful remained resolute as I decided to acknowledge his comments with a question. I made an effort to keep my voice even and asked, "Would you like to explain that to me, Dad?" He seemed to become enraged, which made me stay even more steady as my mind tried to keep ahead of what was happening so I could find my next answer. My heart was pounding so hard I was sure the whole room could hear the vibrations within me. Despite that, I had also never felt so in control and felt the strength of the Holy Spirit guiding me.

While my brother was out of the room and in a moment of surprise, my dad appeared to fold under pressure and brought up a different subject, admitting that he had taken the gift money from my grandmother to me and had given it to my brother to put back into our LLC. I hadn't pressed him on this issue, yet it came out unprovoked as a full admission in the presence of others of what I believed to be an unethical and gross abuse of patriarchal power. "I had nothing to do with your gift. Your brother decided to take it and pay your loan." When I asked him why my brother acted on it, my father replied, "I told him to do that." He then added that I had "poisoned his grandchildren against him," to which I steadfastly looked at him and calmly said, "I can't believe it feels very good to speak to your daughter this way, Dad. That is incorrect, and I believe you have underestimated me." Just then, my brother and a few others returned, and with that, my father stood up and hastily gathered the papers in front of him and said to those who had returned to the room, "I'm leaving because I can't stand being in the room with my daughter." He then looked at me as he walked out, saying, "You are ill, you need some medical help. Something is wrong with you."

The entire incident was so shocking and upsetting that my former self would have fallen apart in tears, yet I felt steadfast in the power of the Holy Spirit and remained calm. I found myself immediately writing down exactly what had happened on one of the notepads provided by the hotel. Looking over my notes several years later, the logo of the hotel on the pad of paper takes me back to my seat at the table in that room. Rereading his words to me in my own handwriting serves as a painful memory of that moment yet confirmation of what exactly transpired. I might have either blocked it out in my memory or forgotten the nuances of the situation, but putting pen to paper in that moment would later serve as a reminder of one of the last times I was in the presence of my father.

I was calm as he walked out past me but also shaking inside because it was a confrontation that confirmed for me some of my worst fears that my father, whom I had loved and worshipped my whole life, was someone I was suddenly starting to believe might have stolen from me. The man I once knew was gone and replaced with a dark, angry presence. It would take a lot of time before I was able to separate the man whom I loved from the enemy who I believed had settled into his soul to have him behave this way. God's word teaches us to separate the person from evil actions as found in Ephesians 6:12 (ISV), "For our struggle is not against human opponents, but against rulers, authorities, cosmic powers in the darkness around us, and evil spiritual forces in the heavenly realm."

Some who had returned to the boardroom looked understandably shocked by what had transpired as my dad's place at the table was now empty. Yet, among all the chaos, I noticed my brother at the head of the table, shuffling the papers in front of him while keeping the coolest demeanor, literally acting as though nothing had happened. As soon as my father exited the room, my brother called the meeting back to order, and business resumed. I sat there during the rest of the meeting, feeling shaken and very alone.

Several years later, I was told by my mother that my father claimed I had physically assaulted him during the meeting break. She expressed her anger to me and questioned how I could do such a thing, and I was dumbfounded by the accusation. My mother had said as much to my children, which they shared with me, and she clearly appeared to believe it even though she wasn't there when I approached my father to have a calm verbal exchange in the presence of others, not a physical assault for which I was now being blamed. I had a room full of witnesses and yet what she heard otherwise was what she was going to believe.

While I was in Oregon, I had been told by my lawyers that my brother's lawyer had informed them that he would be at the Wild Creek home to do some repairs. The notification came, I assumed, to honor the demand we had in place that no one use the properties during our legal matter. Clearly, he was entitled to maintain the property and keep things running as the General Operating Manager, so the communication seemed in order. I was aware of the short window of dates he had earmarked and hadn't planned to stay at the house as I was the one who had made the demand in the first place. However, as my time in Eugene came closer to an end, I realized I had some personal effects at the property that I wanted to retrieve before I flew back to New York, so I waited until I knew he was gone and planned a day trip to get my things.

The drive along the McKenzie River invoked the memories I always loved and reminded me as it always did of happier times, but there was a sadness over the rift with my father and his anger and the never-ending legal issues with my brother. I just wanted peace. I drove my rental car into the main entrance of the resort and checked into Guest Services to get a code for the security gate. Winding past the familiar main lodge and the lake, then the golf course and homes, I took a left onto our residential road and slowly drove into the area where our family home had been since 1973. As soon as I got to the parking lot, my heart stopped. There was only one car in the lot, and it was my brother's as I noticed the California plates. I had come all this way and was not looking for trouble but did want my things, so I closed the car door and slowly walked toward the house, wondering how I would explain my appearance but even more curious as to how he might explain his.

As I got closer to the house, a large white dog ran out of the front door, which was wide open, and seemed to be defending the place by barking and growling at me. I knew the dog as she was the support dog, Elsa, the loyal companion of my brother's friend, Jeff, who had been at his side during the meeting a few days earlier. I called out, announcing my entrance, and it was obvious they had been caught off guard on a quiet mid-week spring day at the house.

I walked in the doorway and saw my brother sitting at the dining room table with a look of utter shock and surprise on his face. Jeff sat in the nearby chair and instantly turned on the charm, motioning for me to sit beside him. I immediately found this strange since the chair was only big enough for one person, so clearly, it meant I would have to sit on his lap. My previous experiences with him had taught me that he was persuasive this way and it often felt intimidating to me. I declined multiple times as he kept his arm outstretched to me and then kept patting the five or so inches next to him where I was supposed to sit had I accepted his invitation.

Spread out on the floor of the entire living room were a vast array of firearms. I guessed there might have been at least forty or fifty weapons laid out, but I didn't linger to count them. At a quick glance, I noticed what appeared to be rifles, pistols, revolvers, shotguns, none of which scared me. I was no stranger to such things as I had gone target shooting with them before and figured they were cleaning all of their arsenals after an outing. My brother was impeccably responsible with firearms, and he had taken Jaylen and me out years before, and I appreciated his knowledge and respect for the sport. To be honest, I was more surprised to see the two men in the house, apparently staying there for what appeared to be a leisure trip instead of the trip for repairs as I had been told, but I had no way of knowing for sure. I scanned the room and tried to stay calm, but the tension in the air was noticeable. My stress rose when I noticed two assault rifles I hadn't seen before, lying side by side. My mind was running a thousand words a minute, but I didn't say anything out loud about the scene I had stumbled onto. I wanted to get my belongings and leave, so I told them that was my intent, and I headed upstairs to the storage closet. The first three or four stairs had pistols and revolvers on them, again, apparently laid out for cleaning and organizing. There were what appeared to be long black firearm bags stacked by the coat rack between the entry hall and the stairs as I carefully walked upstairs to accomplish my goal.

Once upstairs, I glanced to my left and noticed what I assumed to be my brother's suitcase and clothes in one of the guest rooms. I quickly retrieved my coats and hiking boots from the storage area and headed downstairs. Before I left, I used the downstairs bathroom and saw through the doorway from the end of the hall that apparently Jeff's suitcase and belongings were laid out there. His personal items and medications were on the bathroom counter, so it was obvious to me that they had likely been there for a few days after the meeting, enjoying themselves.

Normally I wouldn't care at all and may have been invited along, but the obvious unfortunate nature of things between my brother and me prevented anything like that again. I could understand that they wanted time together since Jeff's health was noticeably deteriorating, but ignoring my legal demand not to use the property seemed pretty obvious. Truly, had he wanted to stay there to have time with Jeff, I would have been fine with some sincere communication about it, but we were far past that kind of exchange, so doing as he pleased without notifying me as his partner, legal adversary or simply as his sister was just apparently not in the cards.

We had always used this property to enjoy as a family or to bring friends. Since I had made the legal demand months before for neither of us to stay at this place or the condo in Hawaii, it seemed that my request was being dismissed. I decided to let it go and went to the living room to say goodbye. My brother hadn't moved from the chair and said nothing. I noticed a pitcher of what appeared to be margaritas on the table next to him and assumed they had come in from a day of shooting to relax and clean their guns.

"Thanks, guys, have a good time," I said as I turned to leave. My brother asked if I got what I had come for, and I confirmed that I did as I put the storage key back in its place. The blender was out, and there was food on the counters as though they had been there for more than an afternoon. Suddenly Jeff insisted on walking me to my car. He was terminally ill, walked with the help of a cane, and frequently used a ventilator to help him through the rough patches, and yet here he was, trying to get up from the chair and not accepting no for an answer to walk me to my car. It felt strange, and I kept insisting that I was fine, but he got up, grabbed his cane, and escorted me to my car.

The walk between the house and the parking lot was short, but he used it to talk fast. I felt him pandering me with words of endearment and perceived understanding of my family situation, which nauseated me, but what was worse was the admission of his crush on me several years ago when we were in Hawaii working together with my brother. "You know I had a crush on you when we were in Hawaii during that time when we were all working for the family. You've got this (he patted my head like a dog, I assumed, trying to insinuate my intelligence), and you've got a rockin' body, not to mention you're gorgeous. I love you, you're a good person, and I care deeply about you."

And there it was, the admission I wasn't expecting, all neatly wrapped up in an afternoon haze I assumed of tequila, adrenaline likely from his target shooting and the surprise visit by me walking casually and unexpectedly into the house through the wide-open front door. He underestimated me as I was prepared for anything, and I felt he might even be making sure my rental car was empty and I hadn't traveled with someone. The juxtaposition of him being so close with my brother and at times being adversarial with me in emails with our board, now admitting his fondness and attraction for me made me feel sick. There was no question about the growing tension between my brother and me and what side I felt Jeff was on, and yet here he was telling me out of earshot of Gary how much he respected me and found me attractive.

Memories of the trip with my brother in Hawaii and Jeff's inappropriate touches, unexpected and startling kisses on the back of my neck, and emails that questioned me about my marriage went far and beyond the scope of work we had with my brother, and I tried to keep my distance. I was naïve and didn't know how to handle myself then, as I was so committed to helping my brother with the work he had asked me to do that I foolishly put up with the behavior at that time. I knew he was my brother's best friend, and my loyalty to my sibling was stronger than my ability to stand up for myself and call Jeff out in the very inappropriate situation. I remember talking to my mom and dad about it, and I recall their response was unhelpful as they basically both said, "Oh, you know that's how he is, just rock along and let it go."

It was hard to let it go, especially now, but I also realized this could be the last time I saw him as his health was in a severe decline. My head was spinning on ugly words as a backlash, but I kept them to myself. The real feelings I had were how sad it was that he was a terminally ill married man saying inappropriate things to me and still making me feel uncomfortable while seemingly defending my brother and our differences. Behind my brother's back, his emails to me on occasion, and now his words confessing how and what he really thought of me were in direct conflict with the loyalty he constantly showed to him in the workplace setting. The whole incident made me feel sick and sorry for him, as I knew it was likely the last time I would see him alive, but he didn't leave room for me to say much that felt kind, so I stayed silent. It was an awkward parting.

I got behind the wheel of the car and tried not to speed as I left the parking lot. Images of the guns all over the floor and my brother anchored to the chair were etched in my mind. My hands started to shake as I passed back by the lake and the lodge and finally got to the main entrance of the resort before exiting onto the freeway. I knew I wasn't ready to drive the several hours back home along the winding roads through the mountains. Instead of taking a left to head west toward Eugene, I made a right turn onto Highway 20 and drove ten miles to the closest town. I needed to gather myself after the encounter with Jeff and my brother. The urge to cry was suddenly overcome with an unusual calm that took me by surprise.

I rolled into town and went straight to a restaurant to sit down and think about what had transpired. Should I call my lawyers? Did I do anything wrong? Had I violated my own demand by going to the house to retrieve some of my personal belongings? In light of what I saw, I guessed not but still felt the need to roll it all over in my mind. I wrote things down on the notepad in my phone, so I wouldn't forget the conversation with Jeff or the images I saw. It took a while to digest the entire event, as it was truly a surprise for all three of us. I knew it would be something I would think about a lot from that time forward.

I decided to tell my lawyers just to make sure I was complying with everything as it was happening in real-time. After I ate and gassed up the car, I began my drive back to Eugene, trying to process it all and figure out when to make contact with counsel. When I got to my hotel, I decided I would email my legal team the next morning before heading to the airport. I didn't know if my parents were still in town, and the entire state was starting to feel unwelcome to me, and I was glad I would be leaving.

"Good morning. Dena McCoy, please." The phone rang shortly after 9 a.m., and I was getting up and ready to check out. "This is Dena," I answered. The call was from the resort police department verifying that I was a homeowner, which I confirmed. He asked me the last time I had been at Wild Creek, and I told him I was there less than an hour the day before to gather some things from the home, which I co-owned with my brother. Suddenly my stomach dropped, and all sorts of things raced through my mind about the guns. "I've worked at Wild Creek for nearly twenty-five years and, well, I have to say that we have never had a call from the FBI, but we did, and it was about activity at your property." What? What activity? What happened after I left? "We've had a few calls from homeowners in the area who noticed two men carrying what appeared to be large quantities of firearms into your property. Are you aware of this activity?"

I was scared as I didn't want to give any wrong information. I truly believed and knew without a doubt that between Jeff and my brother, they owned a lot of firearms. Neither of them was a hunter, and both were extremely discreet with their target shooting. "Officer, yes, I was at the house and stopped by to pick up some belongings, and I know the two men, and I can also confirm that they own firearms; however, I don't believe anything to be dangerous about them having them in the home." I then asked him what the rule was on the resort for firearms as I wasn't sure, and then I thought I could be getting them in trouble without even knowing it. He confirmed that they weren't breaking any rules but that there had been some concerned homeowners who were doing the right thing when you "see something say something," so they did. The officer was clearly reeling after the contact with the FBI, as was I, so I told him my reason for being on the property and assured him that I believed there was no harm.

We hung up the phone, and my mind was racing again. The officer said every homeowner was getting a phone call like the one I had received, which meant my brother would be getting one too. Suddenly I wondered if he might think I was the one who contacted the police. The officer had said that several people had contacted them over the course of a couple of days, so I hoped they said the same thing to Gary.

I had done nothing wrong, but the fear of insinuation started to grip me. I called my lawyer and explained everything, which instantly made me feel better. I couldn't wait to get out of my own hometown, and my plane couldn't leave the ground fast enough. I checked out and went straight to the airport with the events of the past few days in my head rolling over and over again. If I closed my eyes, I could go back to when things were simple, and there were no lawyers or misunderstandings or angry outbursts of blame or untruths. If I closed my eyes, I could also find peace in a higher place with God, and it became my focus again as I exhaled and sat in the airplane seat, waiting to take off.

Juliet

For God alone my soul waits in silence *and* quietly submits to Him,

For my hope is from Him. He only is my rock and my salvation.

My fortress *and* my defense, I will not be shaken or discouraged.

Psalm 62:5-6 (AMP)

Several years before my maternal grandmother passed away, our conversations often shifted to the subject of my mother. My grandfather had died years earlier, and it allowed for a newfound closeness between my mom and her mother. I knew it was something my mom cherished as she shared her feelings with me about how grateful she was to finally have the time with her mom and to get to know her in a new way later in life.

My grandmother was easygoing and thankful for the relationship and my mom's endless help, but there were times when I was alone with my grandma when she would confide in me and ask questions I couldn't answer. "Dena, what has happened to your mother? Why isn't she taking better care of herself, and why does she talk to the waiter at the restaurant longer than she will talk with anyone at the table?" The questions were out of concern and disbelief over my mom's focus on others rather than herself. I had learned this codependent behavior from her as her daughter, always pleasing others nearly to a fault and not knowing how to stand up for myself. I called it the "pleasing sickness," and during later years of my life, I became more aware of how detrimental it was in my own relationships, so I started to work hard to break the cycle.

I believe my mother is perhaps the most chronic co-dependent person I have ever known, and my thoughts shift between pity and anger, thinking about how many times she would be focused on the neighbors or others instead of my brother and me when we were young. She was a good mother, she worked hard, and we felt loved, but she seemed to always have a deep need to be involved with outsiders instead of those who were right in front of her, much less living with her. This was something my grandma became more and more aware of in her later years and something I believe she couldn't understand. For me, it was all I knew.

I remember the countless times our family dinners would be interrupted because the Fuller Brush Man would knock on the door, and my mom would leave the table and spend an hour chatting and then finally order cleaning products. She became involved in his personal stories and life's challenges when all I wished she would do was just purchase the products at any time other than the dinner hour, but this guy was one of many who knew when and how to access my mother, her open heart, and willing ear to listen and be a friend.

There were so many times my brother and I would retreat to our bedrooms, and my dad would go to his office in the basement because rare family time at home would be interrupted by someone who knew our household had few boundaries. I think this is one reason I have enjoyed living so many years in high-rise apartments in New York City, as the unexpected drop-ins rarely, if ever, happen like they do in a free-standing house. It has made me feel more protected and in control of my personal environment. The door to my childhood home, by comparison seemed to be open at all hours.

An early memory of what I fondly recall as our first and perhaps only mother-daughter trip was when I was around twelve years old. We decided to fly from Eugene to San Francisco together for a few days and enjoy the sights. We stayed at the Hyatt Regency Embarcadero Center, and I remember being mesmerized by the modern architecture of the lobby with a large geometric sculpture in the center of a long fountain. We walked the hilly streets of the city and rode the cable cars and ate at Fisherman's Wharf and did all of the usual touristy things that were necessary for a first trip to the city. We had a great time together, and I enjoyed being with my mom and in the city seeing so many new things. I felt grown-up and special being just with her. She wanted to make sure I had a good time, and I did, but when I think back decades later, two incidents stand out in my mind that I didn't notice at the tender age of twelve as being unusual. But now that I am a mother with my own children, I find the memories a bit sad and unpleasant.

"Would you like to see Alcatraz?" We were standing at the edge of the wharf, looking across the bay at the island with the famous prison. I had heard about it as a child because my father's secretary had grown up at Alcatraz as the daughter of a prison guard, so I knew what it was. I was intrigued and said yes to the offer. My first thought was that we would take a ferry together to the island, but instead, my mom pointed to the helicopter tour and said it would be a fun way to go. I was excited and expected we would do it together, but she only bought one ticket, and I soon realized that if I wanted to see Alcatraz,

I was going to do so by myself from a helicopter. "You'll love it. I will be right here when you get back," she said as I was suddenly strapped in, awaiting liftoff.

It all happened so fast, and I remember sitting next to strangers and seeing my mom wave at me as the helicopter rose into the air for the circular tour of Alcatraz. I was more nervous about sitting next to people I didn't know than being in the air. It was my first time in a helicopter, and it thrilled me, but I wished my mom was in the seat next to me. When I think back on this now, I find it so strange that she didn't come along and instead allowed me to go in the air without her. I don't remember any explanation for her decision to have me fly without her. It's possible she may have said that it was something she had already seen, yet I always felt like it was something we would have done together.

Overall, I recall the experience being fun, and it prompted me to take several helicopter rides later in life, but to think that she chose to stay on the ground while I rode by myself now seems so strange. Not in a million years could I imagine putting my young daughter in such a position without me by her side, and yet there she was, waving and standing there on the dock as she said she would be when I landed. I didn't think anything more about it until I was an adult and then realized how odd that decision was.

At night when we would retreat to the hotel, she would have my dinner ordered to the room, and she would go downstairs to eat and have a glass of wine in the bar. "Dena, be sure you don't open the door for anyone unless you know it's me," she would say as she left. I was nervous about being alone in a big hotel in a new city and felt scared thinking someone would try to find me there, so I tried to keep my mind off of it by watching TV. I couldn't fall asleep until she came back, and I remember feeling my entire body relax once I knew she was in the room.

I look back now and realize it was probably her way of finding necessary alone time, which I understand as a mother and a wife, but also realize the inherent dangers of some of those choices. I don't think for one moment my mother was doing anything other than just finding moments to herself, but on such a trip in a strange city and being so young, I felt vulnerable. I guess it's safe to say that in those instances, I didn't feel protected, and it's something that has taken me years to understand.

When I was around five years old, I felt uncomfortable when one of my parent's friends came to our house to visit. Dave was their "bachelor friend," as they referred to him, and "He loves beautiful women," they would say. Dave would come into the house and tell stories of his girlfriend or his dates, and at a young age, I felt very uneasy. He would talk about his beautiful Asian girlfriend and describe her long black hair and sexy long legs. He would go on and on about their relationship and then would start talking about me and how I had the look of a famous beauty. He told me I reminded him of the dancer, Juliet Prowse, someone I had heard of but didn't know as a child. Comments about how I looked like her and had the beginnings of her famously long legs were part of every visit, and I knew from the moment he would arrive at the house, I would feel put on the spot.

Dave was nice, but he also made me feel creepy, and I recall once coming out of my room after my parents asked me to get ready for bed, and Dave said he would massage my back if I laid down on the couch. Somehow, I ended up there in the middle of the living room after dinner, and Dave was giving me a backrub in my nightgown. At the time, I complied, but I remember feeling uncomfortable, not so much from the act but more from how he seemed to control what was happening in my home and how little ability I had to take charge of myself around the age of five. Again, when I look back decades later and now as a mother, I am absolutely appalled and uncomfortable thinking how unprotected I may have been in that situation, and yet it seemed to be okay with everyone in the house. Everyone was in the living room, as I recall, and I don't believe my parents thought I was in any danger, and I likely wasn't, but what resonated then and now were my feelings of vulnerability and powerlessness that were never appropriately addressed. I didn't want to be touched, and I didn't know how to take charge of my boundaries without the support of my parents, which felt confusing and, at times, unavailable.

One afternoon around my sixteenth birthday, I was home with my mom, and a close family friend of ours stopped by to say hello. My mom and I chatted with him in the foyer as he finished his visit, and as he started to walk down the front steps, he suddenly turned around and walked back to us and said, "Oh hey, I have something for you! Now that you're sixteen, you need to know how to be kissed." Suddenly he grabbed both of my arms and pulled me close, and stuck his tongue down my throat. He pulled away laughing as though it was the most hilarious thing in the world that I had now been "taught" how to kiss. My mom stood rigid and still but laughed and seemed a little surprised, yet she chose to laugh along with him. I believe she felt awkward but decided not to make a big deal about it, thus possibly creating a more uncomfortable situation, which I know now to be classic co-dependent behavior. Sadly, I was left to deal with it alone and not have an adult stand up for me to say how offensive the whole episode really was.

Their reaction made me feel that I was supposed to accept what had just happened, but the entire event made me sick to my stomach. I felt dirty and could still feel his tongue in my mouth as I watched them laugh, and he walked away, saying he would see us another time. My mom nervously laughed, and as she closed the door, I ran to the bathroom in shame to brush my teeth. I felt disgusting inside, but their laughter made me question myself, so I kept silent with the adults. I found the courage later to tell Randy, who had been my boyfriend already for a few months. We were both upset and felt rather powerless. The friend's claim that I needed to be taught how to kiss now that I was sixteen was disgraceful, and I felt violated and let down.

I feel that my mother wasn't strong enough to stand up to say it was wrong and protect me. I was young and had little role modeling for how to handle myself when I felt offended, so I pretended it didn't happen. I did such a good job of it that I forgot the whole incident for years until later, when the pain of more present issues started to arise.

Later as an adult, as I became more involved on a family board, I realized Jeff was not only the financial advisor but also a close social friend of my parents and brother, so the boundaries became blurred. When he secretly made inappropriate gestures and sent emails to me that made me feel uncomfortable, I finally tried addressing it privately with my mother, naïvely thinking that because she was a woman, she would understand. Instead, she just shrugged it off as though it was nothing and something I could handle. If my husband were to have witnessed the behavior, he would have been rightfully furious, yet I would have felt protected. In retrospect, I wish I would have gone to him, but I also realize that I was scared of creating more of a family rift, so I moved on and buried it, which was not good.

I had hoped that my parents and brother would have made me feel protected, but that was not the case. Their loyalty to Jeff seemed to far outweigh my complaints of being approached sexually by this man who was involved socially and professionally with the family. What he seemed to offer them professionally felt more important than how I felt personally, and I started to realize my place and lack of importance. One of my relatives told me that some members of the family noticed Jeff's inappropriate attraction toward me while we attended a family business trip, yet no one seemed to want to get involved, so it was up to me to deal with it, and I resented it greatly.

I struggled with how to address the issue, sadly behaving codependently, not wanting to upset anyone in my world, so I kept silent when I didn't receive the support I sought from my mother or hoped would come from my father. I talked about it privately with a few trusted friends but felt hopeless in receiving the validation I felt I deserved from family. When the issue kept arising, I remember trying to communicate with my parents about it, saying I didn't feel comfortable having to attend family business meetings with this man, and I received nothing but silence. It was then that I began to realize that silence was also an answer and one I would be met with more and more frequently. My comments hung in the air, and my need to be validated and protected was totally ignored. It was my problem in their eyes, not his.

I soon learned that silence could be one of the loudest forms of communication. The lack of a reply to a question could linger and create an abyss of enormous size, calling one to fill it with deceptive thoughts as the mind takes over. Silence *is* an answer, although not one often sought by its inquirer.

One of my greatest fears is to be unheard. It is, therefore, no surprise that silence makes me feel vulnerable, doubted, and questioned by those from whom I await answers, yet silence is where I started to feel a sense of knowing myself better than before. Like Jesus, who spent forty days in the desert, I have found myself alone in the silence when ultimately God has met me there. It is in that sacred place that I have learned to grow and become more comfortable with not having an immediate answer or even one at all. I've realized that there can be peace, knowing that God always hears us and that we are never dismissed by him. It is when waiting on and seeking the answers of man, however, that lingering silence becomes deafening.

I believe one of the cruelest things one can do is to not listen to one another. The attacker suddenly marginalizes the one trying to be heard, and the weapon is therefore invisible, unpredictable, and hard to define. The victim is left with no choice but to finally meet silence with silence, and the echoes of warfare are left only to the mind.

I needed my mother so much in those uncomfortable situations, but it seemed to me that she was unable or unwilling to champion the needs of her daughter, much less confirm the issues, so I had to try to figure out how to deal with them alone. The only response I ever received from her when I pressed the situation one final time was, "I hope you don't raise your daughter with your man-hating ideals."

Anyone who knows me knows I do not hate men, nor have I raised my daughter with such thoughts. My mother's comments cut me like a knife, but I realized that trying to defend myself was a waste of time. I believe that the narrative my parents were seemingly choosing to live by was impenetrable and unwavering. Their outlook on me felt different than the woman I was, and instead of being proud of me and supportive, the silence and hurtful remark created more distance between us.

Missing my mother also made me miss my grandma, and I often cried to God for her, hoping she could see it all from heaven as I asked God how He could help me but, even more importantly, how He could help my mother. These are the frequent prayers I have when I visit the gravesite of my maternal grandparents, feeling close to them through the Holy Spirit as they lie side by side for eternity while my mother is alive in the world, silent and sadly unavailable.

Swimming in Quicksand

The Word gave me peace while the world was giving me trouble.

Creflo Dollar

For a brief time in the spring of 2018, I finally found myself unpacking boxes and attempting to get settled in my new apartment. Months of important paperwork that followed me around in a small grey suitcase that I called "my rolling office" eventually made its way into file cabinets for easy reference. It had been a long time since I had felt a sense of order or permanence, and I took nothing for granted. The simple act of taking clothes out of a suitcase and hanging them on hangers in a closet that was mine almost called for celebration. I had never been so happy to put an IKEA file cabinet together, knowing that it was finally going to create order I could only dream about in my cramped days in the studio.

Endless papers from divorce details, taxes, spreadsheets, family business matters, and legal issues with my brother were all hard to keep organized as everything seemed to constantly be happening at once. Calls between divorce lawyer, mediator, and Randy were woven in between the nearly full-time task of trying to extricate my way out of the bondage I felt from the operating agreement with my brother. The progress was painstakingly slow with everything, and the details of it all were happening simultaneously on two coasts, different time zones, and with different assets and issues spanning five states from Hawaii to Connecticut.

Lily was finishing her senior year in high school, and there were many plans surrounding end-of-the-year events such as prom, graduation, and preparation for college. Normally such milestones would bring the family together, but under the circumstances, the details with my side of the family were very tricky. We always made sure my parents were included in big events. Invitations went to all the grandparents, and we never played games. It was important that even with the family dynamics, my parents knew they were included and welcome.

Regardless, my parents continued to send mixed messages as to whether they were coming and if they could make the drive from New York to Connecticut for the ceremony. My father's apparent fear of driving had caused him to overthink what used to be simple, and now he was emailing Randy and me separately on how he and my mother would get to the graduation. Randy and I remained in close communication, trying to keep things orderly and calm for Lily.

In the past, we would have driven them from New York to Connecticut, and all stayed at our country house, but those days were over. It was entirely inappropriate for me to be in a car with my parents when I believed they were tied very closely with my brother and our business and perhaps our legal issues. For them to ride with Randy would also not be comfortable given our pending divorce. My parents drove all over the country and often made the long road trip between Arizona and Oregon between their residences. Why a two-hour drive from the Upper West Side of Manhattan to rural Connecticut was suddenly an issue I couldn't understand, other than my father appeared to have a growing fear of driving in large urban areas. The onramp to the West Side Highway from their studio was not more than ten blocks away, but it was seemingly a source of stress, so they reached out to a friend they knew in the city through me and secured a car service.

Thankfully Randy and I were working as a team for our kids and were able to compartmentalize divorce issues away from what our kids needed. My unwavering respect for him under these complicated circumstances with my parents stands firm, as he had every reason not to deal with them, but he remained steadfast, and for that, I have always been grateful.

At the same time, graduation details were being organized; my father had contacted his three grandchildren and invited them to a financial summit in the Bay Area not far from where Gary and his family lived. I recall Randy may have been included in some of the details surrounding getting our kids on board to attend in person, but I was neither contacted, invited, nor informed by my parents of their plans. It had been months, if not a few years since my kids had been around their only cousin, my parents, and their uncle and aunt. Apparently, they were all invited to this financial gathering organized by my dad and led by a professional from San Francisco who knew our family and me.

The decision was easy for us, as it was not only unfeasible for my kids to travel to the Bay Area at the end of the school year, but it was also something they didn't feel comfortable attending under the circumstances. The legal rift between Gary and me and the constant mixed messages from my parents to us all was something Lily and Jaylen understandably didn't want to face, so Randy and I agreed they should attend via conference call. Since it was a family call and I wanted to be supportive of my kids, I asked the financial advisor as well as my parents if I could join the meeting via phone. My parents didn't reply and remained silent, but the advisor welcomed me and said the meeting would be nothing more than him offering an educational overview of insurance and financial management that would be age-appropriate for the three grandchildren.

Discussions about money have always been a centerpiece of my immediate family, and this type of meeting was nothing new for me. As the years had gone on, my awareness of what I believed to be a hyper-fixation on wealth and money from my father was starting to create an obvious pattern. His heart always seemed to be in the right place, and he cared, yet there was also a feeling of control, and my newfound infancy of independence away from the immediate family dynamic had given me a new vision of how I felt money was often used as a tool by my father. This meeting felt like an example of that since he seemed to want to get the kids together in person and in California, all for the sake of teaching them about finances. It felt more like a vehicle to accomplish a perceived mission of getting the family together without me. To expect my kids to fly from Portland and Boston at the end of their academic year and to be in the company of my brother, his family, and my parents, all of whom they believed were creating a great deal of stress in my life—in our lives—was simply asking too much.

Endless books on investing and wealth management had been sent to me and then to my kids over the years. My father was smart and had a lot of knowledge on the subject and often some good advice, but as I began to notice past conversations or correspondence we had had, it was always laced with how much he had done for me or for us or the kids and how things felt very measured by his financial intent or involvement.

Don't get me wrong, I have always been grateful for my dad and his generosity and support, but as I matured and gained a new independence away from the inner circle of my family of origin, I began to notice a pattern of how money was a true focal point of most conversations, and it made me uncomfortable. If I didn't read one of the books he sent or manage something the way he had advised, I often felt as though I had let him down. It was something so deeply ingrained into the way I was raised that I was only able to see it once I was living outside the insulated family system I had known my whole life.

My mother finally flew to New York alone to stay in the studio and planned to attend graduation on her own. My dad emailed Lily and said he was too tied up with business matters in Oregon to be able to make it and how sorry he was to miss seeing her graduate from high school. He had hired a car service to drive my mom the two hours to and from New York for the ceremony. His private meeting with the school's director of development he had planned months earlier, which apparently included a private tour of the school grounds, was canceled. I had offered for Lily to tour them around her campus, but he had insisted he had a meeting that would include such a tour on graduation day. Somehow the word got back to me from Lily or from Randy that only my mom would be attending and that my father had canceled his meeting at the school. I heard nothing from him on any of the changes and assumed that silence was his preferred method of communication. I received the message loud and clear.

Graduation was beautiful, and Randy and I sat together with Jaylen and his girlfriend, Sasha, who had both come from Oregon for the ceremony. My mother-in-law, who had also come from Oregon, sat with us. My mom arrived in her car service from the city just in time to sit with the rest of us and see Lily receive her diploma. Photos of the family were taken together, and the awkwardness of it all under the circumstances was set aside, and the rightful focus was on the graduate. I knew the pressure of divorce and family dynamics and the undercurrent of the ugly legal mess had to weigh on my kids, but they handled themselves beautifully, and I can honestly say that the day went exceedingly well. My mother didn't linger as her driver showed up to take her the two hours back to her studio in the city, and we all breathed a sigh of relief that it went as well as it did.

My father and mother were suddenly unavailable in the coming year to attend Jaylen's graduation from college and a family dinner after the ceremony, as well as his wedding to Sasha a year later. To be fair, the outbreak of the COVID-19 pandemic disrupted their original wedding plans, but my parents had declined the invite long before. The pattern of receiving invitations and then not being available for various reasons became something we started to expect, yet we always included them.

Their absences were felt, but in the end, it made for such events to be less stressful. My kids appeared to take it in stride, but in my heart, I felt let down that their grandparents couldn't rise to the occasion and be there for these milestone moments. They were missing the most important moments as grandparents, and it reinforced my feelings that they were very likely more focused on protecting their material world over engaging in life's priceless moments.

My futile attempts to get them to see it that way were often thwarted, but I held a strong belief that they had their priorities in the wrong place, and it was very sad and embarrassing. First Timothy 6:17 (NIV) says, "Command those who are rich in this present world not to be arrogant nor to put their hope in wealth, which is so uncertain, but to put their hope in God, who richly provides us with everything for our enjoyment." We were enjoying the important moment in our kids' lives, and it felt like my parents had chosen otherwise.

Sometimes word would get back to me from friends and relatives that my parents claimed they hadn't been invited or that I was preventing them from having a meaningful relationship with their grandkids. They mentioned the latter in emails and texts to me about how I had somehow poisoned the kids against them, which was untrue. Their unfounded claims were heartbreaking, and yet, I knew that it was not worth trying to defend the truth. After years of crying and tearing myself up trying to be heard, I kept trying to let it go and let God take over.

On June 24, 2018, the check from my grandmother's gifting from the previous January was finally sent to me after months of legal haggling. My father and brother had been instructed to reissue the check originally made out to the LLC back to me. It cost me close to $7,000 in legal fees to receive her intended check for $15,000. It was a small victory to get it into my hands and deposit it into my account. That money could have helped me months before when I needed it to move from the studio, but now it would go to pay off debts and give me a little breathing room.

I had such a hard time believing my father when he repeatedly insisted that he had nothing to do with the operating agreement my brother created or that he was unaware of the day-to-day dealings of the LLC. His name was noticeably still on the bank account alongside mine and my brother's, and I still remembered that being one of the main reasons my brother insisted I sign the new operating agreement before the end of 2015 because he wanted to make sure my dad was removed from the account.

By this time, my brother had already rented out the studio portion of the condo in Hawaii, which was actually a large converted two-bedroom plus a studio made into one family-sized apartment. He had found a renter for one side of the property, and the LLC was taking in income, which meant we were now filing taxes in the state of Hawaii. The rental income was negligible, yet he claimed it was needed. My feeling was that the housekeeper he used each time he went to Wild Creek and the cost of winterizing and storing the boat and other expenditures for his business coach a few years earlier were unnecessary expenses.

The new renter in Hawaii, in my humble opinion, was to tie up that part of the condo so it would be harder for me to bring friends or family. This was my assumption, but the number of unnecessary obstacles being put in the way of going our separate ways in the partnership seemed obvious. We were perhaps six months or less away from closure, and now we had a tenant in the studio in Honolulu and new taxes to file in the state. In my opinion, it was madness.

A parcel of commercially zoned property in South Lane County was sold without my knowledge, and it was only when a family member approached me to ask about the details of the sale (because this family member had the right of first refusal due to a longstanding agreement from the past) did I learn about the transaction. These were my assets with my brother, and that agreement I signed gave him the right to do as he pleased. He didn't owe me any explanation, but the lack of respect I felt from the way he dealt with our partnership continued to bother me deeply. I had to fight my way through it with the lawyers, and because of that agreement, my hands were often tied.

Surely if two adult children whose parents intended for them to share gifted assets and for them to get along in the process, would not those well-intended parents pull their adult children aside and make an effort for reconciliation? I was constantly blamed for not making efforts in communication, and yet my records showed countless attempts to partner, to communicate, and to find common ground. My extensive notes to my counsel in October 2019 in preparation for mediation said:

> Gary's communication with Dena became nearly non-existent. Requests by Dena to have clarity on shared use of the residential properties owned by the LLC were ignored or if at all vaguely answered. Requests by Dena to have reinstatement of a calendar system (which had been in place for years) went ignored. Gary used the LLC properties for personal and professional use, often entertaining his and his father's friend and board consultant, Jeff. Dena's repeated requests for a meeting (even though [Gary] offered to be of service to Dena related to her board "assignment") were denied.

My belief is that finding common ground was not the same goal of my brother nor of my father. As far as I was concerned, my mother seemed to accept whatever she was told and just went along

203

with their plans, regardless of her own ability to think for herself. I had sadly lost all respect for her by this point.

I was still trying to get full distributions for taxes owed on my portion of the LLC from 2017. An error had been made in my filing and on the amount ultimately owed for my share of the LLC taxes. What I owed proved to be greater than what had initially been requested as a distribution from the LLC from my brother. My request to him to distribute the shortfall, which was only a few thousand dollars, was denied. At my suggestion, Randy had even sent a letter about the matter to Gary through an attorney, which was ignored. Several years earlier, this would have likely been a friendly exchange with a positive outcome, but now we were having to make up the difference out of our own pocket to pay for taxes on phantom income. Now every single thing felt like it moved in slow motion. The simplest requests for things seemed to take forever. A friend had overheard my father say that the intention was to "make Dena run out of money by letting things drag out." I definitely felt that the intent was there since seemingly simple matters unnecessarily dragged on and on.

Word had even gotten back to me that my mother had made it clear to a close relative that they "had a plan to make sure they would make it very hard" for Randy and me to divorce. Again, I heard this secondhand, but the relative was entirely reliable, and as far as I was concerned, the way I was being treated matched the comment. It was a complicated mess, and even more so as I was feeling pressure of my divorce and Randy's wish for us to get a financial agreement in place before the end of the year, tax laws would change. To say my plate was full was an understatement.

The demand was still in place for neither my brother nor me to use the residential properties while we were in legal dealings, and yet now my brother was extending an invitation for my kids to visit him at the Wild Creek house, which they declined. Later in the fall, my father offered to purchase plane tickets and take the kids on a trip. He even included Jaylen and Sasha as a couple, which was generous, yet also felt confusing in light of the tension between the generations.

Not long after they thanked him and turned down the offer, my dad, while at a lunch with Jaylen, handed him an envelope marked "confidential" with private communication inside between my mother and me from 2016. Jaylen said he didn't want to see it and knew that his grandmother and I had erupted into an emotional exchange that was between us. It seemed to be something my dad held onto and would resurrect from time to time. That one angry exchange with my mother where I was spewing out my anger and frustration and using regrettable language was something taken out of context so many times that now it was almost laughable. I assumed that single misstep on my part would haunt me forever as it appeared to be used as a way to try to convince others how crazy they thought I was. I figure that may follow me forever, and to think Jaylen had to be the adult in the situation broke my heart.

I believed my father was way out of line, and if he truly wanted to mend fences with the family, I wished more than anything that he could be the mature father figure and take hold of everyone and sit people down to clear up these matters, which were unnecessary and, in my opinion, out of control. His failure to do that made me believe more and more that he was likely involved with the entire situation as it always felt very one-sided. I was constantly blamed for not being communicative, and yet the person I needed and wanted to work with was nowhere to be found and always seemingly in hiding, often behind my dad. The rift between my brother and me was so deep and strong that to expect the kids to be in the middle of it was simply unfair. Randy agreed, and as usual, I was glad we were on the same page.

When Lily started college in Boston that fall, my mother reached out to her and sweetly asked if there was anything she needed. It was a nice gesture, and Lily told me about it. Music students have different needs than regular college freshmen, and on Lily's list from the school were things we hadn't anticipated, including a new mic, a special MacBook Pro that the college required with special software for their curriculum, as well as a mini keyboard for songwriting and a new guitar, not to mention clothes and books and the usual items students needed when starting a new school year.

I told Lily that it was an opportunity to include her grand-mother and let her know that it would be nice if she wanted to con-tribute to her school needs. My mother's gesture sounded genuine, and when Lily responded, my mother started to ask questions about why she had to get a new guitar when she already had one, and the same with the computer and everything else. It became stressful, and Lily just decided to thank her grandmother and tell her she was fine. I agreed, and we decided to move on.

Not long after that, my mother, as the newly appointed trustee to Lily's trust after my brother stepped down from his position, made the decision to take $1000 out of Lily's account to give to her since my mother claimed that she was "short on cash." I had never known my parents to be this short of cash, and while there wasn't anything legally wrong with my mother taking the money from her account, it went against things they had said to her in the past. Lily had been told by my parents that her investment was something never to touch, and she, therefore, reminded my mother that she didn't need the money that badly and that she didn't want it taken from the account that was in her name. Nonetheless, my mother insisted she didn't have much money to give her from her own pocket and that the "gift" she offered Lily would be coming out of Lily's trust. I felt it sent the wrong message to Lily about my mom's intention to give her a gift then withdrawing that money from the account she newly managed for her. Given my parent's more than comfortable lifestyle, it wasn't believable to us that she was short on cash. The real eye-opener for Lily was when months later she received notification for taxes due on this withdrawal from her new trustee.

***

It was a time when, unfortunately, I started to lose my spiritual focus and instead relied heavily on the lawyers. If I wasn't dealing with the issues with my brother, I was working with Randy and our mediator and trying to keep my emotions in check while I was losing my marriage and my family all at the same time. I remember a brief conversation at some point with my mother where I was telling her

I needed her and I wanted my mom, and I missed her, especially while going through a divorce. Her words cut like a spear through my heart. "Well, this is what you signed up for, this is what you wanted. You should have thought this through before you decided to leave your marriage."

Out of respect for my children and for Randy and all of our happy years together, I am not going to air the painful details in my marriage that brought me to that point, yet my mother knows them well, so for her to say this was a verbal slap in my face. These were words I could never imagine saying to my daughter should her life take a turn where she made a difficult choice to move forward on her own. It had been an agonizing decision, and these were not the sentiments I believed she would have said to her sister, who had gone through several divorces and by whom she stood no matter what. This was not the unconditional love of a mother to her daughter, and I felt the darkness of it, and it hurt in ways I may never be able to fully express.

I spent most of December crunching numbers and working on meeting the deadline before the alimony tax laws changed. Christmas that year felt like an obstacle as I raced to the finish line to get my paperwork completed, so the law worked in our favor for our divorce and agreement. I pushed everything I could aside and had to check my attitude as I felt angry, sad, exhausted, and overloaded. As people were decorating trees and shopping for loved ones, I felt I didn't have the time or the luxury of resources or energy to put into any of it, and if not for sending some things to my kids, I would not have celebrated Christmas at all. Papers flooded all of the horizontal spaces in my apartment, and I worked between calls and emails with Randy, our mediator, and my lawyer. It was crunch time, and I couldn't wait until we met the deadline before the new year.

My only outlet was the gym for dance and yoga. I would leave my desk after a long day of excruciating calls and paperwork to arrive at class and feel the exhale I'd been searching for all day. Being with my friends who loved the same activities was healing and bonding, as they helped me forget the stress and the impossible painful situations of my life. My fitness friends were a lifeline to the outside world I had forgotten, and I was always grateful for this community which brought much-needed joy in and out of the gym. We were family.

I would come home with a bag full of sweaty gym clothes and start my laundry and stay up late watching episodes of light TV that didn't create any more stress than I could handle. I stopped following the news because the drama in the government and fighting that was debated every night on the networks was too much. I had enough drama of my own, and the last thing I needed was to hear about the country falling apart. It was self-preservation, and I knew my limit.

One night I fell to my knees in tears and endless sobs, absolutely overwhelmed with trying to find a way out of the mess I was in with my brother and the crushing holiday deadline of the financial agreement for my divorce. I cried and cried, feeling totally helpless and pathetic. "Why is this happening?" I looked up to God, and my heart felt ripped in half, and my attention kept turning to what the lawyers could do to make it go away. I knew better, but truthfully, I had been more focused on the legalities and felt like I was close to a breakthrough when suddenly I hit a wall with the legal process. Everything came to a standstill, and I felt trapped and scared and full of fear, totally falling into the snare of the enemy. I felt I was drifting without protection in the storm, and I finally cried out to God, and that's when the most unusual thing happened.

Never in my life had I had words come out of my mouth that I didn't intend, but in the middle of my sobs, I felt powerful and clear energy come up through my diaphragm and out of my throat, and my voice said loudly, "I don't need a lawyer. I need the Lord!" When I think about it now, it sounds like a funny tagline, but at the time, it was profoundly serious and took me totally by surprise.

And there it was, the truth of the matter. I wasn't yet aware of the power of the Holy Spirit, but I now know, looking back, that He was speaking the truth of what I needed to hear within me. I didn't form the thought or the words, and yet I said them loudly. I was changing direction with my legal team and felt vulnerable in the process, and yet God was right there telling me that He had me no matter what. The lawyers were not in charge—He was.

Matthew 19:26 (AMP) says, "But Jesus looked at them and said, 'With people [as far as it depends on them] it is impossible, but with God all things are possible." His steadfast love and commitment to His followers are stronger than what I was seeking from the lawyers, and it had been easy to fall into weakness and believe that my victory could only come from them. The words upon my lips were not mine and the memory of that moment served as a reminder of the super-natural power God has to make what we believe to be impossible possible. That declaration from the Lord was what I needed instead of putting all of my faith in the lawyers. It was the message I required at the right time to put God first. I still believed very much in my legal team but decided to pray for them instead of worship them, and the shift made all the difference.

When I looked around, I had reminders all around me of God's grace and His promises to me. My beautiful new apartment was a miracle as I had just crawled out from the depths of the studio and into the light, and I gave thanks for it often. There was gratitude for my guardian angel, who helped support me through my legal efforts, and other angels; the one who shared her mother's studio with me and the other one who generously helped me secure my new apartment. Their giving hearts and helpful hands to a friend going through a crisis was something I will never forget, and taking stock of the wonderful things God was doing in my life was more important than focusing on the battle I faced each day. I thanked God over and over for His amazing proof of what He was doing and for my ability to provide a home again for my daughter.

Looking around my apartment, I was comforted by familiar things that belonged to me that were no longer in boxes or shoved away. I had my health, and my children were strong and happy, and Randy and I were peaceful and respectful throughout our mediation. I was blessed, and I knew the people I could trust, and I had family from both Randy's and my side who still loved me and showed me respect.

I had new eyes on my troubles, and although they didn't go away, I was committed to reminding myself to put God first and not the lawyers nor the angels. How easy it had been to wake up each day and ask myself what side of the country I would be dealing with and what lawyer would contact me first and what obstacle I may have to address. The truth was, I appreciated the legal team I had and was in awe of their expertise, guidance, and incredible patience. I would have been lost without them, and I knew God had selected the right people to help me through these ordeals. Ultimately God was with me, was in charge, had never left, and I was grateful to have the reminder. He literally put the words in my mouth, and it was a moment I would never forget.

Choreography of Silence

The thief comes only to steal and kill and destroy. I came that they may have life and have it abundantly.

John 10:10 (ESV)

In February of 2019, when the legal process between Gary and me was mounting, and at a critical juncture, my father and brother suddenly left the country for a fifty-day trip together, beginning with a luxury cruise from Florida with several stops along the way to Brazil, their final destination. I was never told exact details of their trip or its purpose, but my father had circulated an itinerary and had emailed photos to my kids with descriptions about his wonderful adventures through the rain forest, their luxury cruise, and the beautiful sights they were seeing. It appeared to be an extended father and son pleasure vacation that made me reflect on my increasingly complicated and nearly absent relationship with my mom.

I couldn't help but feel a tug at my heart thinking that my mother and I had never had a trip for fun together since the one to San Francisco when I was twelve. Something between us felt off limits and had for years. I wistfully saw photos on social media of friends who were enjoying time with their mother, especially now that their children, like mine, were grown and more independent. A vacation alone with my mother seemed an impossibility even during previously good times, but now with the rift in our family, it felt like it would be something we would never share between us. I felt it was almost as if my mom didn't have permission to be alone with me anymore, so the distance just kept growing.

Gary and my father's extensive trip couldn't have happened at a worse time for me as I was working hard for closure with my brother. Gary was silent, with the exception of the vague notification from his lawyer that he would be difficult to reach for a period of time. My father had noted in his handwriting on the extended itinerary that Wi-Fi would be available, but calls might be more difficult. While my father was emailing photos and updates to various people, including my kids, my brother was quiet and claiming connection was limited, if not impossible. I didn't believe him but assumed he was likely managing certain things in the LLC from afar, yet he was mostly unavailable for our legal process, and it slowed progress for a good portion of nearly two months.

Needless to say, I was not happy as it brought communication with the legal dealings down to a nearly grinding halt and also left me wondering who was running things in our partnership while he was away. Later, once the bank statements came out, I learned that Gary had had a rubber stamp made of his signature so someone could sign the checks for the LLC in his absence. Never mind that I was listed on the bank accounts and a fifty-percent partner, I was out, and he was vacationing and still getting paid for his extended time away, and it was yet again another powerless feeling for me. All I knew was that the manager of my assets was apparently off playing in the jungle or on a cruise while I was trying to get closure on our business affairs and move forward.

My goals to break free from the operating agreement and the partnership slowed down considerably, which made me believe that my brother was intentionally dragging me along in a process that was taking far longer than needed and costing a fortune in legal bills. The entire situation called for extreme patience, and that had never been my strong suit, yet I used the time wisely to focus on getting organized and put my priorities in the right place.

Jaylen had recently gotten engaged, and our family was very happy to have something joyous to look forward to in 2020, and I was thankful both of my kids were doing well. Lily was enjoying Boston and her first year at Berklee College of Music, and Randy and I were respectfully working through our personal matters to find closure while remaining strong together as devoted parents.

There was a lot to be grateful for in light of the frustrations, and I was as committed as ever, putting God first and leaning on my growing awareness of Him in my life. I was feeling more support from high places by seeing the good people who had remained in my life and some new ones who had entered and offered unconditional love and communication. Incorporating gratitude into my daily life started to become easier as I realized I was surrounded by good, and all I had to do was focus on God and accept that change was happening in His time, not mine.

My mornings became very important as I restructured the way I began each day, and it was making enormous changes in how I felt and how I faced what was on my plate. When I lived in the studio, I woke up feeling buried and in distress. Rising now meant knowing before I went to bed what would happen the moment I opened my eyes in the morning. Putting God first at the onset of waking up became a necessity as well as a privilege. There was a new order to how I approached the day and what I could expect or not expect, and how I would handle challenges. Recognizing the endless resources available to me through the word of God, I also appreciated the stabilizing force in my world that had previously felt rudderless at times.

I often identified with Christian author and speaker Joyce Meyer, who once said something about how when she woke up each day, she felt the enemy already putting thoughts in her head about how hard this or that would be for the day. Like me, she felt the attacks coming the moment she opened her eyes. "I have to have caffeine and the Word of God before the anointing kicks in," she said on one of her shows, and I laughed because I understood.

Luz had sent me a devotional that I committed to every day. Instead of skipping over the scripture references at the end of the message, I made a decision to look each one up in the Bible. The shortcut would be to Google the scriptures on my phone, but I realized that I was missing an opportunity to learn more and to receive God's Word for me on that day. By looking it up in the Bible, I was learning where in the Bible I could find a scripture and in what order things could be found. There was value in the process and not just getting to the actual finish line. Rushing meant robbing myself of the message and the intrigue I felt by searching for it in the different books of the Bible, which was emotionally fulfilling.

Sometimes I would read the daily scripture and find myself reading the entire page or more. Sure enough, I got into the Bible, and I started to actually look forward to it and really understand when people talk about "getting into the Word." I realized the powerful shift that was taking place in my life just by making time with God first thing every morning. This meant setting my alarm fifteen minutes early to do so, and as I got into more of a routine, I really started to feel the benefit of this ritual. It wasn't long before I started to set thirty and then sometimes sixty minutes early on my alarm so I could watch a half-hour of Christian programming and read the Word. The benefit of making this change to my daily routine was calming and noticeable. Instead of dreading mornings, I looked forward to them. I learned to put my concerns into prayer and ask for guidance and discernment before I ever put my feet on the ground or left my apartment.

The feeling of being attacked over the past few years had been so intense that I seemed to live in a perpetual state of fear and anticipation of what would come next. This new morning routine slowly started to change those emotions, and I felt I was finally really walking with God. I was tapping into His power and the enormous protection and guidance of the Holy Spirit, something I had never learned as a lifelong Christian. I devoured scripture that sustained me and particularly leaned on Jeremiah 29:11 (NIV), which says, "For I know the plans I have for you,' declares the Lord, 'plans to prosper you and not to harm you, plans to give you hope and a future.'" It's one scripture that I have displayed on my desk as a reminder not to fear the future but to have hope and to remember that God's desire is to protect and provide a way in all things. This was something I needed to hear more than ever as the messy, unfinished worldly matters of my life seemed to lie in the hands of lawyers as well as the general operating manager who was on an extended vacation.

There were times in my life since college when I would check in with a therapist from time to time to work on different issues, most of them being family dynamics. Since Randy and I separated, my parents apparently kept telling friends and relatives that I was mentally ill, unstable, and sick. These comments got back to me frequently, and they agitated me greatly because they simply were not true. Because of this, there was a part of me that didn't want to go to therapy for support during my divorce and legal matters with my brother. I felt judged and watched, and it was a sickening feeling. There was likely never a time in my life when I needed that objective outside support more than during these past painful years, but it was something I couldn't afford at the time, and it was also something unavailable to me for some reason. My previous therapist, who had helped me overcome my panic and anxiety, became very busy and unable to add me onto her schedule, and even if she could, I wasn't able to meet the financial obligation as I had before.

Starting over with a new therapist felt daunting as my life was happening faster than I could bring someone up to speed in an hourly session a week. Every time I said to myself, "I really could use someone to talk to and help me sort this out," I started to feel there was a reason beyond the obvious for why I wasn't connecting with a therapist. I began to realize that God wanted to be my therapist and the place I turned to first. He knew exactly what was happening, when and how things would end up, and there were no invoices, appointments, or moments to recap what happened since the last session. God was handling it, and as soon as I recognized that, I began to feel comforted in a new way.

I'm not saying that therapy isn't good or that people who believe in God no longer need to seek support from a mental health professional or other medical doctors. I believe God puts the right people in our path who He wants us to know, as long as we are in prayer first, so we can find comfort that our priorities are in the right place.

What struck me so much during this time was how often I wanted to see a therapist to get advice and even go back to those who knew my family history, and every avenue seemed to be closed. I also stayed away from it because I was tired of seeing outside support being used against me by the accusations from my family that I was crazy. Truth be told, most of my sessions were about trying to figure *them* out and how I could co-exist in the complicated family dynamic I had been born into, but God had me. God made it so clear that He had me that I stopped seeking therapy for the time being and focused solely on the power of the Holy Spirit to guide me.

The realization that God was holding my hand, leading the way, and really overseeing everything in my life became necessary for me to trust as the year unfolded. This was the fourth year of the legal process with Gary, and my divorce was dragging on not far behind. Closure was something I wanted and needed so I could put my energy into being productive with other things, like earning a living instead of trying to keep my head above water in the legal turmoil.

Some people asked me why I didn't just walk away from the issue with my brother, and I had one answer: taxes. As long as I was a partner with him, I would owe taxes on my half of the company. He held all the decision-making power on our joint assets and earned the majority of his income from his role as general operating manager. The six-figure discrepancy in the capital accounts was a big enough blight for me to want to remedy and to feel as though I was being punished for invoking my rights—the few I had—in that agreement was too much to be associated with long-term. I had to get out, and it was my main focus to do so and to accomplish it with dignity.

I believed that if my dad or mother had been in the same situation with their own siblings, they would have fought to break free from the control a sibling business partner might have over them. It was something I definitely believed my father would never tolerate. To be constantly criticized for standing up for myself to gain my financial and emotional freedom felt like adding insult to injury.

In late March, when the long Brazil adventure was over, my patriarchal grandmother, Joy, started to become very feeble. She was living in a nursing home in Eugene, just steps away from the apartment my parents rented. When my parents were in town from Arizona, they said they checked on my grandmother and ran errands for her. Other family members who lived in town were available to her on a more regular basis, and she received the best care available in the area. When I would come in from New York, I would always visit her and sometimes bring my kids if they were with me. Grandma Joy was fun, even in her elderly years, and though living in the memory wing of the nursing home, she still had a sharp sense of humor and was always happy to see us.

Sometime during the stressful divide between my parents and brother, I paid a visit to see my grandmother and dropped by the nursing home before I left town. As I entered the wing of the nursing complex where she lived, I was told that she was on an outing with a small group of residents but that I could go to her room and leave the gift I had brought for her. I walked down the hallway toward her room, which was the last door on the right. As I got closer to her room, I noticed the door was open, and someone was inside.

I assumed it was housekeeping or a nurse, and when the woman looked up, we startled each other. My mother was on her hands and knees going through what looked like clothes and stacks of papers.

"Oh hi, what are you doing here?" she said, very surprised to see me. I asked her the same, and we exchanged a nervous laugh and some small talk trying to find a way to alleviate the obvious tension between us. The lines had been drawn for several years, and we both knew which side we were on, and they definitely weren't the same.

It was immediately uncomfortable to be alone with her, and I couldn't remember the last time we had found ourselves in such a situation. I told her I was bringing a gift before leaving for the airport in the morning. She told me she had been working hard trying to clean out old things in my grandmother's room while she was away on her afternoon outing. I agreed that the place needed a little attention and also mentioned some of the clothing items my grandmother had asked for, which my mother said she had purchased. I asked where Dad was, and she told me he was at their apartment. We made some more small talk before leaving together, and she asked if I wanted to walk across the street to the nearby restaurant for a glass of wine. I felt she was sincere in wanting to see me, and I also recognized that she was more herself without my father around. I declined as I knew from experience that when we drank together, problems would escalate if our conversation turned emotional. Under the circumstances, with the division and legal issues, I felt it was not wise for us to engage.

Two memories flashed in my mind when things had gotten really out of hand between us while under the influence of alcohol. Both times Randy was with us and saw us both get into heated discussions over things I'm sure none of us could remember but each time managed to end unfavorably. Neither my mother nor I are big drinkers, and I can't speak for her, but I will say for myself that it doesn't take much before I feel my guard let down and whatever emotions I may be holding in come out if provoked. I often felt that my mother knew how and when to push my buttons, and it was best for me to remain in control of my feelings.

There was the time at Ridge Winery in the Santa Cruz Mountains in California when I was first married that things went awry. It was a favorite area for Randy and me to pack a picnic to enjoy after wine tasting. We brought my mother along on a sunny afternoon before we were to drop her at the airport for her flight to Oregon later that evening. I believe the wine, the sun, and somehow the conversation started to mix poorly, and the next thing I knew on the way home, my mom and I were fighting and carrying on to the point that Randy pulled the car over to the airport and dropped my mother off hours earlier than we had planned. Some sort of teary, angry, and unfortunate goodbye took place, and when we both felt better later, we called each other apologizing and not really understanding how we got there, but we did. We both laughed but also felt bad and embarrassed, and it was especially hard on Randy, who had to make the decision to drop his mother-in-law at the airport when I'm sure he would have liked to leave us both at the curb.

The other unfortunate incident took place when I was in college, and we were vacationing in Hawaii. I remember my great-grandmother being in the family condo with my mother, Randy, and me. One night we all enjoyed a beautiful sunset dinner cruise. There was dinner and dancing and, of course, cocktails. The last thing I recall about that night was my mom, Randy, and me being on the lanai of our 29th-floor apartment. My great-grandmother had likely gone to bed, and my mother and I had escalated into some sort of argument, and the next thing I knew, I woke up alone on the lanai in the early morning, shivering and holding my eye, which I soon realized, was black and blue. I had no memory of what had happened, and neither did my mom. Randy recounted the story of how he had to break us apart from fighting, and the next thing he knew my mom swung around and punched me. I don't know why I wasn't moved inside and didn't ask, and my mom, of course, felt terrible, and so did I.

These are stories I'm not proud of, and I would venture to assume neither is she, but I remember these moments as the likely effects of high emotion, too much to drink, and neither one of us listening to one another. We were both to blame. I knew that accepting an invitation to drink, albeit one or even two, under the current circumstances was completely out of the question.

We walked outside to the parking lot of the nursing home, and I expected my mom to continue walking the 500 steps or so to her apartment, but instead, she walked over to a brand-new Lexus SUV and said she needed to drive back. She had been running errands and drove to my grandmother's place. She seemed to stumble over my sight of the beautiful new car, and I told her it was very nice. In the back of my mind, I was reminded of what she had told Lily of being short on cash or how things were tight. I never believed it and accepted it as a failed attempt to hide the lifestyle they lived, which was one I knew well, having been raised comfortably by them.

"Where is your car?" she asked. She was looking around and seemed to want to know more about where I had come from and where I was staying. I was staying with friends and had borrowed a car and didn't want her to follow me because, by this point, I sadly didn't trust her anymore. I felt watched and judged and hadn't anticipated running into her.

I waited until she got into her car and drove the impossibly short distance, which was literally under 600 feet, to her own apartment and then walked to my car and drove away. It was the last time I remember having a civilized one-on-one moment with my mother, and I was sad thinking how much it would have meant to actually sit in the restaurant and talk as mothers and daughters do. I also knew well enough that even if we were only drinking water, the conversation would likely escalate. Declining her invitation didn't only mean turning down a glass of wine, but it also meant avoiding the likely turn in conversation to blame and anger. It was strife, and I wanted no part of it. I think we were able to keep the peace just long enough when we discovered each other in my Grandma Joy's room, but I was uncomfortable seeing her there going through things, trying to organize them without my grandmother around. I chose not to engage in conversation about it or anything that could become controversial.

As I learned from other family members that Grandma Joy was becoming very frail, I was reminded of my last visit with her in early March. I had no idea it would be the last time I saw her, but I was glad Jaylen and Sasha were with me. They were newly engaged, and it was so fun to see them share the details of their engagement and show off Sasha's beautiful new ring. We took lots of photos, and Grandma Joy especially loved petting their labradoodle, Cedar. She adored animals and perked up around the site of Cedar, who loved the attention.

I brought a few small gifts for her to enjoy as I was so surprised on an earlier visit to see that this once very glamorous woman who always wore lipstick and had her hair fixed had little to nothing left in her makeup drawer. She didn't have a daughter to dote on her in her later years, and it had bothered me that she was without such simple yet necessary things that I knew she loved and counted on to feel pretty. I had brought several lipsticks in bright colors and a gold compact with powder along with a little box with a sparkly rhinestone bracelet that easily slid onto her wrist. You would have thought I was bringing her the crown jewels; she was so happy, and I knew that just a little bit of sparkle and color would bring her a lot of enjoyment. She was thrilled.

Finally, I gave her a large print Bible with a bright pink cover and a devotional, also in large print that was the same one I had at home and read every morning. I had been so surprised that this faith-filled woman had ended up in the nursing home without a Bible or anything to feed her spiritually. I was reminded of the Bible she gave my grandfather on Easter in the 1950s, which sat in the dresser drawer of the guest room in the Hawaii condo, and her porcelain Madonna and child figurine that was in the master bedroom of the Wild Creek home since the early 1970s. She wore a cross and loved going to church to see friends and sing the hymns and pray. It just struck me that it was important that she had a Bible, and maybe it was something to make myself feel better before I left, but at any rate, I made sure she had one.

The minute she received the Bible, she opened it up and started reading out loud. I watched her and felt comforted knowing that she was finding the Word of God again, and I could see how quickly it brought her to another place. She became engrossed in the reading and nearly forgot we were there. I heard her say under her breath between scriptures, "Oh, I feel better already." For some reason, I must have known this would be my last time seeing her or close to it, and I happened to capture her reading from the Bible on video, and it's brought me so much happiness when I watch it now.

We left saying our goodbyes after lots of hugs, photos, and prayers, and it would be the last time I saw my grandmother as she passed away exactly one month and one day after that visit.

In early April, calls came to me from extended family that she was near death. I was back in New York and knew I wouldn't be able to get to her in time to say goodbye. A couple of very thoughtful relatives called me from her bedside and Face Timed with me, so I felt like I was in the room with her. Jaylen made the decision to drive from Portland to Eugene to see her one last time. I never heard anything from my parents but knew they were in contact with others in the family. Again, it reminded me of when my grandfather had passed away just two years earlier and not a word from my parents. I felt sick and sad that the rift over family business issues, money, and an operating agreement we disagreed on appeared to be the catalyst for silence. Even when the matriarch of the family was on her death-bed, I felt the underpinnings of strife.

By the time Jaylen arrived, it was late, and some members of the family who had been there for hours had gone home, knowing he would come to make sure she wasn't alone. He called me when he arrived, and we talked and prayed together while he sat near his great-grandmother. I was so proud of him, knowing he was there and wanting to be there out of love and respect for her. Grandma Joy adored Jaylen, her first great-grandchild, and it was somehow fitting that he was at her side. She was on morphine and sleeping and quiet, and he sat with her for hours. He finally called me and asked if he could go since he felt she was peaceful and he needed to get some sleep. I told him that, of course, he should go as I knew the next day he had to get back in the car to drive the two hours to Portland for work.

Jaylen kissed his great-grandmother goodnight and then fell asleep at a nearby hotel. When he got there, we texted a bit before he went to sleep. We reminisced about his great-grandmother's long life and how he was born in Santa Monica, where she grew up, and all the memories he had with her. I told him how proud I was of him for representing his generation and for being there when I couldn't be, and he drifted off to sleep.

A few hours later, he woke up to a floor lamp in the hotel room flickering on and off incessantly. He told me later how strange it was and although he was very tired, it woke him up and he knew it wasn't normal. When he got up the next morning, the nursing home had notified the relative in the family who was the power of attorney that my grandmother had passed away. When Jaylen and I spoke later, we both agreed that it was possible that the flickering light was her way of saying thank you for being there with her and for being the last one in the family to see her before she ascended to heaven. I was at peace knowing she had had a beautiful long life and was now reunited with my grandfather, whom she adored and loved more than anyone. I also knew that a part of my heart went with her. Her unconditional love was the most priceless gift and one that I miss every day.

Since a phone call with my dad was out of the question, I decided to text him to say how sorry I was to hear that his mother was gone. I also told him that his grandson was the last person in the family to be with her and how proud I was of him. I heard little from my father and even less from my mother, whom I also chose to reach out to, but only he thanked me, and that was all I heard.

Somehow, I had a vision of my mother as a prisoner being told what to do and how to act because this wasn't the mother I remembered. Her silence spoke volumes to me, and the entire situation appeared choreographed and sad. I felt that even a death in the family was still not enough of a reason for a connection between us and that it resonated as part of the conflict that existed between my brother and me. The strong hand of the enemy seemed to be on their side, and it made me stand firmly at the side of God, who I knew would protect me, and who I knew I needed now more than ever.

Joy

So with you: Now is your time of grief, but I will see you again and you will rejoice, and no one will take away your joy.

John 16:22 (NIV)

"Color always makes me happy," I could hear her say as I looked through my closet for what I would wear to my grandmother's memorial service. What I wanted to wear in her honor was different than what I knew I should wear out of respect, especially since I had been asked by the family to give a eulogy. Most of my wardrobe was black anyway after living in New York for over twenty years, and I knew it was a wise choice, but my eye kept going to a colorful floral silk print dress I hadn't worn yet and thought this might be the time to do so in her honor.

I finally decided to be simple and chic with a timeless respectable little black dress with an appropriate hem and neckline for church with just enough of a little décolletage and a well-placed yet fashionable slit in the skirt that my grandmother would have loved. She always kept a little sex appeal in everything she wore, even when dressing conservatively. She made sure her personality showed in her choices. I selected Italian black patent leather slingback heels and minimal jewelry. As I got ready, I thought of her and the training she afforded me as a teen to go to finishing and modeling school, both of which are a bit old-fashioned now. I always felt grateful for what it taught me about style and poise. I would need to lean greatly on those past lessons as I tried to pull myself together to speak in her memory and pay my respects publicly.

I was her eldest granddaughter and the only woman in the family who would be eulogizing her, and I wanted to make sure I made her proud. To say I was honored was an understatement. The respect my uncles showed me by asking me to speak and the coming together of our family in her memory as well as my grandfather's was special. The irony wasn't lost on me that this was taking place at the little Presbyterian Church in Cottage Grove where my parents had gotten married, my brother and I had gone to nursery school and been baptized, and where I attended service with my grandparents and my children in later years. It was a time to show respect and to come together as a family in my grandparents' honor. Since there had never been a formal service for my grandfather, it was decided that this memorial would be for them both.

On May 5, 2019, the community of family and friends packed the little church, and it had been years since I had seen most of them. My aunts, uncles, cousins, Jaylen and Sasha, all sat together as a family in the front, showing unity as a family. My mother was not able to make it as my father had shared with various friends and family that she was too busy remodeling one of their two homes in Tucson. I had also overheard him talking to people after the service, saying that my mom wasn't feeling well and was exhausted and may have been suffering from heart trouble. The messages seemed to contradict each other, as she was apparently working hard on a home project but was also rundown and needing medical attention, so without hearing from her directly, I just assumed it was an excuse for her not to be present. Most of the people I knew she had been in contact with said she was working hard on their home and was just very tired. Nonetheless, it seemed odd not to make every effort to attend the memorial of one's in-laws for over fifty years.

My brother and his family did not attend and, to my knowledge, hadn't been heard from, so my father attended his mother's memorial alone and chose to sit in the back of the church by the door. His choice felt blatantly noticeable in the tiny church with the well-known community, and I was suddenly embarrassed for my son and his new fiancé because the rift in my own family was felt and, I believed, was very visible. People later asked why my father chose to sit in the back and asked where my mother was, and it was hard to know how to answer, so I didn't. There was room for him to sit with his siblings and the extended family, but he anchored himself in the back of the room alone.

The day was for my grandmother, regardless of the sad divide between my brother and me and the side I believed my parents were talking with him. Just before we took our seats, my mother's sister came rushing up to me and gave me an enormous hug. We weren't close anymore, and it had been some time since I had seen her. She was dramatically gushing and complimenting me on how well I appeared and asked if I was feeling better, which I didn't understand. She then looked me in the eye and asked me how I felt about my parents owning another home in Arizona. The questions seemed very odd and out of place.

It was the strangest encounter of the day, and others witnessed it and commented to me about it later. I really didn't know what to say to her other than I was feeling well and that I was happy for my parents and whatever they were choosing to do. At that time, they had never once told me directly about their new second home in Tucson. I noticed I had not been included in their news updates about their lives for quite a while, and I felt like she was seeking a reaction from me, for which I had none other than to tell her it was nice to see her and excuse myself to be seated for the service.

As I sat on the pew waiting my turn to speak, I steadied myself not to cry and to be strong and not only make my grandmother proud but also my family. My mind was racing with so many emotions and unanswered questions, and I knew I needed to just focus on the moment and honor my grandparents with love and peace. With the grace of God, I gave my eulogy and spoke from the heart, as my uncles had before me. I tried to deliver an honorable, heartfelt message from the little girl I once was to the woman I had become, and I was thankful for Grandma Joy's example in my life.

I was thankful for the unconditional love and family pride I felt and had learned from my grandparents. To stand before their community, one I had known as a child, was one of the greatest and most humble moments of my life. I subtly extended my love as best as I could through my words in hopes of touching my father and showing love for him as he sat away from family in the back of the church. I hoped he would be proud of me in some way that I was honoring his mother and doing my best with grace under pressure, yet all I felt was his blank stare and distance. It was as though he didn't see me, and the tears I felt burning my eyes were almost more for the absence I felt of my father than that of my grandparents, who had finally gone to be with the Lord. It's true that the love I felt from them in heaven was far greater than the love I felt from my parents, who were still on this earth. Reconciling their behavior was something I hadn't yet come to terms with, so everything felt raw and painful.

I felt so many complicated emotions in that sanctuary, yet I let love lead the way. The powerful love of a woman who treated me like a daughter and taught me how to paint, cook, laugh, and be a lady, was what was important to share. I was enormously touched by the outpouring of love by every corner of the beautiful community who had come to honor her and say such heartfelt things in her memory. When the service was over, we all moved into an adjacent room for refreshments and to receive the guests who had come to pay respects. Before I stood in the receiving line, I walked over to my father, hoping to speak with him and have a moment in his mother's memory. It was noticeably clear that his physical distance from me was felt by all who were standing close by. He appeared uncomfortable and not willing to converse with me, so I excused myself and went to greet the friends who had come to share in our loss.

Large easels with my grandmother's beautiful watercolor paintings had been erected around the perimeter of the room so people could remember Grandma Joy's art and enjoy her beautiful world through her eye for color. A slideshow of my grandparent's long lives together and with the family repeated on a long loop in the center wall of the room for all to enjoy. Yet even with the flowers and the paintings and the kind words of loving friends, I felt the distance and silence of my father, and so did others.

Darkness was felt lurking in the room, and I believe others noticed it as well. A few relatives came over to me to comment on the huge display of emotion from my aunt before the service. There was so much history there that I just couldn't let it upset my day. I wanted to remember the moment as being respectable and beautiful. Some family friends asked about my mother's absence, while others told me they had received calls from her saying she wouldn't be in attendance. I had heard nothing from her. The disintegration of my family of origin felt evident, and even if others didn't notice it, I believed there was a spotlight on where we all should be, especially during such an important time of loss of our beloved family matriarch. I also felt my grandparents looking down on us and being very unsettled. As I slowly walked alone to my car and drove away from the church, I experienced a newfound disconnect and isolation from everything and everyone.

***

A few days before the memorial, arrangements were made for me to meet a family member at the local jewelry store in town for me to receive my grandmother's wedding ring. I received a nice note from the relative in charge of her estate, who said, "Grandma Joy, during her last weeks and as we spoke, asked that it be given to you, which I will honor. Your dad asked about the ring, and I explained that she asked that it be given to you…" I was deeply touched to learn that she wanted me to have it upon her passing, and shortly before she died, her wishes were followed by her power of attorney, who recounted her intention in writing and put the ring away for me until I was ready to receive it. Since I was returning to New York, I wanted to have it looked at by a jeweler before I left town.

Upon inspection, it was discovered that the center brilliant cut diamond was actually a cubic zirconia. The surrounding diamonds on the band and engagement ring were all real, but the nearly five-carat center stone was not a real diamond. The relative with me was as shocked as I was as we knew this was a ring my grandmother loved more than anything she wore, and not in a million years would she have replaced the diamond in that ring with a fake. Certainly, there had to be an explanation.

I asked the jeweler if they had records on this ring, as my grand-parents had been customers for decades, as had most of the family. Suddenly, I had a terrible feeling come over me as we awaited the jeweler's return from his back office to the desk where we were sitting. Something was wrong, and I was about to find out. I wanted to know what repairs, if any, had been done and the last time the ring had been in the store.

Records indicated that on November 8, 2015, the ring had been brought in with instructions noted:

10.5 mm diamond ring with baguette diamonds
and wedding band, Tasks: change center to synthetic cubic zirconia and return large loose diamond to customer. Price for services upon pickup
$80.

The receipt listed my grandmother's name and address as the
owner, but the phone number alongside the information was my
mother's cell phone. Further verification with the jeweler who assisted
in the transaction confirmed that the customer was my mother, who
had come in to drop off and pick up the ring once the noted task was
completed.

Years earlier, when my patriarchal great-grandmother was alive
and becoming frail, it was decided that her large diamond ring would
be replaced by a synthetic as well. It was something we all sort of knew
in the family, but this replacement in my grandmother's ring came
as a surprise to me as well as other relatives. There was no question
that the same sort of idea to keep the valuable diamond protected
was the common practice of well-intended family with elderly people
who live in nursing homes, but when this took place, my grandfather
was the one who was undergoing surgery, and my grandmother was
living with him in a senior home, and they were still together. At that
time, they were in transition to the nursing facility they would finally
move to in their final years.

The relative in the family who was power of attorney during the
time of the diamond removal and replacement had not been told,
nor had anyone else in the family. That person was selected by my
grandparents to be in charge of all decisions related to their welfare.
Four years after my grandmother passed away and upon inspection
by a respected jeweler, we learned that my grandmother had been
wearing a five-carat cubic zirconia for the last years of her life unbeknownst to her power of attorney or anyone else in the family except,
apparently, my mother and possibly my father.

We learned this information about the diamond switch just days
before the memorial, and I decided it wasn't appropriate to discuss it
with my father and mother until after we had laid my grandmother

to rest. Those in the family who learned about the situation shared in my shock and frustration, yet we all knew it was something to deal with later. My mother's absence at the memorial and my father's distance from the family added to the feelings of sadness and disbelief over the choice that had been made years before without consulting anyone in the family, much less the power of attorney.

I tried to keep an open mind about the intent of the decision around removing the diamond and decided I would approach my parents about it and did so respectfully as I hoped that they had very likely just wanted to protect my grandmother's valuables. Now that she was gone, and her wishes were in writing, and all of her personal effects had more or less been distributed, I wanted to know what to do next and where this diamond might be.

A few days after the memorial, while I was still in Eugene and assumed my father was too, I emailed my parents and included the rest of the family in the email. My father immediately replied to all and insisted that he believed he was supposed to receive the diamond as he claimed his mother told him it should go to him so that he could be the one to give it to Lily. This made absolutely no sense to me or to others. Why would my grandmother want to skip a generation and also not allow me to enjoy this piece of jewelry before passing it appropriately and in a timely fashion to my daughter? His tone felt defensive, and he dismissed the inquiry saying that the ring had been "inadvertently" given to me by the power of attorney and that he would try to remember where it was.

At the time of this writing, the diamond still remains lost, according to my father, who says he can't find it anywhere and would be more than happy to return it, but says it's nowhere to be found. My father is one of the most meticulously organized people I know. I remain hopeful that he will be able to locate it so his mother's diamond can be reunited with the ring she loved and wore for over seventy years of marriage.

In the meantime, the beautiful ring belonging to the matriarch of the family, my grandmother, whom I loved and respected dearly, has a five-carat cubic zirconia surrounded by smaller diamonds in its original setting. It is still a beautiful ring, and I have recently taken it to a jeweler in New York to have it evaluated and to have the prongs repaired. The recent history of the original diamond shows that it had been carefully removed in 2015 and later verified by a GIA report done in August 2016. Nonetheless, we know that it was thoughtfully replaced by a synthetic yet still remains lost, according to my dad.

***

Shortly after the email exchange about the diamond, my parents announced that they would not be attending Jaylen's graduation from college. As it turned out, my grandmother's memorial took place a few days before his scheduled graduation, so it was another opportunity for the family to gather, and this time for a happy celebration. My mother emailed Randy telling him she had pain in her back and was unable to travel and how sorry she was. My dad messaged me saying my mom had a heart issue and couldn't fly and that they were sorry to miss the ceremony. Everything surrounding family events seemed to include some drama around my mother's health, and many of us were noticing a pattern.

I heard from others who my mother had spoken to that she was just very tired from working on her two homes, so it was evident to me that she would not be making it to her eldest grandson's graduation, much as she had missed her mother-in-law's memorial. Whatever the reason, either sickness or exhaustion, the messages appeared to be mixed, and it felt obvious to me that she was likely choosing to or perhaps not even allowed to travel to Oregon. The more I thought about it, the more I believed that my father was likely orchestrating her containment in Arizona and away from all family events regardless of life, death, or a graduation.

My father was in Eugene, which was an easy two-hour drive away from the college where Jaylen was set to graduate. It seemed inconceivable that he wouldn't get in the car to drive the familiar distance to Portland he had driven hundreds if not thousands of times before for such an important event. Education was a very big thing in my family, especially to my dad, and I couldn't believe that he was going to miss the graduation of his first grandchild. We left the door open and the invitation for the ceremony and after-dinner open to him, but he declined.

I remember contacting Jaylen to discuss it with him, as he was disappointed. I reminded him that it wasn't his fault. The main thing was that the people who wanted to be there were doing so with enthusiasm. Lily and I would meet in Portland with Randy and his side of the family, who all came together as families do for such events. Once again, the absence of my parents was blatantly evident, but we all agreed that it was just as well that they didn't come because we were all tired of drama.

A couple of days before graduation, I got a notification that Gary had unexpectedly appeared in the Springfield office with my father and that he was going through files. He had the right to do so, but what was most surprising was that he notified the bookkeeper, who managed the books of our LLC as well as other family entities, that he was relieving her on the spot of her duties. Not long after, I noticed that funds in the bank account for the LLC were withdrawn. The account couldn't be closed without my consent, but the majority of what was left in the cash account had been taken out, and, I would later find out after more forensics, money had been deposited into an account in California, where my brother lived. There was nothing I could do. My hands were tied as the silent partner in the LLC, and all I could do was notify my legal team so they knew what was happening. It was not lost on me that my brother was taking action on things he apparently wanted to accomplish while the family was busily distracted by other events like a funeral and a graduation.

Later that night, after business hours, my brother was apparently back in the office going through even more files, as witnessed by the bookkeeper whom he had let go only hours before. She and her husband were in the area that evening when they noticed an unusual light on and decided to stop by not only to see who was there but to retrieve some of her personal items. She claimed she had caught him going through some of her personal belongings as well as shredding papers, and she felt she had caught him red-handed. Later she said she believed Gary had even tried to open her desk drawer. It was extremely shocking to me that he showed up just days after missing our grandmother's memorial to fire a longstanding bookkeeper and later rifle through files and apparently other items that may not have been his in the office.

As a silent partner, according to the operating agreement, he didn't have to notify me of his actions in staff changes or movement of files or accounts. I believed these to be very bold actions in light of the fact that we were engrossed in a multi-year legal matter over the partnership and having a witness finding him that night after hours with his car backed up to the office going through things seemed appalling to me. I was helpless to change any of it. The continual feelings I had of being victimized and attacked were overwhelming, and my frustration at my inability to stop it seemed to grow.

A day or so after graduation, I accompanied my children into the financial offices of our family investment team in Portland. My grandmother had willed to my father and his siblings the bulk of her estate, and my father generously decided to skip a generation and pass it along to his grandkids. I understood that it was a wise tax decision but didn't expand on that to my children. On our way to the office for them to sign the paperwork, I was notified that Gary was also a recipient of my father's generosity, but he had noticeably left me out. I respectfully accepted the information and went into the office with my kids, where they signed the papers, which were similar to that of their cousin and apparently my brother.

I gracefully yet sadly received nothing, and to this day, I remain the only one in my generation who didn't receive material or monetary inheritance intended to me from my grandmother, who left this world believing that she had equally remembered everyone. For me, it was less about the material and more about the principle that her wishes felt tampered with and incomplete. I couldn't help but feel as though the decisions that were made by my father were executed in a way to make me feel punished. For what? I was an adult who loved my family and was wanting to lead my own life. Desiring that felt like there was a huge price to pay over and over again.

There were those in and outside of the family who sincerely sympathized with the situation yet were unwilling or unable to stand up to my father directly to make him fully accountable on issues that seemed blatantly wrong and unethical. I have come to understand that those who apparently wield the most material and financial strongholds can often try to intimidate and overpower others. I felt that most people were just too afraid or simply didn't want to get involved. Everyone was entitled to their own reasons for not holding my dad accountable, but to me, it was clear. Lack of follow-through with my father had seemed to open the door for repeated incidents of deceit. It felt as though my father knew he wouldn't be held accountable by anyone, so it appeared as though he seemed to continually act without fear. To acquiesce was to enable him and give him the power to continue. I was not afraid of my father, rather frustrated and exhausted from it all and disappointed by the lack of accountability.

I also realized that I felt a sense of quiet personal satisfaction because I had God and the truth on my side. My continued wish for the family to powerfully band together and insist my father do the right thing never materialized, and it soon became apparent to me that I needed to reach higher. This was something only God could fix, and to put hope on others who were not willing or equipped to take it on was fruitless. Sympathy came from behind the scenes, but action came from me, and I learned to accept that even I was not strong enough to change things and that only God could ultimately be my vindicator.

The precious unconditional relationship with my grandmother and grandfather that would last me a lifetime was empowering and forever comforting to me. The memories I had with them were priceless and whatever anger was being taken out on me now was something I had no control over. I just knew I was seeing a pattern of behavior by my dad and brother, who continued to claim that they were not working together, yet appeared to be, and I didn't like it.

I felt blessed with clarity and vision and saw things for what they were. I am not saying that I didn't have support and people who cared, because I did, but when it came to the possibility of the majority of the family, family friends, or those associated with the family business coming together in some way to confront my father, who I believed in this instance was a wrongdoer, it just didn't happen, and the only thing that I can surmise is that God, the God of justice, had another plan. Justice would not come from lawyers, family, or others who could fight for what was right, it would ultimately come from a higher place, and when that would be, only God knew. My work was to learn how to become more patient and to trust that God had a plan. One thing I knew is that God doesn't like evil, and there appeared to be enough of that to go around for Him to be noticing.

***

There was enormous pride in seeing Jaylen graduate from Lewis & Clark College surrounded by loved ones. It was a moment I will never forget, sitting by Randy and his family and later attending a dinner in our son's honor generously hosted by them and then another one the following evening by a kind and thoughtful relative on my side of the family. It was clear who was standing with us and showing up for Jaylen. He deserved family to be there, especially with all of the challenges of his parents divorcing and the divide between my brother and me.

There had never been a time in Jaylen's life when having his grandparents show up to an event would have been more meaningful, but their absence instead spoke volumes. It felt like it was signaling a true departure by them from the family and their grandchildren. My dad's decision to remain in Eugene with Gary seemed to illuminate his priorities, as they were in town to apparently access the office and deal with business matters together. How Randy and I, who were divorcing, could come together and be there for our son and put our differences aside was a blessing. I was proud of that and disappointed that all my parents could do was to find blame in us and insist to others that they had been poisoned by me toward their grandkids. It was a narrative that kept resurfacing, and I had to just keep leaving it with God and pray that He would handle justice in all of the injustice.

Kaumaha

Behold not with anger the sins of man, but forgive and cleanse.

Lili'uokalani

June 8, 2019, I wrote Proverbs 4:23 (NIV) in the note app on my cell phone. It read: "Above all else, guard your heart, for everything you do flows from it," and served as a reminder of how vulnerable yet strong one's heart is throughout every moment of life. As I was gaining more strength and understanding from scriptures, I found myself keeping notes on those which resonated with me during the busy and often hectic days of my ever-changing world. May had been so busy and such an emotional roller coaster that I found myself writing recaps of each day just to keep the events straight in my mind and in my heart, which was constantly hurting.

I was deeply grieving the loss of my grandmother and the shift in my family, which now meant that my father was the patriarch and someone who I felt was making enormous efforts to disconnect from all of the generations. My grandparents and great-grandparents before them always kept us together for holidays, birthdays, and other gatherings. The image of my father sitting in the back of the church at his mother's memorial and later not attending his grandson's graduation were unlike any behavior I had seen in my family before. I kept thinking there would be a way to connect and to be heard, but the opportunities were less available with the clear and sad divide between my brother and me.

My father and mother insisted, both to my kids and to me through texts and emails, that they were not taking sides and that it was for Gary and me to work out. My parents would email my kids and tell them that one day they would sit them down and tell them the truth of what was really going on. My kids were smart enough and old enough to see for themselves what was happening, and it was heartbreaking to their father and to me.

The short entry in my personal notes a few weeks earlier, on May 29th, described how much everything was affecting me. Death, divorce, graduation, moving, legal matters, family business dynamics, and financial stress were noticeably impacting my health.

"…health report from doctor showing my cortisol levels are off the charts, cholesterol and blood sugar high and a possible kidney issue. Not a good report. Stress very high."

I had never had any of these issues, and to receive this news was alarming. At the same time, I had my first case of eczema appear right in the middle of my face. It was obvious that I was needing to make some serious changes in how the stress was affecting me, so I followed up with a naturopath for further answers and started to make some adjustments to my eating and sleeping patterns. I was prescribed some herbal therapies that also supported the stress load I was carrying and promised to help with the spike in cortisol.

One thing I never knew was how operating from long periods of time in a state of fight or flight mode is very taxing to one's liver as it overloads it with cortisol. This explained the extra weight I was wrestling with as well as my overall fatigue. I was paying the price on every level during this time, and it made me focus even more on breaking free from my brother and this endless legal process.

The whole ordeal left me constantly in a state of nervous anticipation as Gary had control over the assets, and I had no indication of what was happening. As his business partner, I received little to no update on the performance of things and what had been sold, rented, or even purchased. My brother had sporadically offered an annual or bi-annual snapshot in what felt like more of a consolation. But what I was able to learn would often come after decisions had been made, which naturally affected my bottom line. It took a team of lawyers to retrieve the answers any business partner would expect.

Now that files were removed from the office and most of the money appeared to have been withdrawn from the local account, I felt scared and stressed all the time. How couldn't I? Gary had offered me no explanation. On top of it, the legal bills were piling up, and my brother continued to pay his out of his own pocket and then get reimbursed by our company, while mine were my own responsibility. I was constantly fearful because I felt I knew from the patterns of the past several years of this mess that more trouble was coming. I had strong indications that my father and brother were dealing with the Hawaii condos, which meant a lot to us all as we had spent happy times there. After all of the previous decades of family ownership, my brother and I were the third generation in the family to own this special property through our LLC.

Earlier in the year, when my parents rented the condos, my father emailed Jaylen and told him that he had just joined the Oahu Country Club and was excited to be a new member. My grandfather, Carlton, had been a member, and we had enjoyed visiting the club as their guests, but now my dad was making a commitment to be a new member of the prestigious golf club, which I found strange. They lived along a golf course in Tucson, and I didn't even think of my father as a regular golfer, though he did go out from time to time.

My son, on the other hand, played in college and was the avid and competitive golfer in the family. I thought, initially, how nice it was that my dad was joining with a possible intention of taking Jaylen, or even all of his grandchildren along, but that meant we would all need to be in Hawaii, assuming we were staying in the family condos. With the current situation of Gary and me not speaking and trying to work our way through the legal mess, I felt the only way my father would join Oahu Country Club would be if he had a residence there.

My mother was already a member of two beach clubs, and my brother had been given a transfer of membership to the Outrigger Canoe Club by my grandfather when he became too elderly to travel. I remember at the time asking my father why I wasn't considered, as I traveled more frequently to the Islands than my brother and loved that particular club. "Your brother will have the membership, and then we can all use it as guests," he said, which meant that we would also pay higher guest fees. I accepted the explanation and was thankful Gary was kind enough to set up access for me when I would go to Honolulu.

I considered these four memberships between three people and how much they all knew I adored Hawaii and how I was even seriously considering moving there once my divorce was finalized. I expressed all of this to my counsel, who brought up my concerns with my brother's attorney. Again, we were requesting to be notified of any possible rental or sale on the property as a partner of the LLC. We had been more than clear on our demand for transparency. The new operating agreement didn't hold my brother accountable to anything I requested, but still, I wanted it noted that I would appreciate the communication, especially since we were starting to evaluate all of the assets for an eventual split of the company.

Unbeknownst to me until it was confirmed by my lawyers a few weeks later, my father secretly purchased both of the Hawaii condos from the LLC with the help of my brother on July 17th. The properties had transacted with a shockingly small down payment, a thirty-year note, and a balloon payment at the end. For a seventy-three-year-old man who prided himself for years for carrying little to no debt, the whole thing appeared to be a sweetheart deal, and their appraisal of the properties had taken place in mid-February, while my dad and brother were on their extended trip to Brazil. I remembered that my lawyers were notified that Gary would have limited if any access to communication, but this made it more than obvious that business had been transacted while they were likely onboard the cruise ship.

To me, there was absolutely no question my father was involved in what was going on with the LLC, and believing anything else was to accept a lie. He denied it over and over, which was more than ridiculous, given the paper trail that was accumulating on their plans and time together. I felt they took what meant the most to me and did so in what I believed to be an underhanded and spiteful transaction.

My notes to my counsel in October 2019 prior to mediation recapped some of the history of this matter:

> Dena does not believe Gary did his due diligence as a good general operating manager to find the best buyer for the property in Hawaii, nor did he give her first right of refusal on the property after his counsel asked which of the residential properties Dena might want should there be a buyout. Gary was formally notified of her desire to acquire the Hawaii property, whether through a buyout or other means but was never given a fair chance to be considered in the event of the recent sale to their father.

Although totally legal, my brother claimed the reason for selling the property was because it had been operating at a loss. I found this absurd as there had been limited efforts to truly generate much cash flow from the place, and knowing that I was interested in possibly living there and had never been given an option to rent it to offset these apparent losses felt offensive. The rent I was paying in New York City was likely far more than what it would have cost me to rent in Honolulu, and to have never been given a chance for discussion on other possibilities felt clear to me that it was likely a decision made out of selfishness, greed, and spite. I doubted there had been any great push to market the condo for sale other than making a deal with my father, who I believed would likely then hand the place over to my brother once we finalized our legal matters.

Shortly after the swift sale, my mother had mentioned to a family friend that my sister-in-law had traveled to the islands for a vacation with some girlfriends to stay in the family condo, and I assumed it was very likely she had the locks changed. My assumption about this was based on my parent's quick action to change the locks on the studio in New York once I left, as well as their unwillingness to allow me to visit or stay in their apartment in Eugene. I felt like I was being treated like a criminal. My personal belongings, including clothing, Hawaiian Christmas decorations, original art, photos, and items belonging to my kids, have yet to be returned to me from the apartment in Hawaii, and my personal inquiry with my parents for the safe and prompt return of my things was and has still been ignored.

It all started to come together for me even though I couldn't prove intent. I had enough material and patterns of behavior to see what was happening. Because of that operating agreement, which I unfortunately signed, my brother could continue to do as he wished, and very little had shown me over the years that he didn't have the support of my parents. I was only a placeholder, like a king on the chessboard, who was feeling closer to checkmate with each passing day.

What my parents may or may not have taken into consideration with their purchase of the Hawaii property was not only how it made me feel but how it also deeply hurt their grandchildren, who had also spent a lifetime going there. I thought about my grandmother's Bible she had given my grandfather on Easter in the mid-fifties with a loving inscription. It sat in the top drawer of the nightstand in the bedroom. I prayed that she would watch over things from heaven. I knew the place had meant a lot to her too.

The entire situation made me feel sick for days. The Hawaiian word "kaumaha," which means dreary, sad, dismal, downcast, and depressed, was the single word that summed it all up for me, as the deep grief I felt was especially overwhelming with this latest revelation. I cried and cried about it as it felt like the cruelest blow, especially since it confirmed in my mind my belief that my father was involved. I believed it would give my father and brother great pleasure knowing how much this hurt me, and I resisted the urge to lash out. I was devastated and felt it was incredibly mean-spirited and low. Joyce Meyer's wisdom reminded me to remain godly when I heard her say, "Don't let what they did change who you are." The message was clear that I was to rise above their greedy ways and carry on. I knew it wasn't worth being lost in the trappings of material things, yet the compulsive lies from my father and deception by the three of them cut my soul.

When one of my children inquired about the sale with my mother, I remember being told by Jaylen that her answer was, "Well, we had no choice but to save it from your mother, who would probably get it and sell it away from the family." It was another unbelievable statement that was as far off from my intentions as could be. I had made it clear to my parents that if I was the one who acquired the property, I would be more than willing and happy to allow the family to use it again and to do so with the family calendar we had all enjoyed for years until my brother took over the LLC.

When Jaylen asked my mother if he and his fiancé could visit the property one last time, my mother told him she would "think about it" but that he had to promise not to let me come along. I doubt my mother had any idea how that sounded to her grandson and his future wife. My parent's apparent hatred of me was felt without question. It felt clear that my mom and dad, like my brother, were only thinking only about themselves and had lost sight of the greater family and any future together.

The only way I could make sense of all that was happening and how truly unrecognizable my own parents and brother had become was to listen to sermons about strife and evil. I read scriptures that helped me understand and believe more and more that these people whom I loved, yet didn't feel I knew anymore, were being used as tools of the enemy. Creflo Dollar, in his powerful sermon series on strife and spiritual warfare, helped me understand this when he stated, "It's not the person (we are fighting), it's the demonic influence working in their life." My eyes and ears were open for the first time on this subject as it was happening to me, and my focus of disbelief, anger, and hurt was incorrectly being pointed at the individuals themselves.

The spiritual attacks couldn't help but feel personal because of the intense emotional pain they inflicted, and they were ultimately affecting my day-to-day life. However, the more I realized the people I loved and felt I knew were no longer recognizable, the more I sought for new understanding. Again, I returned to Ephesians 6:12 (NIV), which reminded me, "For our struggle is not against flesh and blood, but against the rulers, against the authorities, against the powers of this dark world and against the spiritual forces of evil in the heavenly realms." Remembering this helped reintroduce me to the wisdom that people who worshipped material things over God were opening themselves up to the enemy and would thus become vulnerable to evil.

I believed strongly that the change of behavior in my parents and brother was due to their focus on money, power, and greed. I felt that their goals for happiness were intently directed on the accumulation of material things and that the more they had, the more powerful they felt. Certainly, I felt powerless at the hands of my brother and the operating agreement he had designed, which made me feel trapped. My parent's behavior around money and the excessive accumulation of things and acquiring material possessions didn't feel balanced or normal. It felt clear that this mindset had become more important than valuing family and relationships. The entire situation seemed to me to be driven by avarice, the compulsion for power, and an insatiable quest for material accumulation, all of which I saw as an attempt to remedy some sort of emotional void or vulnerability.

I believed that their apparent chosen path of life to keep focusing on the material would likely not be their best ethical and moral investment as expressed in Jesus' parable of the rich fool in Luke 12:15-21 (NIV):

> Then he said to them, "Watch out! Be on your guard against all kinds of greed; life does not consist in an abundance of possessions.
>
> And he told them this parable: "The ground of a certain rich man yielded an abundant harvest. He thought to himself, 'What shall I do? I have no place to store my crops.'
>
> "Then he said, 'This is what I'll do. I will tear down my barns and build bigger ones, and there I will store my surplus grain. And I'll say to myself, "You have plenty of grain laid up for many years. Take life easy; eat, drink and be merry."
>
> "But God said to him, 'You fool! This very night your life will be demanded from you. Then who will get what you have prepared for yourself?'
>
> "This is how it will be with whoever stores up things for themselves but is not rich toward God."[2]

I felt greed was growing like cancer, and it became the real battle I was fighting within my family. Although I had a brilliant legal team, I realized this part of the fight couldn't be won with the law or in a courtroom. Yes, we could divide the assets and go our separate ways eventually, but a dark, gripping presence seemed to overtake my loved ones and prevented them from hearing, seeing, or speaking the truth. I accepted that it was spiritual warfare and that it was time to educate myself on how to handle this and not only set myself free but possibly my brother and parents. It was time to become a spiritual warrior.

> Therefore, put on the full armor of God, so that when the day of evil comes, you may be able to stand your ground, and after you have done everything, to stand. Stand firm then, with the belt of truth buckled around your waist, with the breastplate of righteousness in place, and with your feet fitted with the readiness that comes from the gospel of peace. In addition to all this, take up the shield of faith, with which you can extinguish all the flaming arrows of the evil one. Take the helmet of salvation and the sword of the Spirit, which is the word of God.
>
> Ephesians 6:13-17 (NIV)[3]

Armed with the Word of God, I began my mission to stand firm against the attacks and not fall prey to the enemy. I prayed for my family, who I saw as lost in the wilderness of worldly goals. What would become of them on their deathbeds? After all, it is said that one cannot take it all with them when they die. My wealth was my increased peace, knowledge, and strength from God and His example. I could only anticipate by trying to break from this generational greed and deceit that new seeds of hope could be planted not only in my own life but in those of the next generation.

A summer day with my grandma Margaret at
her home in Cottage Grove, Oregon.

One of my earliest memories with my great-grandfather, Walter.

I always felt a deep and protective love from
my great-grandmother, Dutee.

With my grandma Margaret in her kitchen in Eugene,
where we spent many meaningful times together.

My last visit to Hawaii in 2006 with my grandparents, Carlton and Joy.
This photo was taken after service at the First Presbyterian Ko'olau, Oahu.

Christmas Eve with my maternal grandparents, Herman and Margaret.

My grandmother, Joy and me after our painting class.

Aloha 'Oe ~ The lei I wore into the ocean, January 2017, when I
said farewell from Waikiki to my departed grandfather, Carlton.

The Holy Spirit spoke to me during this moment in Hawaii, August 2017. I had no idea what was ahead but I remember my heart felt very heavy and sad.

Seeing the cross in the Manhattan skyline every day has given me incredible peace knowing I am right where God wants me to be.

The morning smile from "Waffles" the tortoise.

Cognac captured my heart and soul when I cared
for him in 2018. He is pure love.

Yoga has been an important part of my life since 2010. I
believe our bodies are a temple to the Holy Spirit.

"Rememberance of Fields Past" resounds strongly in my soul
when I find myself here thinking of my great-grandfather.

My journey has created within me the spirit of a
"Graceful Warrior." Photo by Luciana Pampalone,
makeup by @glamgoneviral. New York, 2021.

My son and daughter, walking the beach at sunset at Three Tables
Beach on the North Shore of Oahu, December 29, 2016.

Loved,
Conditionally

All I can say at this point is that the particular brand of narcissism that characterizes evil people seems to be one that particularly afflicts the will.[4]

Malignant narcissism is characterized by an unsubmitted will. All adults who are mentally healthy submit themselves one way or another to something higher than themselves, be it God or truth or love or some other ideal... They believe in what is true rather than what they would like to be true... In summary, to a greater or lesser degree, all mentally healthy individuals submit themselves to the demands of their own conscience... They are men and women of obviously strong will, determined to have their own way.[5]

Such people literally live "in a world of their own" in which the self reigns supreme[6]

—M. Scott Peck, MD

People of The Lie: The Hope for Healing Human Evil

In August, my mother arrived alone in Eugene and spent time moving the majority of things from my father's office. It was the same office where Gary had appeared shortly after our grandmother's memorial. She had reached out to Jaylen to say she was in town and had hoped to get to Portland to see him. Various other relatives told me she was there as it was known by now that we were estranged, and things were uncomfortable between us. My parents still had their apartment near my grandmother's nursing home and close to their former house. I didn't know if she was moving from that location as well but thought it wouldn't be long before they did. As far as I could see, they had been making more and more decisions to be free from all ties to Oregon.

In late September, I arrived in my home state from New York for meetings and business matters. I understood my mother was still in town, so I decided to reach out via text to see if we might be able to connect on some level. My hands shook as I looked up her number on my phone. Even though I knew it by heart, I wanted to make sure. The last time I had reached out was a few months earlier for Mother's Day, and she never responded. For whatever reason, this time it was one of those social media event days called "National Daughter's Day," and although I knew my mom wasn't on any social platforms, I decided to share a photo with her I had posted of Lily along with the following text:

> National Daughter's Day today—Lots of moms posting photos of their girls. This is a recent one of Lily. I'm celebrating Lily. <3 Let me know if you'd like to go to yoga class with me in Eugene as there is a great place I've found in town. I just got in and would love to see you! We could also go up and see Grandma Joy and Grandpa Carlton's new memorial plaque if you haven't seen it yet. Hope you're well mom. Would love to see you. Let me know. Thanks xo D

I spoke honestly and thought if we could connect over an activity or even pay our respects to my grandparents together, it might be a point of authentic connection. Every time I am in my hometown, I make time to visit the resting place of her parents and now my father's parents, who were finally laid to rest in the nearby cemetery mausoleum. I had created a beautiful floral bouquet with a miniature bird and butterfly wrapped a big pink and green ribbon for my grandparents. It gave me so much peace to sit with them and see that their chosen site together looked nice.

I always felt close to my grandmothers, especially when I visited their resting places and somehow hoped my mom would possibly want to meet there or at least go for a coffee or lunch. This time I was hopeful for a reply as I didn't think my father was in town, and I noticed she was usually more herself when she was alone. I couldn't remember the last time I had seen her, and for some reason, I really hoped that a pre-planned face-to-face meeting between us could be a possible step in a new direction. I prayed about it and pushed send. I waited for a reply, and when I didn't receive one, I tried not to focus on the lingering silence, but it was there.

Even though I was starting to accept spiritual warfare and the work of the enemy on vulnerable people, I kept holding out some shred of hope that maybe I would be able to connect with my mother and have a real mother-daughter moment between the two of us, but it didn't seem to be a possibility. I knew if we ran into one another around town, at least she wouldn't be surprised to see me. I wanted to have full transparency and make the effort to truly try to connect.

A date for mediation between Gary and me was finally being discussed between the lawyers. I felt nervous but thankful that an end to this nightmare was starting to look like it may become a reality. I had no way of knowing what would happen to the family after my brother and I would go our separate ways. So much emotional damage had taken place over the years leading up to this that if there ever was a change, it would be a miracle in the making.

I drove to Portland to take Jaylen and Sasha to dinner. They were both working and living in Portland and planning their wedding for March 2020. We were all hopeful for a happier year ahead, and it was like a breath of fresh air to focus on their exciting plans. Sasha was from Newport Beach, but her parents also lived in France, so they were planning a wedding and reception in both places. It was really a sign of hope that there would be some great moments of families coming together instead of ripping apart at the seams like mine was. Their excitement was evident at dinner, and I soaked up every happy minute with them before driving back to Eugene for the night.

The next day as I was wrapping up my short visit home, I needed to drop by the office to pick up some paperwork before heading to my hotel room to pack. I parked my rental car in the half-full lot and saw movement out of the corner of my eye. At once, I recognized my mother as she stepped out of an unfamiliar car from the farthest end of the lot. My heart started racing, and I tried to calm myself as I realized we would soon be meeting face to face, although not in the way I had hoped.

As she walked across the parking lot to the office door, I witnessed something very strange as I noticed her body movements didn't seem recognizable, as though they were not her own. My mother's petite yet strong physique, which had always been impressive for her age, was still the same. I was always proud of how she stayed fit and active, skiing, hiking, biking, and doing her own yard work. Her strength was in her stride, but the movement of her whole body was different, almost animal-like. It was as though someone was walking for her. A chill went through me as I saw for the first time an almost demonic spirit in her movements.

Before I opened my car door, I prayed, "Dear God, I pray to you in the name of Jesus and ask for the power of the Holy Spirit to surround me like a fortress, to protect me and give me strength and calm as I face my mother. I will not fall prey to the enemy and the attacks which are meant for me. I will stand strong in the name of Jesus and bring a spirit of light, love, and peace to this moment. Guide my words, my intention, and allow me to be light where there is darkness. Amen."

As I walked through the door, she was as surprised as I was, although I had had a few minutes beforehand to prepare myself for our untimely meeting. The office manager, Katherine, was there, and the three of us engaged in light, meaningless conversation. My mother stumbled a little over not replying to my text about getting together. The usual excuses being too busy, tired, on a deadline, all came out at once, and I nodded my head and said I had figured as much. I felt authentic in my choice of words and knew under no circumstances would I engage in strife. I felt that the first ten or so minutes of the three of us chatting went considerably well, and then mom invited me into my father's office, which was the room just across from Katherine's desk.

As we stepped into the doorway, I immediately noticed how empty the room was. My mom explained how hard she had worked to get all of my father's belongings packed up and on their way to Arizona. In my mind, I turned over the usual thoughts of how she was always the one to do such work for him while he stayed comfortably away. I kept the conversation light and realized the door to my dad's office was still open, so we were still well within earshot of Katherine, which wasn't unusual as the office was small and it was not an easy place to have a conversation without being overheard.

Suddenly the small talk stopped, and my mother looked at me, and I was instantly struck with how dark, flat and lifeless her eyes had become. There was a barrier between the woman I knew and the one who was standing before me. I realized immediately I was dealing with someone who I believed had been possessed by the enemy.

Her voice dropped, and the enemy within started to attack. "Why are you being so hard on your brother? Don't you know how much he has done for you?" Was she kidding? "You have destroyed the whole family, and you have no idea how much you have hurt us all." Not once had she thought for a moment what it was like to walk in my shoes.

I believed she had been brainwashed with the narrative she had accepted, and I knew it wasn't worth trying to defend any of it anymore. Her world seemed isolated, directed, and contained, and her efforts to look at the other side of things had stopped long ago. For many years I had tried to show her the numbers, the facts, the evidence of what had happened between Gary and me, and it always fell on deaf ears. It was all in black and white and obvious to anyone who looked at the facts that there were serious issues to be questioned. This would be another fruitless attempt at trying to be heard if I engaged, and from painful experiences, I finally knew better.

I felt an unusual strength and calm come over me as her verbal attacks came stronger and faster. I felt aware of a shield of protection around me that I had never experienced before, and I knew God had me. I knew that the Holy Spirit was shielding me from engaging in strife and from feeling the blows.

"Mom, I didn't come here to discuss these things; I'm just happy to see you." Her eyes widened, and she started to get angry, and as I felt her rise to engage, I reached my arms out to her for a hug and said, "Mom, I love you." She immediately pushed my arms away and said, "You don't deserve my love," and walked from my father's office past Katherine and into the conference room in the back of the small building. I stood for a moment and was surprised I had no tears. I felt shocked but also knew I hadn't faced the mother I knew. I believed I had just dealt with Satan himself.

Katherine witnessed the whole thing and was standing at her desk with tears streaming down her face. I smiled and told her I was sorry she had to witness that but was glad to see her and started toward the door, almost totally forgetting why I had come there in the first place. Knowing my mom was in the next room, I didn't think there was anything to be said between Katherine and me since she had seen the exchange for herself and was noticeably upset. I smiled at her with a look of appreciation for her care.

As I turned to leave, I noticed a stack of books under Katherine's desk, and I saw one of the titles jump out as one I recognized. My mom referenced the book often when she used to tell me about people succumbing to evil. I remember her explaining to me that it was a book not to be taken lightly and to use care if referencing people in our own lives whom we may view as evil or misguided.

The People of The Lie was a sort of guidebook on how she seemed to make sense of people in her own life she believed were hurtful or not living their truth. When I pointed to the book, Katherine pointed in the direction of the conference room, indicating that she had received it from my mother. We exchanged a look, and I knew it was time to leave and not a time to discuss why my mom would give her such a book. My mother was still in the conference room, and I had a plane to catch.

Walking to my car, I expected to fall apart but didn't. Remarkably I never shed a tear over that awful moment with my mother. My sadness was instead seeing how sold out to the enemy she had become and how I believed my father was also using her. I was glad Katherine was there to witness everything because it was not to be believed. My mother's choice of words was so telling to me that she was likely directed by something dark and evil. Those words and her actions were the last I have seen or heard from her, and I've thought if she were to die, that would be my last encounter with the woman who birthed me into this world.

Every time I see one of my kids, I pray over them and hold them tight and tell them how much I love them. I can't imagine leaving one of them with the words that they don't deserve my love. September 26, 2019, was the last time I saw my mother when she walked out on me and pushed my love away, telling me I didn't deserve hers. What I want her to know most of all is that I still love her, and I pray for her every day and that I am sorry she isn't living her own life. My strong belief is that she is living hers in bondage to my dad, the trappings of wealth, and the enemy. Her dark, flat, emotionless eyes said it all.

Anticipation

I wait for the Lord, my whole being waits, and in his word, I put my hope.

Psalm 130:5 (NIV)

Their minds had been infected with the evil that had spread across the country, but their *souls* weren't evil. Despite their atrocities, they were children of God, and I could forgive a child, although it would not be easy...especially when that child was trying to kill me.[7]

—Immaculée Ilibagiza
*Left To Tell: Discovering God Amidst
the Rwandan Holocaust*

To know me in the fall of 2019 was to know someone who was battle-weary, sad, yet hopeful for closure and a new beginning. I was well aware that my trusted social circle was likely very tired of hearing me talk about my pain and shock over my family and the almost daily ups and downs of the past few years. If I wasn't talking about it, my eyes quietly told enough of the story of sleepless nights and oceans of tears I had cried as they had created dark circles and deep lines.

Stress and sadness had aged me, and sometimes, when I caught myself in the mirror, I was surprised by how much pain I saw in the reflection. Sometimes I was sad because I also saw my mother's image in me. I felt like I was seeing glimpses of the woman I once knew and from whom I was now estranged. My heart felt constantly heavy, and sometimes I even noticed myself trying to take deep enough breaths just to stay calm. These worldly afflictions caused me to seek my faith more and more as a means to ground and center myself.

I was aware of people who had faded into the background after Randy and I split, some deciding which side they were on and others perhaps feeling awkward at our newfound status as separated and divorcing. There were some who didn't seem to take a side and were friendly with us both, and I appreciated their decision. I never expected to lose friends, but divorce divides, and it's something one is never prepared for in the process. Sometimes there is that longing to clarify things by saying, "You haven't known us long enough for this to make sense," or "You've known us so long this really doesn't make sense." I often said, with much heartfelt honesty, that, "We are good people who still respect and deeply care about one another but just can't make it work anymore." Regardless, people perceive what they want to, and it's something I've had to accept.

It made me reflect on how I may have behaved in the past with friends who had faced the same in their relationship and whether I had faded into the background or made a choice to stand by one or another or both. Certainly, when you go through it yourself, it magnifies your past decisions and those going forward. The shoes I have walked in have taught me a lot about perception, compassion, and the unfairness of judging others.

The rift with my parents and brother was like a second divorce that unexpectedly stole the spotlight away from my marital split and immediately became more painful for so many reasons. Like my separation from Randy, the divide with my brother caused people to fade into the background or to take clear sides, and in this instance, I felt so many of those decisions were based on fear of a backlash by my father or fear of financial hardship if the individual relied on him for support or in business.

I beat myself up for many years over these losses of people I loved and expected to be in my life forever but started to realize that their absence was very likely due to God's plan. The process of pain has taught me that sometimes God chooses to separate you from certain people because they may be in the way of the work He is trying to do in your life, and/or He prunes them away so that He can do important work in *their* lives.

This certainly seemed to be the case with my family, as the clarity I gained by living separately from them illuminated the very clear and sad dysfunction in my family of origin. God not only pruned them away but seemed to do an entire field burning by removing them from my life. I have therefore come to believe that God has selected who would remain and who would leave my life, and that has made a great difference in the way I think about people who have chosen to leave me as a friend, or in the case of my family, a daughter, sister, aunt, sister-in-law, and cousin.

Life had become something I observed from a distance and felt less of a participant in as my focus was on surviving and getting out from what I felt was generational bondage. Exhausting the ears of even the most patient friends and family who stood by me didn't always feel good, but there were times I just needed to feel the unconditional love I no longer had from my parents or brother. I was grateful for anyone who would listen and that I had a handful of extremely loyal and caring friends whose support meant a great deal to me and still does today.

Pain had brought me a lot of clarity on life, on what was important, and who had stood by me during the worst of times. I wanted to be free from the legal entanglements and the tiresome, painstakingly slow process to the finish line that I believed to be orchestrated by my father and brother to cost me nearly everything. My legal bills were costing me hundreds of thousands of dollars and growing, which made my head spin. I knew I was borrowing and spending some of what I was hoping to receive in a settlement, but it was the necessary price of freedom from the chains I felt on my life. I was, therefore, grateful when both parties finally arrived at a date for mediation. It was a day I had prayed for and hoped for, and now it was solidly on my calendar. November 5, 2019, was on the horizon, and the count-down had begun.

My relationship with God had grown immensely during this time, and it was becoming more evident to me that my pain had a purpose. It steadied me during the storms and gave me hope when all seemed lost. Finally, having a place to live to call my own after all I had been through was always reason enough for me to see how far I had come when so many odds were against me.

Even with the pain, loss, and frustration of the legal process and my divorce still on the horizon, I felt newly grounded. I had lost a lot, some material and some of it personal, but what filled the empty places was my faith. It filled me to capacity far more than the petty material things that so easily ensnare us into emotional bondage. I searched scriptures constantly and prayed with a newfound belief that I was not going to fall. God had kept a roof over my head, food on my plate, and my health steady even during the absolute worst of times.

My struggle to be patient felt like it might be coming to a partial end as the mediation date was confirmed. I didn't know exactly what God's plan was for me, but I was absolutely positive He had one. I felt it deep in my soul, and I also felt my pain would not be wasted. Somehow, in all of the turmoil, I heard God's plan and His hope that I would recognize how much my hurtful journey might help others. It was the beginning of the calling for this book, and that message was one of grace overcoming greed. The seed was planted, and now it was time to pray for direction. Getting through mediation and on the other side to freedom was all I could think about.

Patience continued to be a challenge as I produced more facts for my legal team and painstakingly went over every detail I could remember or found in my notes. When asked for a written review of my position on my past few excruciating years in the partnership with my brother, my fingers couldn't type fast enough. A twenty-five-page timeline and summary of events emerged, and I wrote it as much for me as for my lawyers. It felt good to review and organize things and also see how far I had come. Above all, it was a strong reminder of how steadfast God had been throughout the ordeal, and I knew I would not let this nearly five-year battle go without recognizing it as a shift for something better in my life.

Scriptures reminded me how to accept the process. "But these things I plan won't happen right away. Slowly, steadily, surely, the time approaches when the vision will be fulfilled. If it seems slow, do not despair, for these things will surely come to pass. Just be patient! They will not be overdue a single day!" (Habakkuk 2:3, TLB)

I was getting prepared for what to expect during mediation or, more specifically, shuttle mediation which meant that my brother and I would be in separate rooms at opposite ends of an office building with our own lawyers, while the mediator would go between the two rooms to negotiate a settlement and hopefully close the outstanding matters between the partners. It was unbelievably sad to me that I was at a place with Gary where we couldn't even be in the same room with one another to sort out our differences, split our assets, and go our separate ways. Never in a million years did I think I would be in such a situation with my only sibling, but the date was upon us, and the meetings to prepare for that day were in full swing.

In the months leading up to mediation, my brother had sold well over a million dollars' worth of property assets without informing me until he was forced to do so during our discovery process. His new operating agreement didn't provide that he had to, but basic decency, in my opinion, didn't seem to exist. My father was the new owner of the Hawaii property, and several parcels of valuable commercial property had been sold to an outside buyer. I believe if my dad had not bought the condo in Honolulu, Gary would have likely wanted the Wild Creek Resort home and I would have desired

Hawaii. Because my dad purchased one of the assets out of the company prior to mediation, the process for splitting things down the middle appeared to me to be more complicated. As far as I was concerned, I felt my brother and father had already cherry-picked what they wanted. My father's repeated claims that he was uninvolved and that the company was solely a matter between my brother and me were absolutely offensive to me by now.

As I was thinking about the enormous legal bills I was to pay back to my guardian angel, I knew my brother would not face the same. It made me feel like I was sort of paying for us both since his reimbursement checks dwindled the value of the LLC.

As my best friend, Georgia, would often say to me when I would tell her about the situation, "Dude, there is no fair!" While I always laughed when she called me, "Dude," I knew her statement was right. I mulled that over in my mind as I looked back over the past few months and years. I was especially still hurting over how Hawaii was handled and just incredulous over how my parents seemed so insensitive about it and how it affected my children and me.

I listened to Joyce Meyer often about God being what she called "a God of justice." I reminded myself, as did my lawyers, that this would not be an opportunity to get even, rather one to get out and be free. As Proverbs 20:22 (NIV) says, "Do not say, 'I'll pay you back for this wrong!' Wait for the Lord and he will avenge you."

Preparation for mediation meant hours of pouring over documents, appraisals, financials, and other details with my legal team. For me personally, it also included praying for my brother and father. Trying to practice spiritual maturity, I had learned that praying for one's enemy was a way to open the eyes of the one who has hurt you and thus allow God to work on them instead of trying to force the issue of right and wrong. "But I tell you, love your enemies and pray for those who persecute you, that you may be children of your Father in heaven. He causes his sun to rise on the evil and the good and sends rain on the righteous and the unrighteous" (Matthew 5:44-45, NIV). I was living what I believed and trying to put all of my fears with God. In doing so, I felt empowered, protected, and more peaceful than ever. My former self would have been paralyzed by fear, but I felt steady and prepared for what was ahead, knowing I was not alone.

I believed my brother was being used by the enemy as a weapon of destruction, and I was ultimately embarrassed and sad for him. It was the only thing that made sense to me as it did with my mother and father. I no longer felt that I knew these people who had at one time been my family. They were strangers and their focus, as far as I believed, was solely on power, money, and greed. I saw it as the work of a dark, demonic force that took three otherwise good people and blinded them from truth and love. Family, relationships, and love appeared to have been pushed away in a quest for the material. Their apparent fixation on greed caused me to search instead for grace. As Joyce Meyer once said, "You'll never have peace if you don't have grace."

The fact that several years of agonizing legal back and forth had transpired and my brother and his counsel still had ignored repeated requests of documentation and simple answers to straightforward questions related to my brother's job description was still unacceptable. The use of his title as "General Operating Manager" in the ill-fated operating agreement appeared to garner an enormous swath of leniency in any direction that might hold him accountable to me or to my share of assets. I saw him holding onto a job title and our father's lawyer from San Francisco for his redemption. I valued and respected my incredible legal team and knew I was in amazing hands, but God was my ultimate counselor and vindicator. I prepared for mediation, knowing that my priorities were in the right place, and believed that God already knew the outcome. All I had to do was show up and trust Him.

Remembrance of Fields Past

She is more precious than rubies; nothing you desire can compare with her.

Proverbs 3:15 (NIV)

Two days before mediation in Portland, I found myself driving along familiar roads in Cottage Grove. I knew the efforts to divide most of what was left of the remaining assets in the LLC would likely focus on properties we owned in and around the town, and part of me wanted to look at things from a business perspective while the other part of me embraced the growing nostalgia that was tugging at my heart. Everything we still owned here had been acquired decades before by our great-grandparents, and I couldn't help but think of how they likely never imagined part of their legacy ending in a legal battle between siblings.

My early childhood always floods my memory every time I take the southbound exit off of Interstate 5 into town, and this moment was no different. I circled the little town, driving by familiar landmarks, remembering happier, easier times. I passed by my father and mother's childhood homes, the Presbyterian Church where my parents were married, and I went to nursery school, family businesses developed and sold or still owned by other relatives. I went by the grade school where I attended first grade and the nearby pool where I learned to swim, all not far from my childhood home on a dead-end street which bordered a large parcel of land now owned by my brother and me.

I drove down Main Street, which was once the setting for the parade scene in the movie *Animal House*. I remembered my Grandma Margaret taking me there the day the big finale scene was being filmed and how small I felt standing in such a large crowd. That little girl never knew she would one day live among 8 million people in New York City, and I smiled, thinking of how innocent she was clinging to the hand of her grandmother, who wanted to see the exciting activity around the filming of a movie.

I drove south on old Highway 99, heading out of town, passing the Dairy Queen where I used to get ice cream on hot summer days. On the southern part of town, just outside of the city limits, I took a left as the road wrapped around part of the Weyerhaeuser Company Lumber Mill, originally built, privately owned, and operated by my great-grandfather. The tall smokestack bearing our family's last name had long been torn down, but the memories of a log pond full of enormous timber and log trucks going in and out of the mill yard were still vivid in my mind, along with my great-grandparent's nearby home where I spent many happy years.

As I saw the sign for Cottage Grove Lake, I felt drawn to drive the three or so miles southeast to the shore to reminisce about the fun times I used to have with my aunts, uncles, parents, cousins, and brother on lazy summer nights. Fond memories of the family taking turns on my uncle's boat to water ski or swim, followed by dinner around a campfire at one of the picnic areas, seemed like a lifetime ago.

The lake also reminded me of beautiful afternoon drives I would take with my great-grandmother and uncle just for something to do. "Let's go to London today," she loved to say as we packed a lunch and got into her car. London, Oregon was not far from the lake, so we often took trips to London, where she fondly remembered an old nearby mill house that she used to call home before it burned to the ground.

Instead of going to the lake, I took a left and headed north in the direction of the south entrance to the large parcel of land owned by the LLC. Before I arrived, I recognized on the left side of the road a very nice little mobile home park that had been there for years, and as I glanced to the right, a sign for Torrington Road sparked a memory I had forgotten until then. My mind suddenly started to replay images from my past, so I quickly pulled to the side of the road and caught my breath. Tears started to well up as memories I hadn't revisited in a lifetime suddenly became very vivid. I was immediately overwhelmed with emotion and found myself sobbing uncontrollably, which took me by surprise.

Torrington Road used to lead to a produce farm where my mother decided I should work one summer. I recall carrying a sack lunch and a thermos of water to the site where my mom would drop me off in the morning to pick strawberries. She used to tell me that when she was a little girl, she picked beans in the fields and often turned the bucket upside down so she could sit and reach up to pull the beans from the stalks. "It goes fast and is very easy to pick beans, and strawberries should be fun too," she would say, trying to spark my enthusiasm. I was always happy picking vegetables and berries with her in the large garden in our backyard, but suddenly I was left to fill large flats of strawberries by myself. Looking back, I realize she was trying to teach me the value of working hard and earning my own money, but I was happier at home earning money shining my father's shoes or helping her around the house.

Working in the strawberry fields was painstaking work in the hot sun as I remember being given a flat to fill and long low rows to harvest. Instead of looking up as my mom did picking beans, I was hunched over the low-lying strawberry plants looking for ripe berries, and my neck not only got sore but sunburned as well. At lunchtime, I would sit alone and eat the peanut butter and honey sandwich on wheat bread, which was my favorite. Carrot sticks, a green apple, and maybe a homemade cookie were likely in the bag as that was my standard lunch when I was in first grade. I don't think I could have been more than seven or eight years old. I just remember I was young and felt vulnerable as I vividly remember the disappointment one day of having the berry checker walk through one of my rows to find berries that were still ripe enough to pick. For some reason, I felt an enormous letdown as though I had done a terrible job when in fact, I thought I had done my best. When my mom came to pick me up that day, I was still going over the row trying to make up for a job I had thought done well and suddenly couldn't wait to get in the car to go home.

Thinking about that time in the strawberry field made me sad as I couldn't imagine sending my daughter or son to do the same at such a young age. The world is different now, I admit, but it's a job I didn't like, mostly because I remember feeling scared and alone in a field with strangers and no sense of time or when my mother would come to get me. I know my mom had good intentions at the time, but the truth of the matter was that I had buried that memory for decades because it was unpleasant. It wasn't until this day, when I was in a nostalgic state of mind and drove by the area, that I suddenly felt the juxtaposition to my recollection of what had happened in the mobile home park on the other side of the road.

My Grandma Joy had signed up for a four-week oil painting class with other adults taught by an artist who lived in one of the mobile homes. She had asked me if I wanted to learn how to paint, and my agreement led her to take me with her one day a week for four weeks, where I was the only child in the class sitting at an easel learning the techniques of oil painting. A set of new brushes, oils, turpentine, and canvases were given to me. I felt so excited and proud as my grandmother sat beside me while we followed the teacher, who instructed us how to paint a snow scene with evergreen trees and a river flowing through the middle of the painting.

Each week we would paint a different seasonal scene, and I tried so hard to make mine look as good as my grandmother's, but she had decades on me with her talent and technique. She gave me praise and shared hints on different brushstrokes to create realistic shadows and light. She taught me how to look at things with a critical artistic eye, and to this day, I have never forgotten some of what she taught me.

I never realized it at the time, but now that I was a mother, I could see these events in several ways. On one hand, my own mother was likely trying to teach me the value of hard work and how to earn money, yet my laboring in a strawberry field all day also meant she had one less child to deal with at the time, and it was likely a welcome break. My grandmother had three grown boys, and I imagined she wanted to share this type of activity with her granddaughter, so looking at it through my eyes as a mother, I understood why she would have enjoyed inviting me to a class with her.

I couldn't stop crying as I sat in the car, feeling the little girl inside of me come alive. She was shy and eager to please yet scared and alone. Afraid to voice how she really felt yet wanting to please and to do the right thing, I saw her again in each place on different sides of the road and knew it was important to remember her and her feelings.

The sun was lingering in a late afternoon fall sky, and I knew what I wanted to do before I got back on the freeway to Eugene. I wiped my tears and started the car to drive the short distance to the entrance of the property that always brought back happy childhood memories. It was a beautiful, vast stretch of undeveloped land that went alongside the river and had a grove of old-growth trees on the top of the hill at its northern end. I drove to the end of the road, where the gate secured with a heavy-duty lock made me stop. Ironically, I co-owned these beautiful open fields just on the other side of the gate but had never been given a key. My brother may have had the key, but I held the memories.

Thick blackberry brambles, which had reached the end of their season, were wildly overgrown on one side of the gate near the adjacent fence, while on the other side of the gate stood an abandoned house once belonging to my great-grandmother's eldest sister, Jeannie and her husband, Morton. An inner cyclone fence wrapped around the perimeter of the now dilapidated house, memorializing it as the last vestige of residential property on the farmland that was now boasting cattle and horses for grazing. I stood at the gate and stepped both feet up to the lower metal bar feeling like a child peering into a closed playground. The road continued beyond the gate onto the property, and I stared at it for a long time until an image from the past appeared in my mind.

Like a scene from a movie, I saw my great-grandmother behind the wheel of her golf cart with me sitting in the passenger seat. Her nearby home sat between the Coast Fork of the Willamette River and a manmade lake that was part of her estate. The golf cart was used often to navigate around the property and sometimes cross the private bridge over the river to visit her sister, Jeannie. The tiny gravel rocks crunched under the wheels as we headed toward her sister's house. In the scene, the blackberry vines, livestock, and gate were gone and in its place was manicured green grass, which was the fairway of my great-grandfather's private golf course. The gravel road wound along the river's edge and passed between the fourth and fifth fairway. Her sister's farmhouse stood neatly and proudly among a grove of oak and apple trees with a beautiful lilac bush on the south side of the yard. As the golf cart appeared to come closer, I saw the joyous anticipation on our faces and a large basket full of something likely homemade on the seat between us as we arrived at the entrance to the house.

My eyes started to focus again on the present moment as the past image of the golf cart and my great-grandmother and I disappeared like a fading mirage into the afternoon sun. I stepped away from the gate and immediately felt a quick-moving strong wind kick up from the ground and rise into the trees. As I looked up into the long hanging branches of the old oaks near the house, I could hear the wind rustling the leaves as an unusual calm came over me. The hint of a whisper said, "this land will make everything okay," as it seemed to touch all of my senses at once before blowing away with the traveling wind. I was aware of my feet firmly grounded on the land beneath me as I felt the air become still again. As I looked toward the house one last time, I suddenly noticed the beautiful purple lilac bush that had appeared in the past was still there.

There were deep memories here of family history and images in my mind that had long been dormant. The heavy metal lock didn't keep me from accessing the splendor of what was on the other side of the gate, or at least what I remembered to be there. I knew I belonged at that place at that moment, and I said a prayer thanking God for the people who came before me, for the love they shared, and the good things they did in the community and the family they created that I was fortunate to call my own.

I felt the enormous power of the Holy Spirit envelop me in love and a knowing that no matter what would happen in the legal process, I would be okay. I felt the arms of my great-grandparents and grandparents in the limbs of the trees and the tangled bushes that at first glance seemed foreboding but now served as the living reminder of their essence, which kept watch over me. I was one with them as they were with me. Nothing mattered besides their love, and I felt God enlightening me as I stood in the middle of the gravel road.

The material possessions from their lives earned out of grit, hard work, and a desire to make a difference didn't outweigh who they really were. The homes, the golf course, the businesses, and worldly things that were acquired through years of sacrifice and taking risks had mostly been divided or sold, but who they were as people with heart and integrity was priceless and lasting. What was left here now were remnants of their dreams, and this land was a part of that. Whether I would walk away from the negotiating table with it or not didn't matter because I realized I owned the most priceless thing of all, which was their unconditional love and happy memories of them as my wonderful family.

Standing on the road near my rental car, blocked by overgrown shrubs, gates, and fences, didn't keep me from knowing who they were and who I was to them. The wind in the branches of the old trees sent a message to me, confirming they felt my presence as I did theirs. God was showing me that I was to them as they were to me, more precious than rubies. I smiled, thinking about the scripture from Proverbs, remembering that my great-grandmother once owned a very rare set of rubies that were one of only two sets like them in the world. She only wore them for extremely special occasions, which were much fewer as she got older. I had only seen pictures of them and heard her talk about how they were her favorites.

Before my wedding day, I had stayed at her home, seeking solace and wanting time alone with her. I felt peace in her home and was comforted by her presence. I remember needing that time with her before I got married and moved away. Looking back now, I am so grateful I created that precious time, which means more to me now than ever. Her gift to me had been the wedding dress of my dreams, and I remember feeling like a princess. A baby blue silk-covered button from her own wedding dress had been hand-sewn in the seam of the inside skirt of my gown, and it symbolized the "something blue" from old-fashioned wedding traditions. She enjoyed seeing my excitement as the day drew closer, and I realized how lucky I was to have my nearly ninety-year-old great-grandmother attending my wedding as the guest of honor.

She loved the color pink and strawberries and often stitched needlepoints with strawberries and had little pots of strawberry pink lip balm near her reading table, which was fun to find as a child. She had personalized notepads with her name on them in pink with a strawberry motif. When we were young, she would say to us that she was the strawberry lady or the pink lady, and I smiled, thinking of those silly happy memories. As the matriarch of the family, she was loving and genuine to all of us. Division between the generations was unthinkable as we were undeniably a united, proud family and one she held dear.

As she and I talked about my wedding day, she spoke about it as though she was attending Queen Elizabeth's coronation. Never mind that she actually attended that event in London years and years ago. We all knew it, and some of us had a copy of an article she had written for the local paper about the experience, but she rarely spoke about it, and instead, she wanted to know about each of us and what our dreams were. When we asked about her past, she reminisced about the good old days and shared stories of another era. Growing up around her and in this part of the state was unforgettable. Her land became our land as each one of us in the family came to have our own special memories. Her love was unconditional, as family love should be. Her words still ring true today when I think of her saying, "Family is everything."

Finally, after careful consideration, she decided what dress she would wear to my wedding and when she told me, she looked up and said with a smile, "I think I will also wear my rubies."

Epilogue
The Choice

Resolution is not an event, it's a decision.

Steven Furtick

November 5, 2019, was the last time I saw my only sibling. Our mediation took place in an office in downtown Portland, and although we did not formally meet, we briefly passed one another from a large distance in a hallway during an unexpected moment. Our eyes met awkwardly before I looked down at my feet while I kept walking with my legal team as we returned from lunch. I said a prayer in my mind for peace, healing, and closure as we walked by each other, realizing I may never see Gary again in this lifetime. The sudden awareness of that brought a sad relief but a greater emptiness to my heart. Family business had become something I loathed. No one was going to win at this game, and I couldn't help but wonder how my parents were feeling. I could never ever imagine my own two children going through what my brother and I were facing. No parent should ever see their children get to this point of division. I believed that it all could have been avoided, but our partnership goals seemed to be very different.

Although I cannot disclose the details of the mediation, I did write the following to myself shortly after the long day came to a close. Writing has always been healing, and I didn't know it at the time, but the following words may have been what led me to ultimately write this book. Here is the emotional note I wrote to myself just a short time after leaving the legal mediation. I never expected to share it with anyone, much less include it in a published work, but now it seems appropriate to do so here, especially as I can see what walking in deeper faith has done to strengthen my soul:

> *After four years of being at odds with my brother, this nightmare has an end today. My heart is very heavy as my only sibling and I finally divided what we owned together. I am so thankful to God for giving me the strength to get through this painful ordeal. It has not hit me yet that today is the start of a new beginning. Today I begin my life without being tied to my dad or my brother... I do not wish them any harm, but I do want justice, and I believe that God is a God of justice, and He sees all.*

I am eternally grateful, and I give all the glory to my Lord and Savior Jesus Christ... God certainly was with me, keeping me calm and guiding me through this process with grace. Through this entire experience I learned to stand on my own during the past few years without my family of origin or their support... I am eternally grateful for putting all of my trust with God, and I will continue to pray for my parents and my brother, for I believe they have such darkness on them, and I believe their inability to function in the world as loving honest people has taken over the goodness of their lives.

As I sit in my car in the garage of the legal office with tears streaming down my face, there is a surreal feeling of love and hope for the future but sadness for what has been. I continue to ask God to guide me in each new day of this new life that he has bestowed upon me, and I am so grateful for the freedom that he has given me today from the bondage I feel I have been living under for so long.

There is much to process. My mind is racing, and my body feels heavy. My heart is broken, and my lungs want to exhale fully but are in a state of paralysis. It is as though I have been holding my breath for almost five years and I have forgotten how to exhale. Through this experience, I learned to trust new people God brought into my life when I needed them most. I am grateful for my lawyers, my CPA, friends, and members of the extended family who stood by me.

Thank you, Holy Spirit—thank you for working within me today to do my best and to be an honorable person working through the most difficult chapter of my life. I hope to do good with what I have experienced and hope somehow that I can create healing within my family. My heart is broken in so many ways, yet I also know that there will be a time to heal. I am forever grateful for this day because I never thought I would see it come. I have been so fixated on the trouble this has caused and the pain it has caused my family. I hope somehow that healing can begin.

Nearly eighteen months from the date of mediation, I am finishing this memoir feeling thankful for the process, as it has allowed me to untangle years of emotion and start the long journey of healing my soul. Sadly, my family of origin remains estranged from me, and I understand their narrative may be different than mine, but I stand firm in the truth of my experience and, more importantly, in the Word of God.

My father has since formally removed me from his medical directive as he added Jaylen in my place and, in doing so, told him that he would be listed third under my brother and sister-in-law. My father also quite possibly removed me from his will, which is, of course, up to him. I find his decisions around his estate planning often appearing to be emotionally driven and punitive.

Jewelry gifted to me in 2011 by my Grandma Joy is still believed to be in his possession. Even though my father claimed in an email to me that his siblings got everything and he received nothing, there were relatives present who witnessed otherwise. My mother communicated to me several years ago in a text that they had "a couple of pieces" of her jewelry after I had inquired about the gifting debacle. He also still insists that the nearly five-carat diamond belonging to my grandmother's wedding ring given to me is lost. Friends and relatives tell me that my father continues to say he no longer has a daughter. Sadly, I believe he has chosen to live in anger, thinking he has been done wrong. As Dr. Martin Luther King Jr. famously said, "I have decided to stick with love. Hate is too great a burden to bear." I also wish not to bear such a burden going forward in my life.

I miss my dad, but I realize his feelings may not be the same as mine. For him, material things seem to be more important than a relationship with his only daughter. That is a tradeoff I would never make with my own children, so I pray for him as he must be living with some sort of deep anguish to make such an unfortunate choice. It is my true hope that he can overcome what I believe must be excruciating pain and heaviness in his soul. That unresolved pain has likely spread to my mother and brother as well. I refuse to carry that with me or allow my children to live in emotional bondage to power, greed, and money.

I remember in earlier years, my father saying to my mother and me how much he regretted passing on his unresolved anger over his early family issues onto my brother. I do believe whatever has been unresolved for my father was planted as a seed in Gary only to grow into a fiery torch that later severed our relationship. I believe my father's seeming inability to deal with whatever hurts him has spilled over to hurt the generations that follow him, and to me, that is disgraceful and sad. I believe the enemy has been using him for a long time, and I pray he can be released from that darkness.

The estrangement from my mother feels borne out of decisions we both made as different kinds of women. I decided to honor my desire for independence, clear consciousness, and a refusal to be marginalized, and her choice seemed to come from what I believed to be her blind, loyal allegiance to my father through what I view as her chronic codependence. In her 2018 New York Times best-selling memoir, *Educated,* author Tara Westover explains the complicated relationship with her mother, which resonated strongly with me:

> I could have my mother's love, but there were terms, the same terms they had offered me three years before that: I trade my reality for theirs, that I take my own understanding and bury it, leave it to rot in the earth. Mother's message amounted to an ultimatum: I could see her *and* my father or I would never see her again.
>
> She has never recanted.[8]

The price of personal pain has given me the gift of clarity and has also helped me grow enormously in my faith. I do not wish to live a lifetime of anger toward my parents and brother. My anger has instead turned to pity and sadness, for I see them now living with all of their material possessions while also living in what I believe to be spiritual isolation and darkness. I believe prayer to be the most powerful tool in releasing darkness that is beset upon people acting out of anger, greed, or strife. It is, therefore, a daily prayer of mine to lift up my loved ones and trust that in God's perfect timing, they might be released from the grip of the enemy.

Years before the fallout with my parents and brother, I endured an agonizing emotional setback from a different relationship. The events affected my life in many ways and took it off course for several years, deeply devastating me. However, I believe there is often something good that rises from the ashes of our challenges, and one thing I learned from that unfortunate situation was that if I held onto the pain and anger, it would have defined me.

Steven Furtick, in a powerful sermon to his congregation at Elevation Church on New Year's Eve 2017, referenced the apostle Paul's agonizing yet freeing message to the Philippians in chapter 1. Paul had waited nearly four years for his trial with no resolution of his situation in sight, yet he refused to let the chains he was in keep him in bondage as he claimed the ultimate freedom of his mind as the love of Christ was being preached and because of it, Paul rejoiced. Furtick spoke at length about pain, reminding his congregation that "You do not have to allow your outlook to be defined by the events that brought you to this point." Had I allowed that to happen years earlier, I would have felt like I was dragging a great weight around with me for the rest of my life. I knew I had to release it to be free.

One day during that early hurtful time, I caught myself while reciting the Lord's Prayer and paused on the words "forgive us our debts as we forgive our debtors," which made me stop and realize the work I had to do was to truly forgive what and who had hurt me. I understood that I could never ask God to forgive me if I was unwilling to forgive others, and so the lesson taught me that forgiveness is truly the gift to self. Matthew 6:14-15 (NIV) says, "For if you forgive other people when they sin against you, your heavenly Father will also forgive you. But if you do not forgive others their sins, your Father will not forgive your sins."

From that deeply painful experience, I also learned that forgiving didn't mean I had to forget. I have remembered it so that what I've gone through can serve as a lesson today that I can and will forgive again. I see that it is important to forgive my parents and my brother and those who enabled them to continue to hurt my children and me throughout this unfortunate ordeal.

Choosing forgiveness allows me not to have that pain as the center of my existence. I have decided instead to use pain for a godly purpose as a tool to help me face the work that must be done to truly have mercy on those whom I believe Satan used as weapons to try to destroy me. In the end, I believe those who willfully inflict pain on others live in the bondage of their own hell, and that is something to pity.

It is written in Luke 17:3-4 (NIV), "So watch yourselves. If your brother or sister sins against you, rebuke them, and if they repent, forgive them. Even if they sin against you seven times in a day and seven times come back to you saying, 'I repent,' you must forgive them." I may not ever receive repentance from my brother or parents, but true to my beliefs, I must forgive them because it is the spiritually mature and right thing to do. Living in anger is a tremendous drain on the life that God has created for us to enjoy.

I recently revisited the pages of a book I had read years ago, which greatly inspired me to forgive. In *Led by Faith, Rising From the Ashes of the Rwandan Genocide,* survivor and best-selling author Immaculée Ilibagiza writes about her struggle to forgive those who brutally murdered her family. She was unable to receive God's true love because her heart was blocked by anger and sadness. "My inability to forgive caused me even greater pain than the anguish I felt in being separated from my family, and it was worse than the physical torment of being constantly hunted… Like naughty children, they needed to be punished, but they also needed to be forgiven,"[9] she wrote. This was something I also struggled with, and I knew that her example was powerful and one I needed to hear again.

In June 2008, I had the honor of meeting Immaculée after she spoke about the genocide at The Hotchkiss School in Lakeville, Connecticut, not far from our family home in Cornwall. The school hosted the Independent School Gender Project Conference with a theme entitled "Sowing the Seeds of Change: Women and Girls Making a Difference in the World." Immaculée's riveting, faith-filled account of survival and escape from her war-torn country and ultimate forgiveness of those who had committed unspeakable atrocities left an enormous impression on me. Shaking this remarkable woman's hand and thanking her personally for her courageous stories was an honor and a turning point in my life, as her example is powerful and unforgettable.

As fate would have it, I met her again just days before finishing the writing of this book. She hosted a beautiful tribute to Mother Mary in Manhattan on the first Saturday of May, the month dedicated to the mother of Jesus. The intimate event was held in a small church in Kips Bay and attended by many in her own prayer group. I was honored and pleased to be amongst such godly women. I had the opportunity to thank Immaculée once more for her courage for writing and sharing her stories of forgiveness which helped me once again during my own personal hardship. It was also an honor to tell her I was writing a book with the hope of turning my personal pain into purpose to help others as she had through her own experiences. It was a gift to cross paths with this angelic woman of faith and inspiration, especially as my work on this book was coming to a close. She exhibits what Jesus wants for us, which is to truly love one another despite the painful circumstances.

As I sought healing and inner peace, sadly, mediation was not a true day of immediate closure on the events that took place between my brother and me. While it may have served as a formalized legal ending of our business partnership, the pain and repercussions of my brother's actions leading up to and shortly following the close of our LLC continue to be felt. My legal bills on the matter have followed me well into subsequent years as cleanup over loose ends continues. Wounds continue to be reopened as I struggle to heal and move on, but I know in due course I will. My past experiences and firm standing in faith have proven to me that I will succeed.

On a Friday in late February 2020, my brother was seen by someone who recognized him parked outside of the Springfield office on a day that was the office manager's usual day off. He was seen talking with a professional mover who had brought a large moving truck into the office parking lot. Gary had rightful access to the office, having apparently borrowed a new key and given permission to enter by a well-meaning family member who was told he seemingly just wanted to access some personal files for my father. However, when the office manager returned to the office on Monday, most of the files related to the history of the LLC, as well as some large file cabinets holding some of those files had been removed. As soon as I was notified, I contacted my lawyers because the tax files Gary removed were supposed to remain at the office under my management and not to be moved without prior notice. My brother would later confirm through his lawyer that the files and file cabinets were relocated to my parent's home in Tucson. To say that I was shocked was an understatement, as I was reminded again of my father's continual insistence that he had nothing to do with the LLC or the matters between my brother and me. Now he was in possession of extensive company files.

Since that event, access to some needed information has often been challenging. Important history on assets I acquired, contacts, accounts, and some information that would have made my transition easier were not made available to me. The unfinished business that I believe was left for me feels like a "scorched earth" exit and one that has continued to feel malicious and borne of evil.

One account I acquired continued to call me during the transition, saying that they felt my brother had tried to "sabotage" a certain property by demanding several times the heat be turned off at the property in the middle of winter, which would have possibly led to pipes bursting. The courteous and common transition of accounts between parties felt far from seamless with us at times, and it has been one that has left me continually challenged to put my pain to rest, yet I try every day to do so.

My parent's exit from Oregon has, I believe, further estranged them from the family, associates, and friends. Although I do not have first-hand knowledge, I have heard from friends close to the family that my brother now works for him, apparently managing his financial affairs. I imagine he also spends time with his family in the new homes recently purchased by my parents in Wyoming and Arizona. My kids have heard as much about the summer and holiday visits from my parents. I believe my brother has found a way to manage his inheritance while getting paid for it, which was what I believe managing our LLC looked like once I began to understand more of what was going on.

My kids and I, along with friends and relatives, believe that some members of the younger generation on both sides of the family have been very isolated from the extended family and sadly have likely not known the whole truth of what created this painful divide between my brother and me. My greatest hope is that truth will prevail, and healing can begin based on faith and access to factual knowledge. As my mother used to say to Jaylen, "There are always two sides to things," and now it may be time for those in the emerging generation to discover the side I believe has likely been kept out of their reach. It is time for them to forge their own lives and hopefully learn from those who came before them to make better choices than those who seemingly put greed, power, and money ahead of family.

My parents often insisted to me early on that they were pushed away from the family by me, but, sadly, I believe it was much of their own doing. Some people who know them likely only see one side of their behavior, but there are many who have witnessed the events of the past few years and have been shocked they didn't see sooner what I believe to be their Jekyll & Hyde personalities.

Those who haven't have either decided to stand by and enable my parents' behavior out of fear, a lack of seeking the other side of the story, a desire not to be involved, or because they may have had financial gain by being in business or association with my father. If they really thought about it, such allegiance has had a trickle-down effect which has deeply hurt me, Randy, our children, and others. Their inaction at times has been extremely disappointing, but one that has given more clarity to the love of money or the fear of power. I am reminded of 1 Timothy 6:10 (NIV), which says, "For the love of money is a root of all kinds of evil. Some people, eager for money, have wandered from the faith and pierced themselves with many griefs."

I believe I lost a close relative who seemingly chose to side with my mom and dad in order to protect the cash flow, likely still going toward one of her parents from mine. Our children were very close growing up, but since Randy and I parted ways, her relationship with me seemed to erode, and her allegiance with the source of money appears to have prevailed. Regardless, it has given me great clarity on the importance of standing up for myself, even if it is uncomfortable and even if I must stand alone. To choose the side of truth can often be a lonely place, but an important one. Joyce Meyer rightly says, "When you know who you are in Christ, you don't have to work hard to convince others who you are."

When I think that my father is the patriarch of a once very tight-knit and proud family but now appears to keep his distance and rarely, if ever, engages with the extended family, I realize it is very counter to how his parents and grandparents behaved when they held that role. Instead, blame, anger, misunderstandings, and false narratives seem to have taken precedence with him over truth, peace, healing, and love. I believe my grandparents would be disappointed beyond words to think that the family they raised has been seemingly so affected and neglected by their eldest child. Despite my father's absence, my extended family remains loving, close, and proud.

I still hope that one day my dad might see clearly and search his heart to remember the daughter who looked up to him and loved to hike and ski with him and genuinely enjoyed him as a father and not as someone who owed her an inheritance. For now, I believe it would take a miracle from God for that man to show up again in my life, wanting to be my dad and desiring a true relationship with me that isn't based on power or financial dominance.

My mother remains so distant and disinterested in me or my life that I wonder as she ages whether she might yearn for the love and care from her daughter. For now, I feel dead to her, and it is a feeling I often try to push away before I am lost in tears.

Holidays, birthdays, and life events come and go without contact from my parents, although I did receive an unexpected text message from my father on the second Christmas Eve since mediation. There was no wish of Merry Christmas or question of how I was or even if I was safe during the height of the worldwide COVID-19 pandemic. His words appeared even more starkly on the screen of my phone as I prepared, likely unbeknownst to him, to spend the Christmas holiday alone. "We have many photos of Jaylen, Lily, and you… If you don't want them, we will have them destroyed." He went on to say that he would pay for the shipping to either Portland or New York and that since the kids never contact him or respond, that he wouldn't be offering them any of the photos. He mentioned a second time in the same message that he would be destroying the photos if left unclaimed, then signed it "Dad."

I was speechless but not surprised by his message, which felt clearly like a way to entice me to be concerned over the photos or what I felt was his callous mention of the kids. Not long after the text, he sent me an email the same evening from a new email account I didn't recognize. The email was similar in tone and content yet equally painful and once again met from my end with silence.

A thousand responses formed in my mind as I read the two messages, the first of which was, "Merry Christmas, Dad, let's remember Jesus was born today." There were so many things to say, and yet instead, I chose to remain silent. The seeming threat to destroy family photos on Christmas Eve was something I recognized as an invitation to strife and borne of evil. He has also been told over the years that I moved back to New York from Portland, and he also must know this because he still receives the same family address list, which is updated every year at the family business office.

In January, just a few weeks after his Christmas Eve message to me, an email was sent to Randy and our kids, but this time from my mother. It was a similar message saying they had no room for family photos and there was a threat of destroying them if not claimed. My father surfaced again in March, sending the same messages with a promise to destroy if not claimed to two of my email accounts. My annoyance turned to pity as I believed it was his only way to try to engage me by agitating me over family photos. My father seemed like a broken, angry man, and it made me sad for him.

There are so many reasons why my kids don't reach out to him, the list being too long and too obvious to anyone who has paid any attention to the facts instead of the embellished and outlandish narrative my parents seem to believe. Perhaps the one thing I wish I could say to him would be that after purchasing so many homes and writing these messages to me, likely from his second home and what I've heard to be a large estate in Arizona, he still claims to be short on space to keep a few photos of his daughter and her family. The ranch home in Wyoming, the condos in Hawaii, the two homes in Arizona, and even the small studio in New York apparently don't afford him enough space for such photos anymore, but I believe the real reason isn't a matter of square footage, but rather a lack of space in his heart. It must be painful somewhere inside of him to be reminded of the family that I believe he pushed aside in his quest for the material.

Finally, an email came from him weeks ago, which included screenshots he had taken of the photographs in question with a promise that he would now copy and send them to me in New York. This seemed to signal to me that he actually did want to keep the photos since he would be making copies of them to send my way. I waited most of the day, thinking carefully before I finally responded.

I decided to react to his good behavior rather than bad. Gone was the threat of destroying family photos, and there was no mention of him not having enough room for the photos of his daughter and her family. My response finally felt like the right thing to do, so I kept it simple and thanked him for his kindness. I felt strongly that it was what God wanted me to do, and I was also hopeful that my father was perhaps sincerely missing me, but I didn't know for sure. That was the calling of my inner child, hoping for her dad, whom she once adored, to come back and show a true desire to be her father once again.

A few weeks ago, an enormous and heavy box arrived from my parents with the photos, all in original frames and packaged professionally. As promised, they were sent, but there was no note or anything personal inside except images of their daughter, his parents and siblings and various other family members. It was like he was clearing away layers of his past by sending them to me, and I felt my father's pain in that box and prayed for him to be healed. As I pulled out all of the framed photos, reflecting on happier times, I was sad because our once close family was no longer so. My children, on the other hand, received two similar boxes from my mother last week with cookies, gifts, and old photos of me and estranged relatives with lengthy handwritten notes to each of them, including invitations to their new ranch home in Wyoming for the summer. The mixed messages and blatant ignoring of me is both confusing and painful to me and to my kids and something I believe they both see with great clarity at their young ages.

I hurt for my children, who I believe at one time deserved the unconditional love of their grandparents, aunt, and uncle. These adults once likely knew better than to worship avarice over family, but I believe, have instead fallen prey to the depths and ugliness of greed. I often remind myself that their souls are good but that they have been overtaken by the enemy and subsequently lost.

I remain strong in my faith and lean daily on the word of God to help me through moments that still feel painful, as well as thanking Him for the good things. Gratitude is powerful, and I practice it often. Like Paul, who said in Philippians 3:13-14 (ESV), "Brothers, I do not consider that I have made it my own. But one thing I do: forgetting what lies behind and straining forward to what lies ahead, I press on toward the goal for the prize of the upward call of God in Christ Jesus." I know I am ultimately free.

We are reminded in Romans 12:19 (NIV) how to rise from the ashes of unfortunate circumstances and not take matters into our own hands, "Do not take revenge, my dear friends, but leave room for God's wrath, for it is written: "It is mine to avenge; I will repay, says the Lord." Defending against the attacks of the enemy in Romans 12:21(NIV) says, "Do not be overcome by evil, but overcome evil with good." The fleshly nature of our being often finds us tempted to want to get even and remedy a situation that has been unjust to us.

I recently heard a sermon by Joel Osteen about forgiveness during one of his telecasts on Trinity Broadcasting Network from Lakewood Church in Houston, Texas. I was struck by his powerful words about the price for the human desire for revenge when he said, "God won't give you influence to get even. There is a responsibility that comes with favor. God is testing your character."

The past few years have tested me at times far beyond what I could imagine or desire, but the experience has given me strength and clarity for which I am grateful. Looking back often makes my heart feel heavy as I long for the happier times and people I still love and miss. However, through the Word of God, I am thankful never to be alone and have learned to lean on Him both in good times and in challenging ones.

In a recent moment of deep loneliness and grief, I asked God how I was to live with the pain of circumstances that have felt so unfair and at times still feel unsettled, and He gently whispered to me, "Be the example." I instantly felt the calming presence of the Holy Spirit when I wrote His words down and then smiled, understanding that being the example would always mean choosing to stand on the side of grace.

Acknowledgments

This book would not have been possible if not for the steady prompting of the Holy Spirit, who encouraged me daily to open my heart and to keep putting my journey into words. I thank God for giving me the love of writing and for planting the seed within me that this book should and would be published, as I believe more than ever this has been His plan for me. It is an honor to have accomplished the calling in His name and to do so with Trilogy Christian Publishing and the Trinity Broadcasting Network Family.

A special thank you to my project manager, Jennifer Hudson, and to Terry Cordingley at Trilogy with TBN.

Carolyn Levin, much gratitude for your vetting and thoughtful expertise. Thank you, World Mission Media, for your precise and careful attention to detail.

To my legal team and CPA, whose professional guidance has been invaluable and greatly appreciated.

Sara Corwin, thank you for your treasured friendship and photo courtesy for my book cover.

Thanks to New York photographer and artist Luciana Pampalone, who helped produce my #GracefulWarrior photos for social media and marketing.

To Immaculée Ilibagiza, who so faithfully and beautifully embodies all that it is to live life by being the example God calls us to be. I believe our meetings fifteen years apart between two of the most painful chapters of my life were not by coincidence. Thank you for the lessons of forgiveness which were great reminders during the writing of this book.

A deep gratitude to the father of my children for always standing up for me and our children and for being so supportive of this project. To his extended family and to my in-laws, who have all been strong, present, and unconditionally loving during such challenging times. I respect you all and will always love you.

To those in my extended family who remain at my side and have loved unconditionally, thank you for being so caring, supportive, and inclusive. Family is everything, and I love you.

To my friends who kept encouraging me to find laughter through the tears and to keep moving forward so I could tell my story.

To Kristine Jennings, an angel of generosity and kindness to whom I will always be grateful for offering her hand, as Jesus would, to lift me out of the pit and place my feet upon solid ground. And to her beautiful mother, Nancy Kelley, whose prayers and devotionals have been so appreciated. You both exemplify the mother and daughter relationship I respect and love.

To Andrea Rapaport, my dear friend since college, and to her family. Your hospitality, friendship, generosity, and kindness reached me when I needed to be lifted from the confines and elevated from darkness, and you graciously delivered. I am forever grateful.

My angel sister Minerva Overstreet, who gave me my first modern translation Bible during our freshman year of college and who taught me about the power of the book of Proverbs. Thank you for always being a trusted place to share and grow, especially during the writing of this book. I love you endlessly.

My bestie, Felicia Walker, who has listened tirelessly and been so supportive, inclusive, generous and steadfast. I could not have gotten through this or written my story without you encouraging me. May we fly far again together and break many glasses soon! I love you, friend.

To my soul sisters, Deborah and Brenda Epperson-Moore, and their families, whose precious unconditional love and open doors to my children and me on each coast are deeply appreciated. You have always treated me like your little sister, and I love you dearly. Thank you for being my family. And to Mama Sherry and Daddy Don Pippin, thank you for opening your hearts to me when I needed unconditional parental love.

A special thank you to my midlife co-pilot, talented artist, and BFF, Bianca Pettinari, for all the shared wisdom we discovered those many nights sitting in your garage, talking, learning, creating, laughing, and crying together. Your "Biancaisms," humor, and advice on becoming a stronger woman "galore" through it all has been priceless. And to "special agent drummer" Camille Bernal for joining us for impromptu dinners and much-needed laughs during my Portland days. I could always count on you both for much sunshine during the rain.

Olimpia Filippini for your beautiful presence in our bi-coastal lives and endless wisdom that reaches far beyond your years. We love you.

Much gratitude to Alison Deans for being supportive both on and off the dance floor. Your generous hospitality, valuable advice, introductions, encouragement, and friendship have meant more to me than you'll ever know.

Sang Hong, for your steadfast friendship, support, and kindness throughout these challenging years, which helped me finally get here.

Kim Williams, who planted important early seeds of encouragement within me for this project—thank you from the bottom of my heart.

Ken Leung, for your patience, especially while traveling with our group to Sicily and Costa Rica. You steadied me greatly when I needed it most.

Erin B. & Ali K. for the "pura vida" love and support throughout this journey. I'm so happy to finally share my story with you.

To Oregon friend and artist Nyssa Perrin Clark, who has brought much visual joy through her magnificent paintings, especially "Waves of Grace" created for me during the writing of this book. Our friendship has meant so much throughout the journey.

Tamara Kribs, whose lifelong friendship, honest conversation, and laughs at any hour in any time zone has been so important during this project. Thank you for listening and for being so supportive of this book.

Elizabeth Spence, who has known me the longest and whose friendship and sisterhood are preciously eternal. And to her late mother, Marilyn Holbrook, who always treated me like a daughter. Your mother-daughter relationship inspired me greatly over the years.

To beautiful Audrey Byfield, whose example of inner strength, steadfast faith and friendship have been a priceless gift throughout the years. You exemplify grace in all things and always inspire me.

Merci beaucoup to Alexandre Hague-Mattia, whose longtime friendship, patience, support, and unconditional love from across the pond have been invaluable throughout the past few years. *Je t'aime.*

Rena Hedeman, who came into my life at the perfect time to offer me an opportunity to build my own side business. Thank you for your friendship, example, and encouragement throughout my journey and for suggesting I read Tara Westover's memoir, *Educated,* which resonated with exceptional timing. And to everyone at Team Freedom, thank you for the vitally supportive community.

To Pook's parent, Jan Tilley, whose kindred spirit for peace, art, music, laughs, and anything feline kept me in great and constant neighborly company. Thank you for your fierce support as I navigated my thoughts and feelings onto the written page.

Ivonne Camacho at AbsolutModerne, I am so grateful we could work and create together even during the pandemic. Your patient support while I was writing and when life felt less glamorous was so appreciated because you always made things more beautiful. Thank you for the many opportunities and for your loving and treasured friendship.

Tracy Turco, whose long friendship and gracious invitations to social and business events encouraged me to put my best foot forward even when life behind the scenes felt like it was falling apart. Thank you for your generous spirit and for including me. You're a gem.

My beautiful friend, Marie Leppard, for always adding your special light when I needed it and for being a true sister in faith over the decades. Thank you for listening and encouraging me to keep writing.

To a true gentleman, Vaughn Acord, much gratitude for your kindness and friendship. It is always an honor to visit the best seat in the city, especially during those times I needed some glam and didn't feel my best; thank you for always helping me get there.

Deborah Fields-Newallo, for your daily texts of scripture which uplift my soul and for your beautiful voice and song for the Lord, thank you.

To my wonderful friend, Lori Lewis, whose friendship and selfless mission to others in need has been a strong example of grace under fire. I love you.

And to Michael Colwell, my spiritual brother who understands my journey. You know my heart as we are joined by our past, our present, and, more importantly, in our faithful future and love of God.

To Nadia Zaki, who continues to be an enormous source of inspiration of strength, grace, and beauty in all circumstances and who taught me the power of inner strength through breath, balance, discipline, and consistency. Thank you for your Inner Series community that continues to feed my soul. My life has forever been transformed since we met in Cairo in 2010. And to my amazing, inspiring fitness family including, D'Ann Tollet, Steven Gillespie, Brandon W., Susi Lee, Sandy Trapp, Michelle Ulysse, Felicia Walker, Erin B., Ali K., Diletta Badeschi, Carol Day, Bea Locsin, Jane Carlin, Amy Babcock, Luis E. Ortiz, Rick Talmage, Leslie G., Lindsey Cook, Dede Nazareth, Jenise Crawford, Kimberly Williams, Heidi T., and so many others who share that desire of Education, Love & Purpose. Thank you all for continually encouraging me to write my story.

To James Ervin, for your friendship and special brand of groove. You lead the best "church" of dance on Sundays with the crew, including Ken Leung, Alison Deans, Sang Hong, Julia Vitullo-Martin, JohnPablo Stewart, Hans J. Galutera, and so many others who have given me so much joy when I felt trapped in the studio apartment and needed a community in which to learn, grow and spread my wings. Dancing with you all is my happy place.

To Abby Goldenberg, who I could always count on to make me laugh just as long as I got to class. You have no idea how much your fabulous choreography and sense of humor lifted my spirits during some of the roughest years.

Mahalo nui loa to my beloved *ohana* in Hawaii, Jenn, 'Ilae and Cory Mehau, Kai White, Sue Bliss, Katrina Kaufman Perez and Rick Perez, Dean Powell, Maura Bacon Chang, Bella and Don Faumuina, Jana Zane, Jodi Graham, JoAnn Goldner, Jared Ake, Rebecca Madera, Molly Hagmann, S. Mailelauli'i Naki, Kelly Toguchi and everyone at Street Jamz Werkout and Boogiedown Productions Hawaii. I love you and am grateful for your aloha spirit while on or away from the *'āina*. My heart overflows because of you. *A hui hou!*

Me ka mahalo Nui to the spirit of Queen Lili'uokalani, whose lasting example of grace under pressure forever resonates deeply within my soul to the cries of *'onipa'a*, a word which has carried me through many unjust moments and served as a strong reminder while writing this book.

Thank you, Vega Dance Lab in Portland, a place that gave me a lot of community and acceptance through dance. Evie Graham, for your positive energy and amazing classes and to Daniel Prince, Maki Schwarz, Anna Truxes, and neighbor Erin Gilreath—thanks for the friendship and for making a place for me on your dance floor.

Gus Bembery, for bringing a lot of joy and incredibly happy choreography into my life when things felt hopeless. We met during the storm, and your friendship and inspiring creativity has been a lasting gift. <3

Danielo Mendes, for making a huge impression on me during my challenging studio days through dance, beyond any definitions, adventures, and a fierce attitude. Thanks for the continued friendship and inspiration.

Derek Mitchell, for your positive energy and phenomenal choreography via Zoom, which has energized me, especially during the editing process. You've brought lost laughter and the joy of dance into my living room during an extra-long stretch of alone time during COVID.

To Dr. Leon Abinder for the essential PT adjustments, life wisdom, and laughs throughout the roller coaster years. Thanks for the encouragement during this project and for having my back, literally!

To those who I couldn't mention yet are forever in my heart, I would not have been able to overcome some of the steepest hurdles without you. I am forever grateful.

My heavenly family of great-grandparents, Walter, Dutee, Hadie, Andrew, Nell, P. H., Karl, Selma, and grandparents Carlton, Joy, Herman, and Margaret, who all walk with me in spirit. This book is so much for you as I believe your promptings from above through the Holy Spirit have helped me tell my story. I am honored by the example you gave me of what family and legacy should be, and I thank you for your love, which will be with me always.

To my daughter, son, and daughter-in-law, whose encouraging words, maturity, and unconditional love have carried me through so many ups and downs and whose brave support of this project has made me realize this book is for us all. I love you so much.

And to my rock, Steffen, who inspires me every day to trust God's timing, remain positive, and to never, ever give up. I marvel at your patience throughout my painful ordeal and for your steadfast positivity, which has lifted my spirits so many times. There is no doubt in my mind you were heaven-sent. *Ik hou van je.*

To everyone who listened and cared, you offered me a priceless gift by doing so, and it was that kind of support that helped me move toward finishing this book. God bless you. Grace always, xo Dena.

Endnotes

1 Eger, Edith Eva, Esmé Schwall, Weigand and Philip G.,Zimbardo. 2017. *The Choice: Embrace the Possible. (New York: Scribner, 2017), 183.*

2 *THE HOLY BIBLE, NEW INTERNATIONAL VERSION* ®. Copyright© 1973, 1978, 1984, 2011 by Biblica, Inc.™. Used by permission of Zondervan

3 *THE HOLY BIBLE, NEW INTERNATIONAL VERSION,* Zondervan

4 Peck, M. Scott (Morgan Scott), 1983. *People of the Lie: The Hope for Healing Human Evil, (New York: Touchstone, 1983), 80.*

5 Peck, 78

6 Peck, 162

7 Ilibagiza, Immaculée, and Steve Erwin, 2006. *Left to Tell: Discovering God Amidst the Rwandan Holocaust.* (California: Hay House, Inc, 2006), 94.

8 Westover, Tara, 2017. *Educated: A Memoir.* (New York: Random House, 2017), 322.

9 Ilibagiza, Immaculée, and Steve Erwin, 2008. *Led by Faith; Rising from the Ashes of the Rwandan Genocide.* (California: Hay House, Inc. 2008), 38.

About the Author

Dena McCoy is President of Grace West Properties LLC and Grace Meadow Properties and is the proud fourth-generation trustee and Vice President of her family's nearly seventy-year-old philanthropic foundation in her homestate of Oregon. She has a BA in Humanities from the University of California, Berkeley. Dena also has a background in commercial acting, social media copywriting and online media branding. She is a member of SAG/AFTRA and the Authors Guild. After the birth of her son in Santa Monica, she and her husband moved from California to New York where her daughter was born a few years later. They raised their family in Manhattan and Litchfield County, Connecticut. As an avid fitness enthusiast with a discipline in dance and yoga, Dena has learned that an important part of emotional healing is creating inner strength through fostering a healthy mind, body, and spirit. She hopes to inspire others to break free from their painful pasts through education, self-care, and by finding grace through faith. Dena lives in New York and is working on her second book.

Find Dena at denamccoy.com, and on Instagram @denamccoy.